HOW TO
INCORPORATE

HOW TO INCORPORATE
A Handbook for Entrepreneurs and Professionals

MICHAEL R. DIAMOND
Professor of Law
Antioch School of Law

JULIE L. WILLIAMS
Deputy General Counsel
Federal Home Loan Bankboard

JOHN WILEY & SONS

New York · Chichester · Brisbane · Toronto · Singapore

Library of Congress Cataloging in Publication Data:

Diamond, Michael R.
     How to incorporate.

     Bibliography: p.
     1. Incorporation—United States.   I. Williams,
Julie L.   II. Title.
KF1420.D53 1987   346.73′06622   87-12968
ISBN 0-471-63110-8   347.3066622
ISBN 0-471-85768-8 (pbk.)

Printed in the United States of America

10 9 8 7 6 5 4 3 2 1

Despite the unsentimental nature of this material,
this book is dedicated, with great affection,
to JBDD and, especially, to Rebecca Caleff.
M.R.D.

With love to Don and my mother
and in memory of my father.
J.L.W.

ACKNOWLEDGMENT

Writers of books are often credited with accomplishing the task on their own. In fact, books generally could not be completed without the invaluable but often under-recognized contributions of persons other than the authors. This is surely such a book. We would like to extend recognition and appreciation to Arthur Jackson, a law student at Antioch School of Law, for extraordinary research assistance and to Jacqueline Bruce-Yamin and Patrice A. Britt for processing the manuscript and, more important, for their constant organizational involvement which allowed the project to be managed smoothly. Finally, we wish to thank Gail Elise Ross who shepherded this book to completion.

M.R.D.
J.L.W.

CONTENTS

APPENDIXES   **121**

1

INTRODUCTION

Corporations are among the most visible and most powerful participants in our national economy. When one thinks of corporations, one often thinks of corporate giants such as IBM or Exxon, the Fortune 500, or the New York Stock Exchange. However, of the several million corporations operating in the United States, fewer than 10,000 are publicly traded in any significant way.

The typical corporation, in fact, is closely held, that is, owned by only a small number of persons (known as shareholders or stockholders). The shares of stock they own are not readily transferable from person to person as are, for instance, those of IBM. Instead, the shareholders of the typical company usually know each other and often work together in the business.

Often, the corporations they established were organized and operated without the assistance of a lawyer or other professional. In many cases, that fact is insignificant in the life of the corporation or its shareholders. There are, however, many situations where the absence of professional planning and ongoing professional assistance has had serious consequences. While this book is not a substitute for such assistance, it is designed to fill part of the void between business persons and outside professionals and also to highlight areas where outside assistance is particularly important.

This book deals with the organization and operation of a business

1

corporation. It lays out the legal prerequisites to corporate existence, the choices the organizers of a corporation must make, and the practical implications of the potential choices. The book also discusses the legal and practical realities of operating a corporation, including many of the financial issues likely to be faced by the business's principals.

Stylistically, we have attempted to be straightforward and clear. There are forms, explanations, and examples to take readers through the various issues raised in the text. The appendixes are also intended to give the reader information, or access to information, which is useful in forming and running a business corporation.

Since much of corporate formation involves statutory requirements, and since states vary in their corporate statutes, we have chosen to use as a base for discussion the Model Business Corporation Act ("The Model Act"), which was originally prepared as a research project of the American Bar Foundation and subsequently updated and expanded by the Committee on Corporate Laws of the Section of Corporation, Banking, and Business Law of the American Bar Association. The Act has been adopted in whole or in substantial part by many states, and thus provides the most common link for discussion. Because of statutory variation, however, it is very important that the reader examine his or her own state's law to determine the degree of similarity with the Model Act. The comparison chart in the appendixes is designed to assist in that examination.

Once the statutory requirements are understood, the organizers must make choices both as to statutory possibilities and operational needs. We believe that knowledge and understanding of issues help in the decision-making process. With this in mind, we have attempted to shed some light on the inner workings of corporate formation and existence. We hope this information proves helpful.

2

THE CORPORATION

WHAT IS A CORPORATION?

A corporation is a legal entity, an artificial creation comprised of other entities—human or artificial. Its unique characteristic is that it is recognized by the law as a thing separate from the entities that comprise it, and is frequently treated like a human being. For instance, a corporation is a "person" and enjoys the Constitutional protections against unreasonable searches and seizures, deprivation of liberty and property without due process of law, and denial of equal protection of the law. A corporation is entitled to invoke the attorney-client privilege of confidentiality and may also sue for defamation of its corporate good name. Also like an individual, a corporation is subject to punishment if it violates the law. In such cases, it may be liable for damages or fines or could be prohibited from continuing in business.

For the purposes of federal court jurisdiction, a corporation is deemed to be a citizen of the state (or states) where it was incorporated *and* of the state where it has its principal place of business. A corporation is not a "citizen" within the meaning of the Privileges and Immunities Clause of the Constitution and, consequently, a state may subject "foreign" corporations (those incorporated in another state) to regulations not imposed on "domestic" (those incorporated in that state) corporations.

Generally, an individual is considered to be "domiciled" in the place that he or she calls home. A corporation is considered to have two domiciles—its "legal domicile" in the state where it was incorporated, and its "commercial domicile" where it has its principal place of business. This distinction is significant because it enables more than one state to impose its taxes on a corporation by virtue of the corporation's "domicile" within that state's jurisdiction.*

The most important characteristic of a corporation is the "limited liability" it affords its shareholders (or members), directors, and officers. In the case of a business or a "for profit" corporation, a shareholder's liability is usually limited to the amount he or she invested in the corporation, and if the corporation goes bankrupt, stockholders are not liable for the corporation's debt—they lose only the money they paid to purchase their stock. Or, if a customer slips on a banana peel in a store run by a corporation, the customer may sue the corporation. If the corporation is found to be liable for the amount sought by the customer, the customer may claim the corporation's assets to satisfy his or her judgment but generally may not take a shareholder's personal assets (e.g., car, bank account, etc.). This is true even if the corporation does not have enough to settle the claim. If a stockholder's stock has not been fully paid for, however, that stockholder will be liable to the corporation or to an outsider for the portion that is unpaid.

In a nonprofit corporation, *members* occupy a position analogous to that of stockholders in a for-profit corporation. Nonprofit corporations may not issue stock, and the amount a member would lose if a nonprofit corporation became bankrupt would generally be only the amount of membership dues paid or donations made. In both profit and nonprofit corporations, directors, officers, and other corporate personnel generally are not liable for corporate debts.

The exception to the usual state of limited liability occurs when the corporate form is used to perpetrate a fraud, evade the law, or escape payment of a just obligation. In situations where it would be clearly unjust to allow the corporation to shield the individuals behind it, courts may ignore the corporation and look directly to its shareholders or directors and officers for liability for corporate debts and responsibility for corporate misdeeds. The courts also look behind the corporation or, to use the legal term, "pierce the corporate veil," when the corporation ignores corporate formalities (fails to comply with statu-

---

* This should not result in a double tax. A corporation is generally subject to state income taxes only on the portion of its total activities which are carried on within a particular state. That is, if one-third of the company's activities (property, sales, and employees) take place in State X, one-third of the company's income is taxable by State X. What this does mean is that a corporation may be responsible for filing tax returns in several states.

tory requirements, for example, if its incorporation is defective, if the corporation is merely a shell and is being used solely as a "front" to evade personal liability, or if the corporation keeps inadequate records or follows improper procedures).

Another unique feature of the corporation is its ability to exist for an unlimited period of time. In most states, a corporation must specify the period of its duration, which may be perpetual, in its Articles of Incorporation. Perpetual existence is one advantage of corporations over sole proprietorships and partnerships—the corporation is not terminated by the death or withdrawal of its stockholders or members. Of course, a corporation's existence may be limited in its Articles, and, regardless of a limitation, it may be dissolved at any time by its shareholders or members. Generally, a business corporation may be dissolved by vote of its Board of Directors and a majority of its shareholders present at a shareholders' meeting where notice was given of the vote to dissolve (Section 84 of the Model Business Corporation Act), or, in lieu of a meeting, by written consent signed by *all* shareholders (Section 83 of the Act).

A further advantage of the corporate form is the ease with which interests in a corporation may be transferred. The ownership of a profit corporation is represented by shares of stock which may be sold, traded, or given away by their owners. A shareholder generally may dispose of any portion of his or her stock, or merely the income such stock produces, while retaining voting rights, or vice versa, all without regard to how the other shareholders feel about his or her actions.

Restrictions, however, may be placed on the free transferability of shares, if the shareholders so desire. To protect a prearranged control group structure from outsiders, stockholders of a corporation may enter into a "shareholders' agreement" which may provide that any person wishing to sell his or her stock in the corporation must first offer it to the corporation for purchase, or to the other shareholders, or that upon the death of a shareholder, the corporation has the first opportunity to buy the stock from the deceased stockholder's estate. Absolute restrictions on share transfers, however, have not been sustained by the courts.

CORPORATE STRUCTURE

The control of a corporation is basically three tiered, with the stockholders or members making up the largest group in the corporate hierarchy. Nonprofit corporations are not required to have members, but if they do, these people generally are interested in the objectives of the corporation but not inclined to become involved in actually running it. Stockholders, on the other hand, may be absolutely disinterested in what the business corporation does, as long as it makes a profit and distributes money to them.

Stockholders (or members) generally have few powers in connection with day-to-day operations of a corporation. They usually elect the Board of Directors, they may have the ability to remove the Board, they could be responsible for amending the Bylaws, and they must ratify any amendments to the Articles of Incorporation. In a small corporation, the shareholders may want to give themselves a more significant role by including provisions in the Articles and Bylaws giving themselves broader powers and more direct control over the management of the corporation.

Generally, the Board of Directors is more intimately involved in corporate management than the stockholders. Directors are the corporation's managers. Their legal authority includes decisions of policy, personnel, compensation, delegation of authority to committees, declaration of dividends (in a business corporation), and general supervision and responsibility for all corporate activities.

Pursuant to its power to delegate authority, the Board of Directors may appoint various committees to assist it in its functions. It is possible for the Board to vest virtually all its powers in an Executive Committee composed of a limited number of members of the Board—at least two. This Executive Committee may exercise all the authority of the Board of Directors in the management of the corporation, but the members of the Board may remain responsible for actions of the Executive Committee. (This may include potential liability for improper distributions of corporate funds, guarantees of corporate obligations, liability and fines for acting as a corporation without proper authority, fines for failure to file required annual reports, or prosecution for noncompliance with Internal Revenue requirements.)

The Board of Directors may also create other committees to perform supportive functions such as publicity, charitable contributions, community projects, or designing the corporation's stock certificates. Members of these committees (which do not exercise the authority of the Board) need not be members of the Board.

The officers of the corporation are generally selected by the Board of Directors and generally may be removed by them. Since officers may be directors, directors may select themselves as the corporation's officers. In a small corporation this is frequently done.

Officers carry out the day-to-day business of the corporation, frequently without interference from the Board of Directors, which concerns itself with broader policy decisions. Thus officers are often, in reality, the most powerful group in the corporation. They hire and fire employees, set policy, and make decisions which legally bind the corporation.

The most familiar corporate offices include: President, Vice-President, Secretary, and Treasurer. There may also be numerous assistants for these positions, for example, Assistant Treasurer.

The President traditionally presides at the Board of Directors' and shareholders' meetings and may also act for and obligate the corporation in ordinary business transactions, for example, sign leases, order goods, and so forth.

The Vice-President generally does not have the power to bind the corporation, and his or her duties are usually merely to act in the place of the President should he or she be absent, disabled, resigned, or dead. The Board or the President could, of course, delegate special additional duties to the Vice-President.

The Secretary attends meetings of the shareholders (or members), Board of Directors, and various committees, keeps minutes of these meetings, sends notices, prepares corporate records, and has custody of the corporate seal.

The Treasurer is the chief fiscal officer of the corporation and is responsible for the corporate treasury, that is, for receiving and keeping the corporation's money and disbursing it as authorized, for maintaining financial records, and for reporting on the financial condition of the corporation.

PROFIT AND NONPROFIT CORPORATIONS

Whether a corporation is profit or nonprofit, the previously discussed concepts of the corporate entity (its limited liability and continuous existence) are equally applicable. Obviously, however, profit and nonprofit corporations are not identical and there are differences that are important to recognize.

A not-for-profit corporation is defined, basically, as "a corporation, no part of the income of which is distributable to its members, directors, or officers." This does not mean that a not-for-profit corporation cannot make money. In fact, both not-for-profit and business (for-profit) corporations may make money, but in figuring "profits," expenses are subtracted from the gross receipts the corporation takes in. In a not-for-profit corporation, the money that remains as "profits" after the payment of expenses may not be distributed to the corporation's members, directors, or officers, but must be applied to further the corporation's purposes or to expand its facilities. However, "reasonable compensation for services rendered" is a legitimate corporate "expense" to be subtracted from gross receipts in order to arrive at "profits," and salaries are one way in which members, directors, or officers may receive funds from a nonprofit corporation. (Another instance is if the corporation's purposes incidentally benefit members, directors, and officers as well as the other groups it serves (such as a director of a day-care center whose eligible child attends the center), or if the corporation dissolves and its assets are distributed to its members.)

A business corporation is strikingly different. While a nonprofit corporation may not issue stock or pay dividends, a business corporation may issue and sell a variety of instruments which evidence interests in itself, and may reward the holders of these interests with a portion of corporate profits.

One type of interest in a corporation is represented by shares of stock, the owners of which are, collectively, the owners of the corporation. In addition, a for-profit corporation has the ability to offer for sale a variety of types of stock, each attractive to a different type of investor, and thus may be able to achieve broad investment support.

Stock may be differentiated into "preferred" and "common" types. Preferred stock is so called because its holders generally enjoy a preference in the form of a constant, nonfluctuating dividend payment which is derived from the corporation's earnings, which they receive before the holders of any other type of stock are entitled to receive any portion of profits. Preferred stock is generally considered a conservative investment because of this payoff preference.

Subject always to the Board's discretion, earnings that remain after preferred stockholders receive their dividend payments may then be distributable as dividends to the holders of common stock. The payoff to these stockholders may vary greatly from year to year, depending on the corporation's business success each year. Since preferred stockholders always receive the same fixed amount of dividends off the top of the corporation's profits, in a very profitable year there may be a large amount left over for the common shareholders to receive as dividends, while in a less profitable year, common shareholders may receive nothing. Because of this uncertainty in common stock distributions, common stock is more speculative than preferred stock.

Within each type of stock there may be different "classes" with different purchase prices, rates of dividends, voting rights in the selection of the corporation's management, and so forth. For instance, Class A common stock could pay 10 cents a year per share in dividends but have no voting rights, while Class B common stock pays only 5 cents a year per share, but possesses full voting rights. Those who were primarily interested in financial return would be inclined to buy Class A, while people who wanted control of the corporation would be the investors in Class B.

In addition to stock, a profit corporation may issue a type of interest in itself known as a "debt security." Stock is an equity security because stockholders are considered the owners of the corporation. The corporation has no legal obligation to repay the purchase price of a shareholder's stock. The holders of debt securities, on the other hand, are regarded as creditors of the corporation, that is, the corporation *owes* them money. Debt securities are sold, like stock, for a certain price, paid by the purchaser to the corporation. The holder of a debt security is then entitled to receive interest payments from the corporation based on the value and interest rate of the debt security he or she holds. Thus, if *X* buys a $1,000 debt security, payable at 6% interest annually, the corporation must pay *X* $60 every year until the security's due date, at which time the corporation must "redeem" (buy back, pay off) the face value of the security. Since the redemption price is usually the face value of the security, *X* gets back his or her $1,000 and makes $60 a year until that time.

Unlike dividends, which are paid at the discretion of the Board of Directors, the obligation to pay interest on debt securities continues regardless of the corporation's financial condition.

WHY CHOOSE A PROFIT CORPORATION?

The obvious reason for organizing a business or for-profit corporation is to make a profit. A corporation is an excellent vehicle for a business venture because of the insulation it provides against personal liability for corporate debts and because of the multiple opportunities for personal gain it presents.

As mentioned previously, both profit and nonprofit corporations shield their stockholders or members from liability for corporate debts; however, it is difficult to get rich from a nonprofit corporation. In contrast, the principal motivation of a profit corporation is to make as much money as possible to distribute to its investors. In fact, the managers of a profit corporation have a *duty* to place the business interests of the corporation and its stockholders before any other considerations when making corporate decisions. Thus if undertaking a socially beneficial project was weighed against giving company stockholders increased dividends, absent other factors, it could well be the duty of the Board of Directors to forgo the good deed and attempt to maximize profits to distribute as dividends.

It is the potential for profit that motivates people to create and invest in business corporations. When a small corporation is created, shares of its stock frequently are owned entirely by the corporation's founders. These founding shareholders may provide their company with the money it needs to begin its operations by purchasing interests in it, which are represented by shares of stock. If the corporation does well, the founders' rewards can be very pleasant, for instance:

Three people organize Corporation A, intending to be equal owners of the business. They then decide that the corporation will have 30,000 shares of common stock. To be equal owners, each organizer must now buy an equal number of shares of stock up to 10,000 shares apiece. The price for the stock will be set by determining how much money the business needs at the outset and how much money will come from sources other than the purchase of stock. In this instance, however, let us assume the 30,000 shares are sold for 10 cents apiece. If the corporation is successful and makes a profit, the Board of Directors (elected by the shareholders who may elect themselves as directors) may declare that the company will share its profits with the shareholders. The Board will then declare a dividend of a certain amount to be paid per share of stock.

In this case, if Corporation A made a profit of $3,000 for the year, a dividend of 10 cents per share might be declared. Each of the shareholders would then receive $1,000. If the corporation is very successful, larger dividends may be declared as the stockholders' share in the business's good fortune. However, in the early years of a business's life, profits, if any, are generally plowed back into the business. In any event, corporations typically do not distribute all their profits to shareholders but retain some for growth and reserves.

As a corporation prospers, other investors may notice this success and approach the original organizers with an offer to buy their stock for $2 per share. The organizers may decide to give up their investment by accepting the offer and selling their stock for a gain of $9,000 over their original investment. Of course, had this been a not-for-profit corporation the organizers could not have sold their "interest" in the corporation and would have received nothing.

Returns are rarely as spectacular as in the preceding example, but stock ownership does supply a significant and steady source of income for many investors. The attractiveness of stock as an investment can be a happy circumstance if the corporation decides to expand or if it encounters an unexpected and temporary financial crunch. With the ability to attract new funds by selling stock or other types of interests in itself, all with an expectation of financial return to the investor, a for-profit corporation will be able to weather financial storms more readily than a not-for-profit corporation, which must rely principally on donations for additional funds.

Small businesses, on the other hand, may have difficulty selling their stock and other interests. They are hampered by their lack of recognition, the difficulty in determining the value of their shares (since they are not traded on a stock exchange), and, ironically, by the small amounts of money they need to raise (since investors may prefer large investments because of the potential for large profits).

In summary, business corporations have financial advantages: They are usually able to raise money more easily than nonprofit corporations, and they may generously reward those who choose as their investment a business which becomes successful.

The virtues of a business corporation are not entirely financial, however, for business corporations may be more efficient than nonprofit organizations. This could stem from the desire to make as much as possible by spending as little as possible, thus resulting in cheap, shoddily made goods. However, it may also produce more efficient use of time, streamlined work procedures, and more effective use of personnel. The desire to save money may lead to less expensive manufacturing techniques and materials and less expensive goods. The desire to make money may serve as a spur to research and develop different, newer, and better techniques and products to outsell the competition.

The drive to make money may have an indirect social benefit as well. A business corporation is usually not content to make the same amount of money every year, but tries instead to increase its profits. Making more money may involve improved techniques and products, as discussed previously, but may also be accomplished by an increased volume of business, or both. In order to make more products or perform more services, it is frequently necessary to hire more people, buy more raw materials, and/or invest more money in new machinery and facilities. Thus a successful venture may provide additional jobs and may also contribute to the well-being of other industries by purchasing larger quantities of their products.

DISADVANTAGES OF A PROFIT CORPORATION

There are, however, disadvantages to the profit form. While many non-profit corporations may be tax-exempt, business corporations are not.

State income taxes vary, but federal income taxes currently range from 15% on the corporation's first $50,000 of taxable income to 34% on taxable income in excess of $75,000.

The activities of nonprofit corporations are potentially more flexible than those of profit corporations. Nonprofit corporations need not be primarily concerned with making maximum possible profits, and consequently they may experiment with new products or innovative management, or they may dedicate themselves to helping disadvantaged groups—without being under pressure to make these changes result in increased revenues. Also, through membership in a nonprofit corporation, residents of particular areas may become organized and effective in dealing with community problems. Nonprofit corporations may receive local, state, or federal government grants, and people may give these groups money because they support their activities. This combination of grants, donations, and a subordinated profit motive allows nonprofit corporations to work in fields that profit corporations may avoid because of the high risk and/or low or nonexistent profits involved. Thus, while there is some crossover in function, each type of corporation has its own purposes and fills its own niche in society.

3

CHOICE OF FORM

There are, of course, other forms of organizing and operating a business. One may choose a sole proprietorship, a general partnership, or a limited partnership rather than forming a corporation. Each of these forms has its own advantages and disadvantages. This chapter will describe briefly their attributes and uses.

SOLE PROPRIETORSHIP

A sole proprietorship is the simplest form of business organization. It is really nothing more than one individual undertaking some business activity in his or her personal capacity as sole owner. This does not mean the business must be made up of one person. There may be employees, perhaps many employees. A sole proprietorship involves a one-*owner* business. The proprietor owns the business directly in an individual capacity.

The major advantage of this form of business is the lack of legal formality in its establishment and operation. A sole proprietorship may be established anywhere, anytime, by anyone. There are no requirements for filing organizational documents or, with the exception of tax returns, annual reports with the state. Of course, if special licensing is necessary in order to engage in an *occupation* (such as law or medicine) one must obtain the license regardless of the form of business chosen (i.e., proprietorship, partnership, etc.). There is no additional license needed for a licensed attorney to set up his or her business as a sole proprietorship.

Additionally, there is administrative ease of operation. Since there are no co-owners, there is no need to hold policy-setting meetings or to report to colleagues. Moreover, there is no legal distinction between the proprietor as owner and as individual. Therefore, financial record keeping may be less formal (although as a practical matter, one should be able to account for and distinguish between income and expense from the proprietorship and income and expense from other sources if for no other reason than the tax law treats business expense differently from personal expense).

The proprietor, as sole owner, has the ability to make all business decisions and stands to benefit from business gains. On the other hand, the proprietor is also personally responsible for all business losses. There is no separate identity shielding the proprietor from such liability, thus all of his or her personal assets may be called on to satisfy business obligations.

Similarly, there is no separate entity to be taxed. All gains or losses are attributed directly to the proprietor and are combined with the proprietor's net income from other sources to arrive at his or her taxable income. The proprietor will fill out Schedule C to IRS Form 1040 in reporting business income or loss.

Because there is no entity separate from the proprietor, the proprietorship's existence terminates with the departure, through sale, abandonment, or death, of the proprietor. There is no continuity of life, so if a proprietor sells the proprietorship to another sole proprietor, from a legal standpoint the first proprietorship ends and a new one begins at the time of sale. This fact is legally significant because of the personal liability of a proprietor.

GENERAL PARTNERSHIP

A general partnership is defined by Section 6(1) of the Uniform Partnership Act as "an association of two or more persons to carry on as co-owners a business for profit." Thus, the most obvious (and critical) distinction between a partnership (also known as a *general* partnership) and a proprietorship is that it is comprised of more than one person; there are *co*-owners. By law, this means that each owner is entitled to a say in the partnership's affairs and is entitled to have information about the partnership's business. Often, partners will agree to let one or more (but less than all) of the partners actually run the business. As to the outside world, however, each partner retains his or her right to run and to bind the partnership.

The main advantages of a partnership include its ease of formation and the greater resources it can command. Like a sole proprietorship, there are no organizational documents which require state approval. Unlike a sole proprietorship, however, it is very useful to have a written partnership agreement, that is, a contract between the partners setting out their various rights and responsibilities. This is because there is more than one owner and responsibilities are shared and rights divided.

Again, like a proprietorship, there is no intervening legal entity. The partners stand to gain or lose, in proportion to their partnership interest, from the success of the business, and are personally liable for its obligations. They also are taxed directly for their share of the partnership's income (even if it is not actually distributed to them but instead is reinvested in the business) and may be able to deduct partnership losses from their income from other sources. The partnership pays no taxes (although it does file a partnership information return on IRS Form 1065). It then sends a Form K1 to each partner setting out his or her share of the partnership profit or loss. The partner will transfer that information to Form K and submit it with his or her Form 1040.

This array of tax forms points out the need for good financial record keeping but, again, the relationship between the assets of the partnership and those of the partners is less clear than in a corporate situation. With a corporation, even a one-person corporation, there is a need to distinguish between corporate assets and those of the shareholder. The absence of this distinction, the commingling of funds, is one of the bases on which the protection offered the shareholder by the corporate existence may be lost.

People choose the partnership form for several reasons. As mentioned previously, a partnership is easier to establish and maintain than a corporation. No documents, meetings, or reports are required (although all may be recommended). On the other hand, more capital and resources may be available to a partnership than to a sole proprietor. However, the tax advantages formerly available especially to partnerships and proprietorships (primarily the pass-through of tax write-offs directly to partners or to the proprietor) have largely been made available to corporations through the liberalization of Subchapter S of the Internal Revenue Code (which will be discussed in Chapter 12).

Again, since the partnership is not recognized as a separate legal entity, its existence is limited to the retention of the original partners. If one should leave or a new partner enter, the partnership is said to have "dissolved" (although its business may continue as before). When the business itself terminates, it is said to have been "wound up" or "liquidated."

Finally, as a side note, the definition of a partnership calls for "a business for profit." Thus, by definition, there cannot be a nonprofit partnership.

LIMITED PARTNERSHIP

Section 1 of the Uniform Limited Partnership Act defines a limited partnership as "a partnership formed by two or more persons . . . having as members one or more general partners and one or more limited partners." The limited partnership is a device designed to bridge a gap between the tax benefits available to partners and the liability protection available to shareholders. Subject to the Tax Reform Act of 1986, partners can write off partnership losses against income from other sources but are personally liable for partnership obligations. Shareholders generally cannot write off corporate losses but *are* protected from corporate obligations. The limited partnership allows the *limited* partners to retain tax benefits by permitting some partnership losses to be written off against income from other sources *and* protects the limited partners from liability for partnership obligations.

In exchange for this obviously beneficial situation, the limited partner gives up his or her right to participate in the management of the partnership. This right is left to the general partner or partners who remain personally responsible for partnership liabilities. The limited partner becomes what is colloquially known as the "silent" partner. If a limited partner becomes actively involved in management, he or she forfeits the limited liability enjoyed by limited partners and becomes, at least for liability purposes, a general partner.

A limited partnership has other similarities to a corporation. For instance, it is created by a written document which must be filed with the state. This document is like the Articles of Incorporation for a corporation but is in addition to the partnership agreement which is typically signed by the partners.

Taxation is treated as with any other partnership. There is basically no taxable entity other than the partners themselves. It should be noted again, however, that much of the tax advantage that a limited partnership has over a corporation has been removed with the liberalization of Subchapter S of the Internal Revenue Code.

One remaining tax advantage of the limited partnership is that an S Corporation is limited to 35 or fewer shareholders whereas a limited partnership may have as many limited partners as desired. Thus businesses with a need for greater capital and a need to retain individual tax benefits may perfer the limited partnership route which permits more investors to be brought in than in the more restricted S Corporation. On the other hand, in the limited partnership there always must be at least one general partner and, as such, that partner has unlimited liability.*

The following chart sets out the presence or absence of various attributes and requirements in several business forms.

BUSINESS ASSOCIATIONS

	Sole Proprietorship	General Partnership	Limited Partnership	Corporation
Associates	No	Yes	Yes	Yes
Objectives to carry on a business	Yes	Yes	Yes	Yes
Continuity of life	No	No	Yes, as to the limited partners	Yes
Centralized management	No	No	Yes	Yes
Limited liability	No	No	Yes, as to the limited partners	Yes
Free transferability of interest	No	No	Yes, limited partners' interests in capital and profits	Yes
Legal documents required	No	No	Yes, limited partners'	Yes, Articles of Incorporation
Taxed as an entity	No	No	No	Yes, unless S Corporation

* Efforts to get around this problem by establishing a limited partnership with a lightly capitalized corporation as the sole general partner have not succeeded. The IRS has established an asset-based test concerning corporate general partners. If there are insufficient net assets in the corporation, the IRS will not issue an advance ruling indicating that it will recognize the organization as a partnership. The absence of such a ruling makes it extremely difficult for organizers to attract investors.

4

PREINCORPORATION ACTIVITIES AND INCORPORATION

The first event in a corporation's history is someone's idea to start it. Before going any further, the prospective organizers of a corporation should evaluate their plan and attempt to gauge its potential for success. If the organizers are thinking of a particular type of business, they should consider the success of similar businesses in the community and the need for another venture. (If nothing similar exists, they should ponder the need for the business in the first place.) If organizers decide that their idea has a chance of success, they may then want to begin preliminary planning and establishing business contacts.

PREINCORPORATION AGREEMENTS

Organizers frequently choose to impose additional obligations on themselves other than those owed to the corporation of good faith and fair dealing. Especially if they intend to control the corporation when it is eventually incorporated, organizers may want to enter into a preincorporation agreement to establish mutual commitments to be satisfied after the corporation is formally in existence. They may agree among themselves, in writing, as to who will act as the corporation's incorporators; who will serve on its first Board of Directors; who will purchase what types of stock, in what amounts, and for how much; or that corporate documents that have already been prepared will be adopted by the organizers when they become directors.

This type of preincorporation agreement is helpful to establish organizers' responsibilities and to chart steps to be taken following incorporation, but an agreement can also prove to be especially valuable as an incentive for organizers to fulfill their preincorporation promises.

In addition to agreeing among themselves, organizers may also enter into agreements with third parties on behalf of the corporation to be formed. Common examples include lease arrangements for space that the corporation will use when it begins business, equipment rental agreements, or agreements for the purchase of goods that the corporation plans to resell. Since some things cannot be arranged at the last minute, the organizers may find that they need to assure space, equipment, or merchandise for the corporation before the corporation really exists.

This is potentially awkward because the third party providing the goods or service is actually agreeing to perform for a nonexistent entity—the not-yet-formed corporation. If the corporation comes into being and adopts the contracts the organizers entered into on its behalf, no difficulty occurs. The new corporation, however, is not bound by its organizers' contracts, and should the corporation not be formed, or, once formed, decline to accept a contract entered into on its behalf by one of its organizers, a third party will want to recover money for the goods or services it provided or will want damages for breach of the contract. The question is—the contract with whom? The organizers or the corporation? Very often the answer will be that the contract is with the *organizers* and that they are personally liable for contracts they entered into on behalf of an unformed corporation.

In practical terms, this means that organizers should be cautious in contracting for a corporation before that corporation is formally in existence (i.e., before the appropriate state official has issued its Certificate of Incorporation). A preincorporation agreement among the organizers could provide some protection against this liability if the organizers intend to remain in control of the corporation after its incorporation (as shareholders, directors, and/or officers), if the preincorporation agreement obligates them, as directors, to support the adoption of the preincorporation contracts they arranged.

A more direct technique would be for promoters to have precise written agreements with all third parties they contract with on behalf of the prospective corporation. These contracts could state expressly:

1. The scope of the promoter's potential liability (complete, none, partial, etc.)

2. The promoter's rights and obligations under the contract (e.g., the right to approve the work performed, the obligation to use best efforts to form the corporation, commitment to vote for its adoption as a member of the Board, etc.)

3. The rights and obligations of the corporation (e.g., the right to approve the work performed, a requirement that it decide whether to accept the contract within a certain period of time, etc.)

4. What happens if the corporation is never formed (e.g., promoter liable, contract void)

5. What happens if the corporation is formed but declines to adopt the contract

6. What happens if the corporation ignores the contract

7. What happens if the corporation accepts benefits under the contract

8. An express statement that the corporation is not then in existence

9. A disclaimer of any implied agreements in addition to the terms stated in the contract

PREINCORPORATION SHARE SUBSCRIPTIONS

Another possible preincorporation event is a preincorporation share subscription. This occurs when people (including the organizers) agree to purchase stock in an as-yet unformed corporation. Because the corporation does not exist and the shares are not yet issued, a preincorporation subscription is a continuing offer to the corporation (conveyed by the organizers) to buy a certain amount of its stock. An offer to subscribe for shares is irrevocable (by the person wishing to buy stock) for a period of six months unless otherwise provided in the subscription agreement or unless there is unanimous shareholder consent to the revocation of the agreement by the subscriber (Section 17 of the Model Business Corporation Act). That is, the corporation has six months from the time of the offer to accept it, and the person making the offer may not withdraw it unless he or she *expressly states* at the time of making the offer that it is only open for a specified period of time.

Organizers should require that all share subscriptions be in writing, in order to establish firmly each offer and its details, such as the number of shares to be purchased and the price to be paid.

In a small corporation, the organizers could use a contract for a share subscription as a device to prearrange corporate ownership. As part of the preincorporation agreement, the organizers could promise to subscribe for amounts of stock representing each organizer's agreed future shareholding in the corporation. Working out this agreement may help determine how corporate interests will be distributed, and the contract's existence may help to preserve that allocation in the event of later squabbling.

INCORPORATION

Obviously one of the first things the organizers must decide is what their corporation will do. A corporation organized for any lawful purpose other than banking or insurance may be incorporated under Section 3 of the Model Business Corporation Act. Thus the statute allows a vast array of activities.

Organizers must also decide on a corporate name. The name must include the words "corporation," "company," "incorporated," "limited," or an abbreviation of one of them. This requirement is imposed so that people who are not familiar with the corporation are on notice that they are dealing with an entity in which no individual may be held personally liable if the business is unable to pay debts (Section 8 of the Act).

The corporate name may not inaccurately describe what the corporation does and, to avoid confusion, the name of a new corporation may not closely resemble the name of another corporation that does business in the same jurisdiction.

If organizers have any doubt about whether the corporate name they have selected is acceptable, or if they merely want to reserve the name for 120 days so that no one else may claim it, they may file an Application for Reservation of Corporate Name with the appropriate state official. The official will notify the corporate organizers if the name is available and, if so, that it will be reserved for 120 days (Section 9 of the Act).

The next document to be filed is the corporation's Articles of Incorporation. The Articles must be signed by at least one "incorporator" and "duplicate originals," that is, two fully signed copies must be sent or delivered to the Secretary of State or other designated official, along with the statutory filing fee.

The charge for filing and indexing the Articles varies from state to state. The amount can be ascertained by checking the state's statute or by writing to the Secretary of State. In addition, an initial fee is generally imposed for each authorized share of stock. You should check with the state filing office to verify current fees before submitting Articles of Incorporation or other corporate documents for filing.

Within several days to several weeks the corporation will receive from the filing office a Certificate of Incorporation. When this Certificate is issued, the corporation's existence officially begins.

5

FINANCIAL STRUCTURE

A business corporation may obtain money to finance its operations by issuing interests in itself which are generally known as securities. This term is used to describe all types of interests that a corporation may create in itself and offer for sale. There is nothing necessarily *secure* about a security; the term here refers to an interest or an investment in a corporation.

Securities are of two basic types: debt securities and equity securities (in fact, there are many types of securities, often being anything but basic). "Debt securities" are so called because the corporation is considered to be in debt to the person who holds this type of interest; the person has lent the corporation money and eventually the corporation will have to pay it back—with interest. An "equity security" creates no debt relationship. When a person purchases an equity security, he or she is not lending money to the corporation, but is considered to be acquiring an ownership stake in the business.

DEBT SECURITIES

A debt security generally is created when the corporation (through its Board of Directors) decides that it will attempt to borrow money, from individuals, institutions, or the public. Typical sources of borrowed money are the corporation's organizers (or their families) or a bank. If the money is lent to the corporation by such individuals or institutions, the corporation will issue its note (one form of debt security) to the lender. If, on the other hand, the corporation hopes to borrow from members of the general public, it will issue and offer for sale to the public (usually through a broker) debt securities known either as bonds or debentures (which are basically the same except that a bond is secured by particular property of the debtor while the debenture is unsecured indebtedness). These securities are issued in face amounts of generally $1,000 each. If the bond is sold for more than its face value, it is said to be "issued at a premium." If sold for less than the face value, it is "issued at a discount." Like other evidence of indebtedness, bonds have a maturity date, a specified time when the corporation must pay back the face value of the bond to its holder. The face value is the principal amount owed by the corporation. But a bond costs the corporation more than merely repaying the principal amount for the use of an investor's money. The corporation will also periodically pay a fixed interest charge, calculated as a percentage of the face value of the bond.

Debt securities come in various forms. For instance, mortgage bonds are one type of debt security where the bondholders have a mortgage on the corporation's property. If the corporation fails to pay its obligations, the bondholders may foreclose their mortgage and claim the corporation's property to the extent necessary to satisfy its debt to them.

Unlike a mortgage bond, a debenture is a simple type of debt security; there is no property to which the holder of a debenture has any special claim if the corporation should fail to pay its obligations on the debenture. Debenture holders, and other holders of unsecured debt securities, are instead considered to be "general creditors" (as opposed to "secured creditors") of the corporation.

Status as a corporate *creditor* is one of the important features of a debt security. It means that if the business should fail, the holders of the corporation's bonds may take whatever property secures the bonds. Other creditors (note or debenture holders) then have first claim to the corporation's remaining assets in order to satisfy sums owed to them. The holders of equity securities (stock) are left to divide whatever is left, if anything.

This preferential claim to corporate assets makes bonds an attractive, if conservative, investment. Therefore, issuing debt securities may be one device whereby a small business can make itself more attractive to outside investors who want steady income and less risk. It also keeps voting control of the corporation in the hands of the organizers, since debt holders, as such, are generally not entitled to vote.

The corporation could make a bond even more desirable by promising bondholders that the corporation will take certain steps to insure that corporate assets will be retained and available to satisfy payments due to bondholders. For instance, the corporation could agree to limit total corporate debts, reasonably restrict dividend payments to keep a certain amount of funds always on hand, create a special corporate reserve to pay bond obligations, limit issuance of additional bonds, or restrain the corporation from incurring any *secured* debts which would have a preferential claim to corporate assets above existing bondholders.

As mentioned previously, bonds usually pay a fixed amount of interest per year; for example, $8\frac{3}{4}\%$ on a \$5,000 bond would entitle its holder to payments of \$437.50 each year. The corporation has an obligation to pay this interest regardless of its profits or losses for that year. This is in contrast to dividends on equity securities which may or may not be paid or not (as determined by the corporation's Board of Directors) even though the corporation has sufficient funds to make a distribution.

A corporation may, however, make its obligation to pay any interest conditional on its making a certain profit, and the amount of interest paid could be made dependent on the amount of profits. For instance, in the first case, the corporation would be required to pay the stated interest only to the extent that it had profits with which to make such payments. In the second instance, the corporation would be obliged to pay a fixed rate of interest, say $8\frac{3}{4}\%$, and up to an additional 4% of its earnings if it had sufficient earnings to cover the obligatory interest payment and any portion of the additional 4% payment.

Whatever the terms of payment, they should be expressed in the bond instrument. This will insure that owners of the bond have notice of its terms of payment and cannot insist on other, more favorable terms.

At a predetermined date, the corporation must pay the bondholder the principal amount of the bond, for example, \$5,000 on January 1, 2000. When a corporation is profitable it may wish to pay off its bondholders before that date. This may be done with corporate funds or by issuing new bonds at a rate more favorable to the corporation. In order to be able to do this, the corporation must include a "redemption" provision in the original bond instrument. This provision will state that the corporation has the right to buy back the bond at a certain price, usually a figure in excess of the face value.

As an additional feature to attract investors, bonds may be made "convertible;" that is, the holder of the bond is given an option to exchange it for another type of bond or for types of equity securities. Bonds that are convertible should state that they are convertible, what they may be converted into, when and at what price they may be converted, and so forth. Convertibility is considered a desirable investment feature because the bondholder has a relatively safe investment that he or she may convert into a specified different interest if that new interest becomes more attractive.

EQUITY SECURITIES

The other type of corporate security is an equity security, known as shares or stock in a corporation. Stock is called an equity security because stockholders are considered to be the *owners* of the corporation.

Shares are a function of the wishes of the organizers and of the Articles of Incorporation. A corporation's Articles must state the number of shares and the characteristics of the corporation's stock. When the Articles are approved, the corporation may "issue" all or a portion of its authorized stock. To issue stock is actually to offer shares of stock for sale. The corporation's Board of Directors may control when and to whom the corporation's shares are offered and sold. When issued shares are actually purchased they are known as the outstanding stock and the purchaser is known as a shareholder or stockholder.

Before the corporation authorizes stock in its Articles, the organizers must decide on the types of stock they feel are appropriate for their corporation. There are several choices. Shares may be with or without "par value." They may have preferences over other classes of shares or may be common shares. These terms and their importance must be understood in the planning of a corporation.

Stock may have a par value or may be of "no par value." "Par value" is an *arbitrary* value per share assigned in the Articles of Incorporation, and does not necessarily reflect the true market value of the stock. Because the law is that par value shares may not be issued and sold by the corporation for less than their par value, it is advisable for the corporation to set a par value lower than the estimated market value of the shares (Section 18 of the Model Business Corporation Act). (Once the stock is sold by a corporation to a shareholder, sales by that shareholder to any other person may occur at whatever price the parties deem appropriate, even if it is less than par.)

No par stock allows the Board of Directors (or the shareholders if the Articles of Incorporation have granted them the power) to decide, each time shares are issued, what the price per share will be. Since there is no par value attached to the shares, they may be sold without any restriction on sales price. The Board (or the shareholders) thus has more flexibility to adjust the stock's selling price to reflect the corporation's success or lack of it. (In a very large corporation, the stock might be traded on a public exchange such as the New York Stock Exchange, in which case the public demand, and not the Board, would determine the selling price of the stock.)

Despite the arbitrary nature of par or stated value, the concept has some very practical significance. First, and most basically, if stock is sold for less than par or stated value, the purchaser of those shares may be liable, to the corporation or to its creditors, for the difference between what was paid and what should have been paid.

The second practical consequence is more subtle. The par or stated value is used to determine the corporation's "capital account." This account, which is really only an entry in the books of the corporation, is determined by multiplying the par or stated value of the corporation's stock by the number of shares outstanding. For example: if the corporation had sold 1000 shares of stock which had a $10 par value, the capital account would be $10,000.

If no par shares are issued, the total amount received from their sale is the corporation's "stated capital." However, prior to issuance of no par shares, the Board of Directors may pass a resolution declaring that only a portion of the money received for shares will constitute the corporation's "stated capital" and that the remaining sum will be deemed "capital surplus."

The importance of these accounts is mainly in relation to the payment of dividends. Although Section 45 of the Model Act permits dividends only out of earned surplus (retained earnings) or out of recent profits (even if there is no accumulated and retained earnings), most states provide for a different formula. In those situations, the corporation may pay a dividend so long as the capital account is not "impaired" or will not be impaired by virtue of the distribution. What this means is that a corporation may pay a dividend if the value of its net assets (i.e., its total assets minus its total liabilities) is greater than the amount of its capital account (par value times outstanding shares). If net assets are less than the capital account, no dividend may be paid.

To illustrate the point, assume Corporation X has 1000 shares outstanding at $10 par value. The capital account is $10,000. Assume also that the corporation has $50,000 worth of assets and $25,000 worth of liabilities. Since its net assets ($50,000 − $25,000 = $25,000) exceed the capital account ($25,000 − $10,000 = $15,000) a dividend of up to $15,000 could be declared. If, alternatively, the corporation's liabilities were $45,000 the net assets would be only $5,000. Since this is *less* than the amount of capital account, no dividend at all could be paid.

In those states which permit dividends when net assets exceed the capital account, the excess assets could come from retained earnings (which is the basic test under the Model Act for the legality of dividends) or from a capital *surplus* account (as distinguished from the capital account). We have already discussed the fact that stock may not be issued by the corporation for less than its par or stated value. What happens, however, if it is issued for *more* than par or stated value? For instance, shares of Corporation X have a par value of $1.00 but are sold for $10. From a bookkeeping point of view, $1.00 per share would be recorded in the capital account book while $9 per share would be recorded in the capital *surplus* account book. From an operational point of view, the entire $10 per share may be placed in the corporation's bank account and spent (even the $1 per share in the capital account) for corporate purposes. It is only when the net assets fall below the amount in the capital account book that *dividends* are prohibited.

In addition to distinctions of par and no par value, stock may be divided into different "classes" (Section 16 of the Model Act). For instance, it is possible to create one or more classes of stock whose holders have a preference in receiving dividends before holders of other classes of stock. That is, if the Board of Directors decides to distribute a portion of the corporation's profits to shareholders, the preferred shareholders receive their dividends first (in the order of their preference) and the other shareholders receive their share from the distributable profits remaining after each higher preference has been paid (though the holders of debt securities will be entitled to their payments before any shareholder, and regardless of the corporation's financial condition).

The payment to preferred shareholders is generally a constant amount, phrased as "a preference of $ ＿＿ per share" or "a preference of ＿＿ % of par value." Thus in a year in which the corporation is very profitable, there may be substantial profits remaining to be distributed to nonpreferred shareholders (known as common shareholders).

Preferred shares may possess other attractive characteristics in addition to their payment preference. The corporation may create "cumulative" preferred stock, where the corporation is obligated to pay the shareholder a fixed payment each year. If the dividend is not paid in any year (due to a lack of income from which to distribute dividends or, even if the income is available to pay a dividend, due to a decision by the Board that it would be better to retain the money for corporate purposes rather than distribute it as a dividend) it accumulates, and the aggregate amount of accumulated unpaid dividends must be paid in full to the holders of cumulative preferred stock before the corporation may pay dividends to the holders of other types of stock with a lower preference.

A variation on cumulative preferred stock is "cumulative to the extent earned" shares. The payments on these shares accumulate only to the extent that the corporation had profits from which it could legally have paid dividends, and the holders of these shares are not entitled to dividends from years in which the corporation had no profits to distribute.

Preferred stock may also be "participating." If it is (as determined by the Articles of Incorporation), shareholders receive their preferential distributions and then, when all preferences have been paid, are allowed to share with the holders of common stock in the pool of money remaining. This can be very advantageous, since the preferred shareholders get a constant payment and then a second opportunity to share in corporate profits. It is possible to curtail this benefit by specifying that the common and preferred stockholders divide the profits remaining after the first fixed payment to the preferred shareholders on a $2:1$, $3:1$, $4:1$, and so forth basis, in order to assure the common stockholders the better portion of the remaining profits. Of course, preferred stock need not be participating and would only be made so if the organizers felt it was necessary in order to be able to sell the preferred stock to investors.

Stock that does not possess a dividend preference is known as common stock. Common stock generally is the base of all shareholder power. It typically includes the broadest (often the only) voting rights and the potential for the largest financial gains (although it is also the least secure of the various investments one may make in a corporation).

As with preferred stock, the corporation is not required to distribute its profits to common stockholders, but when the Board of Directors exercises its discretion to distribute profits, the amount available for common stockholders' dividends is determined only after preferred shareholders, if any, have received their distributions. The common stock dividend is usually phrased in the form of "$ ____ per share," and is established by the Board rather than by the Articles. The Board of Directors, in its discretion, may vary the amount from time to time, for instance, taking account of the funds available for distribution as opposed to the corporation's need to retain the money.

In addition to the distinctions between preferred and common stock, stock may also be classified according to other characteristics (Section 16 of the Model Act). In the event of a corporate liquidation (when the corporation winds up its operations and distributes its assets, or their value in cash, to its shareholders), one or more classes of stock may be given a preference in the distribution of the corporation's assets (or their value). One class could be granted the exclusive right to receive all the assets. All classes could be allowed to divide them equally, or a class (or classes) could be granted a preference—a right to receive a certain value before the holders of any other class of stock receive any payments in liquidation.

Voting rights may also differ among classes. One class may be given the exclusive right to vote at shareholder meetings for the election of the corporation's Board of Directors. Other classes could be empowered to vote only on extraordinary corporate matters such as merger or dissolution, or all classes could be given equal and complete voting rights. Many corporations do not give voting rights to preferred shareholders. This may be in recognition that preferred shareholders receive preferential distributions of the corporation's earnings, while the size of distributions to common stockholders depend on the size of the corporation's profit and thus are tied more closely to the skill of the corporation's management. It may seem appropriate, therefore, that the common stockholders are the group responsible for selecting that management.

Classes of stock may also be made "convertible" into stock of another class; that is, the shareholder has the option to swap his or her shares, at a predetermined ratio set in the Articles, for shares of another class of stock or, perhaps, for a bond (Section 18 of the Model Act).

Classes of stock are also divisible into "series" (Section 16 of the Model Act). Shares of a class may be divided into and issued in a series as provided in the corporation's Articles of Incorporation or as authorized in the Articles with the details established by a resolution of the Board of Directors. Different series could pay dividends at different rates, have different redemption rights, terms, and prices, possess varying provisions for liquidation payments, or be convertible at different ratios. For instance, Class A preferred stock may have voting rights and exclusive liquidation privileges. There may be Class A Series A, and Class A Series B, which differ in that Series A pays twice the rate of dividends as Series B.

Whatever the organizers' choices as to the types of shares that the corporation will issue, each share certificate representing stock should state the precise characteristics of the stock it represents. This provides each shareholder with clear notice of the rights, duties, and characteristics of the shares he or she owns.

THE CHOICE BETWEEN ISSUING DEBT OR EQUITY

A small business corporation almost certainly will not utilize all the security interests that have been described. Nevertheless, corporate organizers should consider the characteristics of all types of securities and then select the features most appropriate for their financial needs and anticipated corporate structure. For instance, if the organizers intend to remain in charge of the corporation, they should arrange to control the stock possessing the power to select the corporation's

Board of Directors (which, in turn, is empowered to select the corporation's officers).

If there is a need for more investment than the organizers alone can provide, preferred stock with a good dividend and/or liquidation preference may attract outside investors. Assuming these shares carry no voting rights, they may be issued without diminishing the organizers' control of the corporation's Board.

Bonds also may be attractive conservative investments, and holders of debt securities generally have no say in the management of the corporation's affairs. Debt securities can be complicated, however, and for small business, may be very difficult to sell to outsiders. An easier alternative is probably to seek long-term loans from a local bank or an individual.

Why should a corporation want to go into debt when it can issue such an attractive variety of equity interests, and thus raise the money it needs through equity financing? Surprisingly, there are certain advantages to debt.

When a corporation pays *interest* to the holders of its debt securities, it may take a tax deduction in the amount of interest paid, and thereby reduce its taxable income. (Internal Revenue Code, Section 163(a).) On the other hand, it may not take deductions for dividends paid to its shareholders.

This favorable aspect of debt securities invites corporations to take advantage of them, particularly when the shareholders are also the lenders. As might be guessed, though, there are restrictions on the tax benefits available through disproportionate debt financing. When the ratio of total debt to total equity exceeds 4 : 1, for example, the corporation is $4,000 in debt which is owed to the shareholders and has issued only $1,000 in shares, the IRS may regard the debt as a disguised form of stock and attempt to disallow the corporation's tax deductions for "interest" payments. A corporation may try to avoid such a disallowance if it stays a healthy margin away from the 4 : 1 borderline.

There is another advantage to debt financing which is known as "leverage." In an economic sense, this means using borrowed money to finance the business. If the company does well, the leveraged financing can significantly increase the rate of return the owners get on their equity investment.

Assume a business requires $100,000 to get started and the organizers put in a full $100,000 out of their own pockets. Also, assume the business's operations net a $20,000 profit in the first year. The organizers' rate of return is 20% (they received $20,000 profit on a $100,000 investment).

If, in the same situation, they had used leverage, the results are much more dramatic. Assume that instead of putting in the full

$100,000 out of their pockets, they put in only $20,000 and were able to borrow the remaining $80,000. They conduct their business with the same total cash input, $100,000, and they make the same profit, $20,000. This time, however, they have an additional expense, the interest on the borrowed money. Assume for simplicity's sake that they borrowed at 10% per year. This would result in an interest charge (tax deductible) of $8,000 (10% of $80,000) per year. When the $8,000 is subtracted from the $20,000, a net profit of $12,000 remains.

At first glance, this looks less favorable than the $20,000 earned without borrowing. On closer examination, however, it is clear that the $12,000 was earned on an equity investment—by the organizers—of only $20,000. This works out to a 60% rate of return, far higher than the 20% rate in the absence of leverage.

Thus in many cases where the organizers are able to put in the full amount needed, they *choose* not to. Assume the organizers had $100,000 cash. On a leveraged basis as described in the example, they could buy five companies worth $100,000 each or a larger company worth $500,000. In each case, they would put in 20% of the needed cash and borrow the rest.

Nevertheless, there are serious drawbacks to leverage. The first is practical. The organizers of a new business cannot always find people or institutions willing to lend them or their business the needed money. If the loans are available, they may be at high interest, carry heavy collateral, and/or require the personal guarantees of the organizers. Any of these factors could put a damper on leveraging.

The second drawback is financial. Just as leverage can increase the rate of return when the company does well, it can be devastating when the company does not do well.

Using our original example, assume the corporation makes only $5,000 profit. If the organizers put in the full $100,000, they still have a 5% rate of return. If they borrowed the $80,000, they still must pay the interest of $8,000, which not only wipes out their profit of $5,000 but creates a $3,000 actual (as opposed to paper) loss.

SELLING SECURITIES

When a corporation sells its bonds or stock, it is subject to certain requirements concerning the value it must receive and the type of payment it may accept for their sale.

As mentioned previously, par value stock may not be sold by the corporation for less than its par value; however, once a shareholder has purchased stock from the corporation, he or she may sell it to a third party for whatever price he or she wishes. On the other hand, the purchase price of no par stock, when initially sold by the corporation, is generally set by the Board of Directors (or the shareholders if the Articles of Incorporation has given them this power) and may be adjusted from time to time (as with par value stock, once a shareholder purchases no par stock from a corporation, he or she may sell it for whatever price he or she can obtain). No par stock may not be sold by the corporation for *less* than the stated value assigned to it by the Board. However, since the Board sets that stated value at the time of the sale, this should never be a problem.

Whatever the selling price, the corporation is restricted as to the payment it may accept in the sale. For stock or bonds, it may receive only money, property, or services actually rendered to it. "Money" means cash, including a check. "Property" could be tangible physical property (land, machinery, a car, etc.), or could be intangible property (stock in another corporation, patent rights, etc.); however, "property" does not include a promissory note. "Services" refers to services that have already been performed (not a promise to perform future services) for the *corporation* (generally *not* preincorporation services).

When the corporation receives property or services in exchange for its stock, the Board of Directors has a duty to ascertain the value of the property or services and to determine that the corporation is receiving something of value at least equal to the par or stated value of the stock which will be issued for it. If the value of the property is less than the aggregate par or stated value, the stock is said to be "watered," and if the corporation should ever be unable to pay its creditors, the holders of watered stock may be liable to the creditors for the corporation's debts to the extent that their shares are watered (Section 25 of the Model Act). For example, if land worth $25,000 is exchanged for stock having a par or stated value of $100,000, the shareholder receiving that stock could be liable for up to $75,000 in corporate debts.

This situation can be avoided if the Board of Directors (or the shareholders, if they are responsible for fixing the price of shares), carefully evaluates the value of property or services received for the corporation's stock. If the Board determines in good faith and without fraud that the consideration received is equal to the value of the stock, that stock would not be considered "watered" even if it ultimately turns out that the Board was wrong in its valuation (Section 19 of the Model Act).

An additional question of corporate finance is that of shareholders' "preemptive rights." This is a shareholder's right to purchase new shares (of the same class as he or she currently holds or of securities convertible into such shares) being issued by the corporation, before such shares are offered to other purchasers (Section 26(a) of the Model

Act). The right allows the shareholder to buy shares from the new issue in proportion to his or her present holdings of that class of corporate stock. For example, Jane Doe holds one-fourth of the common stock of Corporation X. Corporation X is planning to issue 1000 new shares of such stock. Therefore Doe has a right to buy 250 (1/4 of 1000) shares before they may be offered to others. If Doe does not have money to purchase the shares, or does not want more shares of stock, the corporation is then free to offer the shares to others.

Preemptive rights are controlled by statute. Some states require preemptive rights while some states prohibit them. Other states leave it up to the Articles, with formulations such as "there shall be preemptive rights unless the Articles state the contrary" or "there shall *not* be preemptive rights unless the Articles state the contrary."

6

DIVIDENDS

A key feature of a business corporation is its ability to issue shares of stock and to distribute corporate earnings and profits to the holders of these shares. Such distributions are known as dividends. Business corporations are authorized to pay dividends, but may do so only pursuant to statutory guidelines (Section 45 of the Model Business Corporation Act). Even where it is legally permissible for dividends to be paid, the decision whether to distribute them or to retain profits is within the reasonable discretion of the corporation's Board of Directors. Dividends are not mandatory simply because they are legally possible. There may be other important uses for the corporation's profits which persuade the Board against a distribution. The Board, however, may not unreasonably withhold dividends from the corporation's shareholders.

TYPES OF DIVIDENDS

A corporation may distribute three types of dividends: (1) a cash dividend, which is a payment of money—in cash or by check; (2) a stock or share dividend, which is a distribution of additional shares of stock in the corporation itself—usually a fraction of the stock already held by each shareholder (e.g., for every 10 shares of stock already owned, a dividend of one additional share is declared)—which may be the same or of a different class or series than the stock already owned by the shareholder; or (3) a property dividend, which is one other than a cash or stock dividend and could include a distribution of tangible property such as the corporation's inventory or portions of its land, or it could consist of shares of stock in another corporation.

FINANCIAL CONSIDERATIONS

Regardless of the type of dividend the corporation would like to distribute, it may not distribute dividends if it is insolvent, or, in some jurisdictions, if its net assets are less than its stated capital. In any case, it may not distribute an amount which would render the corporation insolvent or, in the stricter jurisdictions, reduce its net assets below its stated capital (Section 45 of the Model Act).

The concept of "insolvency" is relatively simple. "Insolvent" means that the corporation is unable to pay its debts as they become due in the usual course of its business. Therefore, a corporation may not pay dividends if it cannot pay its debts or if the payment of dividends would render it unable to pay its debts.

The concept of "stated capital" is more difficult. It means: (1) the par value of all shares outstanding having a par value, and (2) the value received by the corporation for all shares without par value, except any part thereof which the Board of Directors has elected to allocate to the corporation's "capital surplus." For example: Corporation X issues 1000 shares of Class A common stock which the Articles of Incorporation specify shall have a par value of $1.00 each. X also issues 1000 shares of Class B common stock, of no par value, but with respect to which the Board of Directors resolved that 50 cents received from the sale of each share should be allocated to the corporation's stated capital with any remaining money received allocated to capital surplus. Both classes of stock are then sold for $1.00 each.

The account books would have entries which look something like this.

	Stated Capital	Capital Surplus
Class A	$1,000	—
Class B	$ 500	$500
	$1,500	$500

Corporation X may take the $2,000 received and use it to finance its business operations; however, it may not pay dividends to its stockholders if it does not have "net assets" worth at least $1,500, or if the payment of dividends would reduce its net assets below the value of $1,500. Net assets means the value of the corporation's assets (property, cash, and so forth) minus the amount of its liabilities. Thus the corporation must have money or property in excess of its liabilities when added to the amount of its stated capital if it wants to pay dividends. If the corporation is successful and makes profits, this requirement should pose no problem.

When paying a property dividend, a corporation is considered to be making a distribution equal to the current value of the property it is distributing. With share dividends, the amount corresponding to the par value of par value shares, or the stated capital value of no par shares, is the value of the dividend. In either case, the corporation must have net assets sufficient to cover the amount of its stated capital *plus* the value of the distribution. Also, after a share dividend is distributed, the corporation's capital account is increased by the par (or stated capital) value of the shares making up the dividend, while one of its surplus accounts is reduced by the same amount.

Any director who is present at a Board of Directors' meeting and who votes to distribute a dividend that violates these restrictions may be liable to the corporation for the portion of the dividend in excess of the amount that properly could have been distributed. A director may avoid this liability if he or she enters his or her dissent to an improper dividend distribution decision in the minutes of the Board meeting, files a written dissent at the end of such meeting, or after the meeting promptly mails a written dissent to the Secretary of the corporation. This does not allow a director to *change* his or her vote after the decision has become final, however. A director also will not be held liable if he or she voted for the dividend in good faith, relying in determining the propriety of the dividend on a balance sheet asserted to be correct by the corporation's President, Treasurer, or a certified public accountant.

Where directors are subject to liability, they are said to be "jointly and severally liable." This means that any one director who voted for the distribution may be held liable for the entire amount of an improper distribution, or that all directors who voted in favor of it may be held collectively liable. If any director is found liable for an amount greater than his or her pro rata share, however, he or she may sue the other directors to cause them to contribute their portions of the total amount (Section 48 of the Model Act).

STOCK SPLITS

Since dividends are an important attribute of a business corporation and improper dividends (or the improper withholding of dividends) can result in substantial liabilities for corporate directors, it is important for organizers to understand the legalities in this area. It is an area that calls for caution. If any difficult questions arise, especially if there are dissident shareholders, it would be wise to consult an attorney or accountant.

It is also wise to remember that the legalities are only one of many considerations in dividend policy. There are also questions of business judgment (Is a distribution of cash in line with the business needs of the corporation at this time?) and practical realities (Do the shareholders expect a distribution now and what action will they take if it is not made?).

There are, in addition, tax consequences to a distribution (or non-distribution) of cash dividends. Dividends distributed to shareholders are taxed to those shareholders at their marginal tax rate. This imposes a second tax on corporate earnings. For example, assume Corporation X had $100,000 of taxable income (which, for this example, we will assume is equivalent to its profit for the year). This amount would be taxed at the corporation's normal tax rates (15% of the first $50,000, 25% of the next $25,000, and 34% for amounts over $75,000). This would leave the corporation with $77,750 of post tax income (profit). The Board decides to distribute $25,000 of this amount to its shareholders. Shareholder A receives $1,000 of this distribution. Assume A is a 28% taxpayer. This $1,000 will be taxed to the shareholder at 28% leaving A with $720 ($1,000 − $280). This scenario would be repeated for each shareholder, thus reducing the amount left in his or her hands. Remember, this same pool of money—the corporation's profits (from which this distribution came)—was first taxed at the corporate level. At the shareholder level it is taxed a second time. (See Chapter 11 for a further discussion.)

In addition to dividends, a corporation may make another type of distribution to its shareholders through a "stock split" whereby the corporation splits each share of stock into a larger number of shares, usually in order to lower the price per share and thus make its shares more marketable. For example, Jane Doe holds 10 shares, then selling for $40 each. The corporation decides that it will split its stock at a 4 : 1 ratio. After the split, Doe has 40 shares, (i.e., 4 x 10) worth $10.00 each. The total value of her holdings has not changed (10 shares @ $40 each was worth $400; 40 shares @ $10 each is still worth $400). Neither has her relative position of ownership changed. Assume there were originally 100 shares outstanding. Her 10 shares represent 10% ownership.

If all those shares are split 4 to 1, she now owns 40 shares of the 400 outstanding, still a 10% interest.

Because a stock split is only a process whereby the same corporate interests are represented by a greater number of shares, the problems of calculating stated capital and the needs for a reserve of net assets or cash are not present. A corporation generally may split its stock regardless of its financial condition.

7

CONSIDERATIONS OF CORPORATE CONTROL

As mentioned in Chapter 2, a corporation is basically a three-tiered creation consisting of shareholders, directors, and officers. Each of these groups possesses unique characteristics which can be important when corporate organizers are shaping their organization's management structure.

SHAREHOLDERS

A corporation "authorizes" the issuance of its stock in its Articles of Incorporation. Its Board of Directors then determines how many shares of stock will be offered for sale. When these shares are purchased they comprise the corporation's "issued and outstanding" stock. For example: Corporation X, in its Articles of Incorporation, is authorized to issue 10,000 shares of stock at $10 par value. It decides that it does not need the full $100,000 which it would receive if all the shares were sold, but that it does need $50,000 to begin business.*

* It is important to keep in mind here that a corporation may sell its stock for *more* than its par value (although it may not sell it for less). We have equated the par value and sale price in this example merely for convenience.

Therefore, the Board of Directors votes to offer for sale only 5000 of the 10,000 shares. When purchased, these 5000 shares are the corporation's "issued and outstanding" stock.

Especially in a small corporation, shareholders have a potentially significant role in corporate management—the election of the corporation's Board of Directors. The Board determines corporate policy and selects the officers who carry out this policy on a day-to-day basis. Shareholder power to remove directors, adopt and revise corporate documents, and to ratify extraordinary corporate events such as merger, consolidation, or dissolution may be reiterated in the corporation's Articles or Bylaws. Shareholders may also be granted additional which powers involve them more intimately in the management of the corporation.

Unless the Articles of Incorporation provide otherwise, each share of stock possesses one vote. Organizers may want to deviate from that arrangement, however, in order to protect or accommodate particular aspects or needs of the corporation. For instance, to prevent an excessive concentration of voting power, the Articles could take the drastic step of providing that no individual may own more than a certain number of shares or a certain percentage of the corporation's voting stock, or that despite the number of shares a stockholder owns, he or she is limited in number of votes he or she may cast. In order to implement a restriction of this type effectively, it is advisable that all the shareholders execute a shareholders' agreement containing the limitation and that such restriction also be noted on each of the corporation's share certificates. This will discourage any shareholder from making a transfer which would result in a prohibited accumulation of shares. It would also put any buyer of the shares on notice of the restriction.

Cumulative Voting

Another device used to affect voting rights is "cumulative voting." Many states' statutes require or permit this concept for the election of directors while some states prohibit it (Section 33 of the Model Act). This type of voting is basically a protection for minority stockholders and provides each share with as many votes as there are vacancies on the Board to be filled. The shareholder may distribute these votes among candidates as he or she sees fit. This allows the holders of minority share interests to cumulate their votes in their attempt to elect representatives (although not a majority) on the Board. For example, assume Jane Doe owns 10 shares of stock and there are five positions on the Board to be filled. With cumulative voting, Doe would have 50 votes which she may cast however she chooses.

For instance, if Doe owned 10 shares and Mary Smith owned the remaining 15 shares of a 25-share corporation, Smith would, in the absence of cumulative voting, always elect the entire Board. If there were five directors to be elected, she would cast her 15 votes for each of her five choices while Doe casts her 10 for each of her five choices. *With* cumulative voting, however, Doe would have 50 votes and Smith 75 (15 shares times five directors to be elected). The important feature is that Doe can use her 50 votes however she chooses. Therefore, she might cast 25 each for only two candidates. If she does this, she is assured of electing two Board members because no matter how Smith divides her votes, she *cannot* mathematically have more than three people with as many or more votes than Doe's two people. If she gave any candidate 26 votes, she would have only 49 left for remaining candidates. If she gave a second candidate 26 votes, she would have only 23 votes left. Doe's two candidates would *have* to be among the top five vote getters. Of course, Doe could miscalculate and give a greater number of candidates fewer votes each, but if she does so she minimizes her choices for representation on the Board.

Algebra has produced a formula for maximizing representation. That formula is:

$$X = \frac{(S \times N)}{D + 1} + 1$$

where X equals the number of shares needed to elect a certain number of directors

S equals the total number of shares which will be voting (in person or by proxy) in the election

N equals the number of directors a shareholder wishes to elect

D equals the total number of directors to be elected in the particular election

Plugging the numbers in our hypothetical situation into this formula, we see that the number of shares Doe needs to elect two directors is:

$$X = \frac{25 \times 2}{5 + 1} + 1$$

$$\text{or} \quad X = \frac{50}{6} + 1$$

$$\text{or} \quad X = 9.3$$

Since Doe has 10 shares, she can elect her two directors. If she wished to elect three directors, the formula would indicate the impossibility unless Smith misapplied her votes. To elect three directors a shareholder would need

$$\frac{25 \times 3}{5 + 1} + 1$$

$$\text{or} \quad \frac{75}{6} + 1$$

$$\text{or} \quad 13.5$$

shares, more than Doe controls.

It is important to remember that cumulative voting, if available at all, is *only* used for the election of directors and not for other issues which may be brought before the shareholders for a vote.

Classes of Shares

If a corporation has more than one class of stock, its Articles may provide for "class voting." In class voting, each class of shares votes separately and elects representatives to the Board of Directors. For instance: Class A, Class B, and Class C stock are held, respectively, by the three organizers of the corporation. Since each class has the exclusive right to elect one member of the Board, each organizer is assured that he or she will always have a seat on the Board of Directors. This is *class voting for directors*—to be distinguished from *classes of directors*. The latter means that some directors have different powers or varying terms of service, and so forth.

Another use of class voting is to allow a certain class to elect proportionately more directors than another class. For instance, the organizers might want to provide Class A stock with rights to elect seven directors out of an 11-person Board, with Class B electing the remaining four directors. This could be true even if there were more Class B shares than Class A. If the organizers want to insure that they retain managerial control, all they need do is buy a majority of the Class A stock, thus assuring the election by them of a majority of the Board. Of course, if capital must be raised by the sale of shares to outsiders, the outsiders' willingness to invest in a situation such as we have described is a consideration. The shares must be made marketable.

Class voting may also operate as a veto if the Articles require unanimity among the classes for shareholder actions. For instance, if a particular action needed a majority of Class A *and* a majority of Class B shares, the smaller class could stop corporate action even though a majority of the total shares supported the action. This is a drastic method of protecting minority interests and has the disadvantage of possibly paralyzing shareholder action.

It is also possible to provide for a class of stock with "contingent" voting rights, that is, shares with voting rights only under special circumstances. A corporation may limit the voting powers of shares of any class. Thus shares could, for instance, be entitled to vote only when the corporation had not paid them dividends, or if sales fell below a specified level. At any given time, however, at least one class of shares must have voting rights so that the corporation's directors may be elected and other shareholder functions may be performed.

Disproportionate voting rights may also be used to allocate corporate power. This may be appropriate, for example, when two or more classes of stock exist and the stockholders have paid different amounts to purchase their shares. The more expensive class of shares might be given multiple votes, for example, every share of that class counts as two votes while the other classes enjoy only one vote per share. Or the system could be used to assure that a particular group of shareholders, usually the corporation's organizers, maintain control. The organizers could issue the multiple voting stock to themselves, and sell the other types of shares to outsiders, thereby obtaining disproportionate voting strength. As already mentioned, the outsiders might be less willing to invest under these circumstances and thus the ability to market the shares *must* be considered by the organizers in making decisions about the attributes of shares.

It is also possible to create classes of nonvoting shares. This type of stock might be intended to attract investors and could pay bigger dividends to compensate for its lack of voice in corporate management. Most forms of preferred stock fit this mold.

Classes of shares may also be used to equalize voting rights and still reward shareholders who contribute extra money to the corporation. Although voting rights of all shares could be equal, the class of stock issued to a large investor could pay dividends at a more favorable rate, or an investor could be issued another, separate class of nonvoting stock which pays dividends. In the latter case, the shareholder's economic interest in the corporation would accurately reflect the amount he or she had invested, but his or her ability to control the corporation (through voting power) would not outweigh that of any less affluent organizers.

Quorum and Vote Requirements

Minority shareholders' interests may also be protected by fashioning shareholder quorum and voting requirements to guard against oppression of minority interests. A quorum is the number of shares that must be present at a shareholders' meeting in order for that meeting legally to transact business. The purpose of a quorum is to prevent a small number of shares from deciding questions in the absence of a more representative number of shares. Usually, it is required that the holders of a majority of the corporation's outstanding shares be represented, whether in person or by proxy, at a shareholders' meeting in order for the meeting to be properly constituted and able to take valid and binding action. If a quorum is not present, any actions taken by the shareholders are subject to attack by disgruntled shareholders—who could seek to have a court declare that the actions taken at such a meeting were invalid.

To protect minority interests, the quorum requirement could be increased to two-thirds or three-fourths or other majority level. Minority shareholders could then purposely absent themselves from, and thus prevent a quorum at, a shareholders' meeting scheduled to vote on matters they opposed. Less drastic would be to provide that a greater-than-majority vote is required for passage of shareholder motions. This allows the shareholders to have a quorum, yet enables minority shareholders to cast enough votes to prevent a matter from passing unless a large majority exists. This type of greater-than-majority vote requirement must be specifically authorized in the corporation's Articles of Incorporation or Bylaws (Section 32 of the Model Act).

Both greater-than-majority quorum and vote requirements have the potential for producing shareholder deadlock if the holders of minority shares are uncompromising or irrational. A high quorum is probably the more dangerous, however, since a stubborn shareholder could block all shareholder action by preventing the presence of a quorum and thus the legality of a meeting. A greater-than-majority vote requirement at least allows the shareholders to confront each other, discuss their differences, and pass on to other matters.

Shareholder Agreements

Another method of obtaining shareholder cooperation, one which should not cause shareholder paralysis, is for shareholders to enter into a shareholders' agreement. This is a contract pursuant to which the shareholders bind themselves to do, or refrain from doing, certain things. Among them may be agreement as to the election of directors and, often, a dispute-resolution mechanism. In addition, there is often a share-transfer restriction which is intended to allow shareholders to be able to choose their colleagues. Reasonable restrictions on share transfers preserve an established corporate shareholder group and management structure and protect against intrusions by new shareholders and interests with the ambition to take over the corporation.

An absolute restriction on the transfer of shares is considered to be against public policy and will not be enforced by the courts, but many nonabsolute restrictions have been held to be valid. The most common restriction requires a shareholder wishing to sell his or her stock to offer it first to the existing shareholders in proportion to their current stockholdings and/or to the corporation. If neither the corporation nor the existing shareholders choose to purchase the offered shares, then the selling shareholder could sell this stock to outsiders.

To assure representation of each shareholder on the corporation's Board, a shareholders' agreement also generally provides that shareholders will vote to elect certain persons as directors and will continue voting for them as long as they can properly perform their duties to the corporation. In a small corporation this could take the form of the shareholders promising to elect each other to the Board.

Finally, a shareholder's agreement can provide for a dispute-resolution mechanism. This is a valuable device, since it allows shareholders to set a procedure for dispute resolution *before* a dispute arises and each side seeks a mechanism favorable to themselves. Among the common choices is third-party mediation or a third party given one share with which to break a tie.

Notice of the existence of a shareholders' agreement should be placed on share certificates held by the parties to such an agreement. This puts any potential buyers on notice of restrictions, including transfer restrictions, attached to those shares, and helps to prevent claims that stock is owned by a new shareholder in violation of a share-transfer restriction.

Voting Trusts

"Voting trusts" are another form of control device that consolidates shareholders' voting power in one person or a small group of persons who vote the shares of all the shareholders participating in the trust (Section 34 of the Model Act). Any number of shareholders may form a voting trust by executing a written voting trust agreement, transferring their shares to a voting trustee or trustees, and receiving in return voting trust certificates representing each shareholder's interest in the shares held in trust. The voting trust agreement contains terms which confer upon the trustees the right to vote the shares held by the trust, frequently in a designated manner (such as the names of certain persons to be selected for the corporation's Board of Directors), and usually provides that the shareholders are entitled to continue to receive dividends and other corporate distributions, except stock dividends. The voting trustee keeps a record of the holders of the trust certificates and provides the corporation with a copy of the agreement, including the names and addresses of all the parties to it.

If the terms of the trust do not instruct the trustee(s) how to vote on a particular matter, he or she may vote the shares held by the trust according to his or her own best judgment.

Voting trusts are an effective way to concentrate power in a few individuals; however this result is somewhat at odds with the public policy of encouraging broad participation in corporate control. For these reasons, voting trusts are typically valid only for a specified period of time, often not more than 10 years. After the 10-year period, a voting trust is unenforceable—but the trust may be renewed for successive 10-year periods if the shareholders who participated in the trust sign another voting trust agreement (Section 34 of the Model Act).

Another common use for voting trusts is to protect creditors of a corporation from having management make decisions which put the creditors' loans in jeopardy. Under such a scenario, the creditor demands, as a prerequisite to making a loan, that a majority of the corporation's shares be placed in a trust with a nominee of the creditor named as trustee. The trust instrument normally leaves general management to the Board, but allows the trustee to act on fundamental financial questions.

DIRECTORS

Directors are the corporation's managers and are elected by the shareholders. They are responsible for determining corporate policy and insuring that such policy is properly carried out by the corporation's officers. Directors' responsibilities may also include determining a corporation's products, services, personnel, prices, salaries, corporate finances, and dividends. In larger corporations, these powers are not usually exercised by the Board except in the most general way. The day-to-day decisions on these issues are typically delegated to officers and managerial employees.

In smaller corporations there is often a greater overlap of owner, worker, and manager. This means that shareholders often work in the business and manage it. When a company has more than one shareholder, each of whom wants a say in the company's affairs, problems may arise between majority and minority interests. The result could be that the majority attempts to exclude minority participation on the Board.

There are several devices that could assist minority shareholders in thwarting any such effort by the majority. One is a provision, if legally available, for cumulative voting. Another is a shareholders' agreement committing shareholders to elect certain persons to the Board. The first two were discussed in the preceding section of this chapter. A third device is the classification of directors, discussed briefly in the preceding section.

The Model Business Corporation Act (Section 16) permits shares to be divided into classes. The Articles of Incorporation could establish these classes based on the right of each class to elect one or more directors. This would mean that if there are three shareholders, three classes of shares would be established, one for each shareholder with each class entitled to elect a specified number of directors. All the other rights and obligations of shareholders could be equivalent and all directors would have the same power and responsibility. This device, however, would guarantee equal (or proportional) representation for each shareholder.

As an example, suppose John Carpenter owned 100 shares of Corporation X while Mary Smith owned 75 shares and Jeffrey Jones owned the remaining 25 shares. They had decided among themselves that, despite the differences in share ownership, they each would have equal voice on the Board. If they chose the classification method to accomplish their goal, they would draft Articles of Incorporation creating three classes of stock. Each shareholder would obtain stock of a different class from the others and each class would be entitled to elect one director. Thus, Carpenter would vote his 100 shares of Class A stock for his choice as director. Smith and Jones would each vote their Class B and Class C stock, respectively, for their choice as directors. Each would have one director and equal representation.

Suppose, in this example, the group had decided that Carpenter, due to his greater number of shares, should have more representation on the Board. The Articles could be drafted to give Class A shareholders the right to elect three directors, while Class B could elect two directors, and Class C one director. This could be designed to maintain on the Board the proportion of interest each shareholder has in the stock of the corporation or to create any representational system the shareholders deem advisable.

Just as minority shareholders may feel in need of protection from the majority, the minority directors (chosen by the minority shareholders) may want some assistance as well. One means of protecting minority interests on the Board is a greater-than-majority quorum and vote requirements—the same device that can be used to protect minority shareholders. With respect to directors, a high quorum will protect a "minority director" (a director representing minority shareholding interests) by allowing him or her to block unfavorable decisions by being absent from Board meetings and preventing the presence of the quorum required for the meeting to transact business. On the other hand, the absence of a director for the purpose of defeating a quorum has negative implications relative to that director's duty to the corporation as a whole.

If the organizers choose a high-quorum requirement for Board meetings, it should be coupled with a requirement that directors be given notice of the proposed agenda of each meeting. Thus absences may be strategically planned rather than being indiscriminate.

A greater-than-majority vote requirement is another method to protect minority directors. Such a provision could simply state that a three-fifths, two-thirds, three-fourths, and so forth vote was necessary to carry a motion at a Board meeting. If minority directors muster enough votes to prevent that mark from being reached, they may block Board decisions unfavorable to them.

Both high-quorum and high-vote requirements risk a Board of Directors' stalemate which would be detrimental to the corporation, but these provisions are nevertheless an effective way to force directors to be responsive to all the interests represented on the Board. A greater-than-majority vote requirement is probably the safer feature, however, since it at least allows directors to appear and debate issues, giving them the opportunity to decide uncontroversial questions and compromise on others.

It may also be important to preserve an agreed-upon Board composition by preventing a majority faction of shareholders from increasing the number of directors and filling the vacancies with their own selections. To block "packing" the Board, the number of members may be established by a provision in the Articles of Incorporation or Bylaws, which may be made subject to amendment only upon receipt of a higher-than-majority (two-thirds, three-fourths, etc.) vote of the shareholders. Also, whenever the Board has a vacancy caused by the resignation, death or incapacity of a director, the power to fill that position could be vested exclusively in the shareholders acting by a greater-than-majority vote. If directors were elected by classified shares, the vacancy could be filled by the class of shares that elected the previous director.

Another safeguard of minority interests is a Bylaw provision that directors may be removed only by a greater-than-majority vote of the shareholders and then only for "cause," that is, conduct which is detrimental to the best interests of the corporation. This protects against removals for purely personal reasons. However, even purely personal reasons may interfere with the smooth operation of a corporation and so removal without cause may be appropriate.

OFFICERS

A corporation's officers are responsible for carrying out its day-to-day affairs and are selected by the Board of Directors. Some states allow the shareholders of small, closely held corporations* to select the corporation's officers directly, instead of requiring officers to be selected by the Board.

A device that would protect incumbent officers is greater-than-majority quorum and vote requirements where the Board of Directors votes whether to dismiss an officer. Requiring a greater-than-majority vote would make a hasty dismissal difficult to obtain. (However, consider whether the officer may deserve to be banished as soon as possible.)

A further protection for officers are employment contracts with the corporation. Each officer could be hired by the corporation pursuant to an employment contract specifying standards of performance, salary, and grounds for dismissal. The contract could not prevent the Board of Directors from dismissing an officer, but if the Board did so without adequate grounds, the officer would be able to sue the corporation for damages and, perhaps, reinstatement.

---

* A closely held corporation means a corporation owned by only a small number of shareholders whose shares are not traded publicly and, in fact, are generally subject to rather broad transfer restrictions.

8

ARTICLES OF INCORPORATION

A corporation is created by its Articles of Incorporation, which define its essential characteristics and basic structure and must be submitted to and approved by a designated state official, often the Secretary of State, before the corporation's legal existence begins. Section 54 of the Model Business Corporation Act sets forth the required contents of the Articles.

HEADING

The Articles of Incorporation should begin with a heading such as:

ARTICLES OF INCORPORATION
OF
_____

    TO: The (Secretary of State)
           (Jurisdiction of incorporation)
           The undersigned acting as incorporator of a corporation under the Business Corporation Law of the State of _____ , adopts the following Articles of Incorporation for such corporation:

FIRST ARTICLE—NAME

The organizers must set out the name of the corporation in the first section of the Articles. This name must include the word "corporation," "company," "incorporated," or "limited," or an abbreviation thereof, and may not inaccurately describe the nature of the corporation. The name also may not closely resemble the name of another corporation doing business in the jurisdiction. The organizers can check on this latter point by inquiring of the office of the Secretary of State whether another corporation of the same or a similar name already exists. As mentioned earlier, organizers may reserve a chosen name by filing an Application for Reservation of Corporate name with the Secretary of State.

SECOND ARTICLE—DURATION

The second section must declare the period of the corporation's existence. The organizers may select any duration, but unless circumstances are very unusual it is best to designate a perpetual existence. When the duration is perpetual, there need be no worry that the corporation's authority to do business will lapse while it is still active. Should that occur the corporation could be fined or otherwise sanctioned for operating after the expiration of corporate authority, and would be forced to reincorporate and incur additional expenses. It is also possible that the shareholders would be exposed to individual liability during an interim period.

Selecting a perpetual existence does not, however, mean that the corporation *must* go on forever. It may dissolve at any time by recommendation of its Board of Directors and either written consent of *all* its shareholders, or by the *vote* at a shareholders' meeting of two-thirds of its shareholders entitled to vote.

THIRD ARTICLE—PURPOSE

This section must express the purpose or purposes for which the corporation is organized. A business corporation may be organized "for any lawful purpose or purposes, except for the purpose of banking or insurance" (Section 3 of the Model Act).

If the purpose of the corporation involves any restriction concerning the making of maximum profits, that should be expressed in this section of the Articles, particularly where the corporation intends to combine business with a more altruistic purpose, for example, on-the-job training of unskilled workers. Expressing a unique motivation of this type helps to define the scope of the business and the results considered important. Also, because outside investors will probably assume that a corporation's only motivation is to make money, the inclusion of this type of purpose may serve to warn outsiders that they are dealing with a corporation concerned with goals other than making maximum profits.

FOURTH ARTICLE—STOCK

This section should describe the corporation's stock. It must state the number, how many per class (if there are classified shares), and the par value (or that the shares are without par value) of all the stock the corporation authorizes.

In a small corporation there may be no need for a large number of shares or division of shares into classes. For instance, four organizers of a corporation may decide that their corporation will issue 100 shares, all of the same class (having voting rights), and that each organizer will buy 25 shares to represent his or her one-fourth ownership interest. If the organizers intend to remain in control of the corporation and expect no one else to become an owner, there would be no need to authorize more, or another class of, shares to be offered to outside investors. However, it is generally wise to plan for contingencies, including the possibility that more capital will need to be raised through the sale of shares. Therefore, the organizers might authorize 1000 shares even if they will only buy 25 each. The authorized but unissued shares (the 900 remaining shares) are not "owned" by anyone and are not voted or entitled to dividends until they are sold. Whether and when such a sale takes place is in the control of the Board of Directors which, in our example, is comprised of all the preexisting shareholders.

An important decision in such a closely-held corporation is how much the corporation's shares will cost. Generally, a corporation should sell its stock for a price which, in the aggregate, equals the amount of money the company needs to begin business. In the previous example, if the corporation needed $10,000 to purchase assets and pay expenses, it should offer ("issue") its stock for a total price of no less than $10,000, for example, $100 per share if there were 100 shares. Each of the four organizers would then have to pay $2,500, transfer $2,500 worth of property, or perform $2,500 worth of services for the corporation in order to acquire his or her one-fourth ownership interest.

If the organizers were unable to supply enough money or property for the corporation to begin business, they may increase the number of shares the corporation offers for sale and offer the additional shares to outsiders. (As noted previously, if this happens, the organizers must carefully consider whether federal or state securities laws are applicable.) Since the organizers' voting power would be diluted if outside investors bought and held the same type of stock as the organizers, an outside offering would make sense only if the organizers did not require 100% control of the corporation. (The organizers would not lose control of the corporation if, as a group, they retained 51% of the voting stock, especially if they entered into a shareholders' agreement promising to elect each other to the Board of Directors.)

Where additional money is needed but dilution of control is a problem, a corporation could issue a second class of stock, financially attractive to outside investors, but with no voting rights to endanger the organizers' control of the corporation. A class of preferred stock, or nonvoting common stock, could fill this need. The corporation could also seek loans to satisfy its need for funds. As discussed earlier (in Chapter 5), there are several advantages to this route, assuming it is available, but also some drawbacks.

If the organizers intend to divide the corporation's stock into classes, this must be stated in this section of the Articles. As described in the previous chapter, classification of shares may be used as a device for assuring each organizer a role in the corporation's management, as well as for accommodating outside investors without granting them too much power. That is, the corporation could issue as many classes of stock as there are organizers planning to remain active in management of the company's affairs, each organizer could buy all the shares of one class, and the Articles of Incorporation could then provide that each class shall elect one director to the Board of Directors. Thus each organizer is assured that he or she may elect a person (usually himself or herself), to represent his or her interests on the Board. It should be noted, however, that such elaborate devices are not common and have tax consequences which will be discussed later (Chapter 12).

Finally, the organizers must decide whether their corporation's stock shall be of par or no par value. The significance of setting a par value is that stock may not be sold *by the corporation* for less than its par value. Shareholders may transfer stock (par or no par) between themselves and others at whatever prices they choose, however. A par value is basically an arbitrary value assigned to the stock in the corporation's Articles and does not necessarily equal the market value of a share or the amount of money actually paid for the share. Rather, the par value (which, if it is used, must be stated in the Articles) is used to determine the corporation's capital account.

No par shares are more flexible than shares with a par value because the corporation's Board of Directors, or the shareholders if they have been granted this power in the Articles, may determine the selling price of no par stock from time to time to reflect the corporation's success, or lack of it. That is, if the corporation is not doing particularly well but needs additional capital, the Board (or shareholders) may reduce the corporation's selling price for no par shares to the point where the shares are salable. Par value stock, on the other hand, may not be sold by the corporation for less than its par value. Thus if the market value of the shares (the value an independent third party would pay for the shares) is less than par, the corporation has an obvious problem in its attempt to raise new capital.

FIFTH ARTICLE—CLASSES OF SHARES

If the corporation has divided its shares into classes, this section must name each class and describe its preferences, voting powers, limitations, restrictions, qualification, and special or relative rights with respect to the other class(es) of shares. This is important because unless the Articles of Incorporation provide otherwise, all shares enjoy equal rights to corporate dividends, to assets on the corporation's dissolution, and to vote. Thus, if the organizers would prefer a different distribution of power, they must express it in the Articles.

A frequent distinction is that one class of stock possess a preference to dividend payments. This may be expressed as a "preference of $____" or "____% of par value" per annum (payable yearly, semiannually, quarterly, etc.). A preference entitles the holders of the preferred stock to dividend payments of a certain amount before the holders of any other stock with a lower priority (preference) may receive any dividends on their stock.

In addition, preferred stock may be cumulative or cumulative-to-the-extent-earned. Normally, a dividend is declared on a yearly basis. If it is not declared in any year, it generally is lost forever. Thus, if the corporation earned money which could have been used for a dividend but the Board decided not to declare one, the shareholders would not retain any right to receive payment for that year's dividend. On the other hand, if the dividend were cumulative, the right to payment would not be lost. Rather, the amount of the unpaid dividend would be added to the next year's dividend and the holders of cumulative preferred stock would have to be paid all accumulated dividends before holders of lower priority shares would receive anything.

Cumulative-if-earned stock is similar. The difference is that if the corporation has earned money from which a dividend could be paid, the dividend is cumulative. If there are not such earnings in a particular year, the dividend is lost for that year (but not for the others). Therefore, cumulative preferred stock may make a very attractive investment for some shareholders. However, because no other shareholders may be paid dividends until the accumulated unpaid dividends from past years have been paid to the holders of cumulative preferred stock, the lower preference (including common) stockholders could suffer a long spell without dividends.

Preferred stock may also be participating or nonparticipating. Nonparticipating preferred stock receives no dividends beyond the amount of its dividend "preference." "Participating preferred" receives its preferential dividend and then, once other preferences have been paid, may share the remaining portion of available funds with the common stockholders. This may also make a very attractive investment, since these stockholders get a constant dividend payment before dividends are paid on any other shares, and are also able to share in additional corporate profits.

If a class or classes of shares is to enjoy a preference to the assets or proceeds upon dissolution and liquidation of the corporation, the Articles must also provide for this preference. This may be phrased as "a preference of $ _____ ," " _____ % of par value," or "Class 'A' will get twice (three, four, five, etc.) times per share the amount of Class 'B'." Thus, if the corporation dissolves, sells all its assets, pays its debts, and distributes the remaining proceeds, a certain portion of the money received will go to the holders of shares with a "liquidation preference," and what money remains after all preferences have been paid will be equally distributed among the holders of the common shares.

Unless the Articles provide otherwise, all shareholders have the same voting rights. The organizers may want to alter this situation by providing for class voting for directors to insure representation of various interests on the Board (e.g., to assure representation of minority interests on the Board). In addition, there are other voting right variables such as contingent voting rights (perhaps contingent on not being paid dividends), or classes of stock with no voting rights at all (in fact, preferred stock frequently does not possess voting rights).

Class voting might also be weighted according to classes; for example, Class A shares count as two votes on any issue while Class B and C shares count as only one vote each. This is another method of allocating power to the holders of a certain class or classes of stock. Similar to this device is a provision whereby one class elects proportionately more directors than any other class; for example, Class X elects five directors out of a seven-person Board, Class Y elects the remainder.

There are also financial considerations in the configuration of shares. For instance, after the corporation is established and accumulates an amount of money, it may be desirable for it to buy up its preferred shares, retire them, and issue common shares or new preferred shares that pay shareholders at a lower rate. In order to be able to do this there must be a redemption provision in the Articles allowing the corporation to buy back its own preferred shares from their owners whenever the corporation chooses to do so (Section 54 of the Model Act). The Articles must include a redemption price, for example, "$____" or "____% of par value" (110%, for instance), specify if there is a time limit on the corporation's exercise of its redemption privilege, and prescribe the procedures for accomplishing the redemption. A corporation may not redeem any of its shares, however, if the payments would reduce the corporation's net assets below an amount sufficient to pay all its debts and known liabilities, or below the aggregate amount of liquidation preferences payable to shareholders.

Similarly, if one type of share may be converted into another type or into a debt security, the details of this privilege must be included in the Articles. The Articles should specify what shares are convertible, into what other shares or debt securities, at what ratio (e.g., 1 : 1, 2 : 1, etc.) and subject to what time limitations.

As discussed in Chapter 5, convertibility is an attractive investment feature, since it holds out the possibility that investors may exchange their shares for shares of another series or class, or for debt securities (or vice versa), whenever those other interests become more attractive to them than the stock they currently own. Organizers should be aware, however, that if shares or loans held by outside investors are convertible into a type of stock with voting rights, the outsiders could convert themselves into voting power. At the least, the allocation of voting power established among the organizers could be disrupted if one security holder converted another type of security he or she held into stock with voting rights.

Debt securities, bonds, debentures, notes, and so forth do *not* have to be specifically authorized in the corporation's Articles of Incorporation. They do, however, have to be authorized by the Corporation's Board of Directors.

SIXTH ARTICLE—SERIES OF CLASSES

It is possible for the corporation to issue classes of stock in "series"; that is, the Articles may provide that a portion of a class of shares may be issued with a certain dividend rate, redemption privilege, liquidation preference, conversion privileges, and so forth, and that another portion of shares of the same class may be issued with a different dividend rate, liquidation preference, and so forth (Section 54 of the Model Act). The corporation need not sell each series at the same time. The details of each series could be specified in the Articles of Incorporation, or the Articles may authorize the Board of Directors to issue shares in specified series, and leave the details of each series to be determined at a later date in a Board resolution. The latter method is more flexible, since the Board is not bound by features of a series until it files a statement with the Secretary of State.

SEVENTH ARTICLE—PREEMPTIVE RIGHTS

Unless the Articles provides otherwise, the corporation's shareholders possess (or do *not* possess, depending on state law) "preemptive rights" (Section 26 of the Model Act). A shareholder's preemptive right is his or her right to buy a portion (corresponding to the proportion of his or her current shareholdings to the total number of outstanding shares) of any new stock of the same class authorized and issued by the corporation. Only if he or she is not interested in purchasing or does not have the money, may the corporation offer the shares to other investors. If there are not preemptive rights, the corporation may offer new shares to whomever it chooses. Where the corporation has issued different classes of stock with different voting, dividend, liquidation, and so forth, rights, there may be difficulties apportioning preemptive rights to new stock.

To the extent preemptive rights are available, Section 26 of the Model Act limits their application, *except* as the Articles provide otherwise, in the following situations:

1. When shares are issued to officers, directors, or employees pursuant to shareholder's vote or to a plan previously approved by shareholders; or

2. When shares are issued for other than cash (i.e., property, shares of another corporation, etc.) Moreover, there is an absolute ban, under the Model Act, on preemptive rights for holders of preferred or nonvoting common shares to acquire *any* shares or for the holders of common shares to acquire preferred shares (unless those preferred shares are convertible into common shares).

State law often provides that, even if there are preemptive rights, a corporation may issue and sell new shares to its employees without the new issue being subject to preemptive rights, if two-thirds of the corporation's shareholders have previously approved the plan. It is also generally recognized that preemptive rights do not apply with respect to: (1) originally authorized stock; (2) stock issued in exchange for property or personal services provided to the corporation; (3) stock purchased by the corporation itself (treasury stock) and subsequently resold by it; (4) shares issued in connection with a merger or consolidation, (5) and share dividends. In a small corporation, the organizers may want to provide in the Articles that preemptive rights exist even in some of these instances.

Another method of protecting shareholders' proportionate interests is to authorize only that amount of stock that will actually be purchased by a corporation's organizers. To create any more stock would require an amendment to the corporation's Articles, and many states' laws provide that amendments to Articles of Incorporation require the approval of two-thirds of the corporation's share. (Although the Articles may impose a higher percentage requirement.)

To protect the proportionate interests of shareholders who may not have enough money to purchase the stock made available through their preemptive rights, or to protect against a majority of shareholders authorizing new stock and providing an unreasonably short period of time during which the stockholders may exercise their preemptive rights (thus making it very difficult to raise the money needed to buy the stock), the Articles could impose a very high-vote requirement for amendments to the Articles, or a high-vote requirement specifically for amendments increasing the number of the corporation's authorized shares. These devices would help preserve the proportionate interests of a shareholder who was unable to muster enough money to exercise his or her preemptive rights but who might be able to muster enough votes to prevent an amendment necessary to authorize additional stock.

EIGHTH ARTICLE—SPECIAL PROVISIONS

This section is optional and may include special provisions for the regulation of the corporation's internal affairs, including: authorization for cumulative or class voting; imposition of greater-than-majority quorum and/or voting requirements for shareholders' and/or directors' meetings; permission for shareholders to determine the selling price of the corporation's no par shares; provision for filling vacancies on the Board by vote of the shareholders and any other important, perhaps unusual, features of the corporation's internal affairs.

This section could also include a provision for indemnification of the corporation's directors, officers, and agents for any liability to which they may be subject as a result of the performance of their duties on behalf of the corporation. This is an important protection for corporate representatives who may find themselves subject to claims because of actions they took on behalf of, and pursuant to authorization by, the corporation.

The reason for including these provisions in the Articles is to give notice to the public of the corporation's special management features, thereby precluding an investor from later complaining that he or she was unaware of, and not bound by, these rules. It also makes it more difficult for these protections to be removed, since it would require going through the entire amendment procedure to make a change.

NINTH ARTICLE—REGISTERED OFFICE AND AGENT

This section must provide the address—including street and number of the initial registered office of the corporation, which need not be its place of business—and the name of its initial registered agent at such address.

The corporation must always maintain a registered office and a registered agent at that address in the state of incorporation and the first such office and agent must be specified in the Articles of Incorporation (Section 12 of the Model Act). The basic purpose of the agent is to receive local service of process in the name of the corporation and to forward such communications to appropriate corporate officers or directors. The agent may be an individual, who must be a *resident* of the state of incorporation, a domestic corporation, or a foreign corporation authorized to do business in the state of incorporation. A corporation may thereafter change its registered office or registered agent by filing a notice of the change with the state.

TENTH ARTICLE—BOARD OF DIRECTORS

This section must state the number and give the names and addresses of the members of the corporation's initial Board of Directors. The organizers may choose any number of directors to constitute the initial Board, but there must be at least *one* (Section 54 of the Model Act, although many states require a minimum of three directors). The initial directors (or any other directors) do not have to be residents of the state of incorporation, nor must they be 18 years of age or older or shareholders of the corporation, unless the Articles state otherwise.

The organizers should probably list themselves as the initial directors since they will then have managerial control from the outset. This can be important, particularly in controlling to whom the corporation's shares are offered for sale. Occasionally, however, to disguise who really controls the business or because there are only one or two organizers, there may be people who serve as directors as an accommodation and take no active part in the corporation's management. Accommodation directors are still subject to directors' duties and potential liabilities.

ELEVENTH ARTICLE—INCORPORATORS

There must be one or more incorporators who may be either "natural persons," or another corporation, domestic or foreign (Section 53 of the Model Act). Incorporators need not be residents of the state of incorporation.

Because incorporators sign the Articles when they are submitted for filing, they are responsible and potentially liable if they have made any knowing misstatement of fact in the Articles. Other than this, incorporators, *as* incorporators, have no responsibility to, or authority over, the corporation.

9

BYLAWS

Bylaws are the internal rules and regulations chosen by a corporation's organizers to govern the company's internal affairs. Bylaws need not be filed with the state and consequently are never "approved" by any official or agency. While Bylaws are more specific concerning corporate affairs than are the Articles, the authority of the Bylaws is not unlimited. They must be consistent with the state's corporation laws and with the corporation's Articles of Incorporation. Inconsistencies are resolved in favor of the statute and the Articles in that order.

The responsibility for adopting, amending, and repealing Bylaws is vested in the Board of Directors unless the Articles of Incorporation expressly grant the power to the shareholders. (Section 27 of the Model Business Corporation Act). In a small corporation, the organizers may want the shareholders to be so empowered so that they will be able to maintain more control over the corporation's management.

Bylaws describe power in the corporation—where it is, who has it, how it is used, and how it is controlled. For that reason, an organization should not adopt a form set of Bylaws but should develop Bylaws that fit its structure and method of functioning. Since Bylaws are not hard to prepare, it is worth the time to tailor them to the specific needs and circumstances of each corporation. The following discussion will trace the contents of, and relevant considerations involved in preparing, a set of Bylaws.

SECTION ONE—OFFICES

This section may describe the location of the corporation's offices. A corporation must maintain a registered office in the state of incorporation, but its principal place of business need not be in that office or even in that state (Section 12 of the Model Act). Therefore, this section could state the location of the corporation's principal office, the location of its registered office, and that it may maintain additional offices as determined by the Board of Directors.

SECTION TWO—SHAREHOLDERS

Generally, this section describes the corporation's shareholders—their meetings and their voting procedures.

Shareholders' Meetings

Meetings of shareholders (to exercise those powers conferred upon them by law and the Articles of Incorporation) may be held either within or without the jurisdiction of incorporation. If the Bylaws do not specify a location, the statute provides that shareholders' meetings shall be held at the corporation's registered office (Section 28 of the Model Act).

Shareholders generally meet once a year to elect the corporation's directors. The time and date for this gathering may be provided in the Bylaws, preferably expressed as "the first Tuesday in June," rather than "June 1 of each year" (for instance), in order to avoid selecting a date which falls on a weekend or holiday. The specific time is a matter of corporate convenience, but many corporations schedule their annual meeting shortly after the close of their business (fiscal) year. This allows the shareholders' meeting to review a completed year's activities.

It is also possible for shareholders to hold "regular meetings," that is, to gather at specified intervals, monthly, quarterly, semiannually, and so forth to exercise their powers and keep in touch with corporate affairs. This type of meeting is optional, and in most corporations such meetings are not held since the shareholders have few powers. Also, in a small corporation where the shareholders are also the directors and officers, it would seem superfluous to convene the same group of people as shareholders when they meet regularly in their other capacities and are well aware of what is happening in the corporation. If shareholders were empowered with significant managerial duties *as share-holders,* it would make sense for them to meet frequently in order to exercise their powers effectively.

A "special meeting" is an unscheduled meeting occasioned by an unexpected event requiring the shareholders' response, for example, the entire Board of Directors resigns, the corporation is considering a merger with another company, and so forth. Such a meeting may be called by the Board of Directors or the holders of at least one-tenth of the corporation's outstanding shares or by such other persons as are empowered to do so in the Articles of Incorporation or Bylaws (Section 28 of the Model Act). These other people might include the President, Chairperson of the Board, the Executive Committee, the Treasurer, any member of the Board, two (three, four, etc.) members of the Board, and so forth. The more people who have the power to call such a meeting, the more likely the shareholders can be legally mobilized to respond to emergencies. It is also more likely that meetings will be called for less important purposes. The organizers should weigh the competing elements carefully.

Notice

In order for shareholders to be aware of shareholders' meetings, the corporation must give notice of these gatherings. Unless the Bylaws express different provisions regarding the period of notice, Section 29 of the Model Act states that *written* notice of shareholders' meetings, describing the date, place, and time of the meeting, and the purpose in the case of a special meeting, *must* be given to each shareholder of record entitled to vote, not less than 10 nor more than 50 days before the date of each shareholders' meeting.

The majority of states require such notice even for annual (or regular) meetings, the date, place, and time of which are expressed in the Bylaws. This reinforces a strong policy in favor of active shareholder participation in the general direction of a corporation. This is particulary true in those small corporations where all shareholders do not have daily contact with the business. Therefore, the organizers may want to provide for special types of written notice, such as by telegraph or computer. Moreover, the notification period established in the statute probably need not be so far in advance for a locally based and owned corporation. A much shorter period, a few days perhaps, should suffice.

Who Is Entitled to Vote?

Obviously, persons who own shares are stockholders. The Bylaws, however, may specify a time within which a person must be listed as a stockholder on the books of the corporation in order to be entitled to notice of, and the opportunity to vote at, a shareholders' meeting. This cutoff may also apply to other shareholder matters such as what shareholders are entitled to receive dividends (which are paid as of a certain record date). The problem arises when shares are sold or otherwise transferred from one person to another. In large corporations where this happens frequently, the corporation needs some method of deciding which persons may act as shareholders on corporate matters. The method developed is that of the "record date." This is the last day prior to some shareholder action that the corporation will recognize a buyer of shares as a shareholder for the purpose of that action.

For instance, assume a shareholder vote is to be held on March 15. The corporation may say that all shareholders of record, that is, shareholders listed as such in the corporate records, as of February 15 may vote. If X bought stock from Y on March 1, Y would be entitled to vote on March 15, not X. To cure this problem, X might demand, as part of the purchase, that Y give X an irrevocable proxy to vote the shares.

Section 30 of the Model Act provides that a corporation's Board of Directors may "close the stock transfer books" for a period not to exceed 50 days; that is, the Board may halt stock transfers on its books within that time in order to determine those stockholders entitled to notice, eligible to vote, or qualified to receive dividends. If the books are closed in order to determine who are stockholders entitled to vote at an upcoming shareholders' meeting, the books must be closed at least 10 days prior to such meeting.

If no provision is made by the Board for either closing the books or setting a cutoff date, the date when notice was mailed will be considered the date of determination of shareholders entitled to vote. It is therefore possible for new shareholders to be recognized up until the moment of the vote—if notice was delivered personally rather than by mail. Absent a contrary provision in the Bylaws, or a resolution by the Board, shareholders listed as of the time the Board declared a dividend are eligible to receive that payment.

The organizers may want to designate one of the corporation's officers, usually the Secretary, to maintain a record of shareholders. In a corporation with few shareholders, this is a simple task. If the number of shareholders is large enough that they are difficult to keep track of, however, it may be worthwhile to record transactions concerning the corporation's stock more closely. This is often accomplished by the use of a professional "transfer agent," usually a bank or other financial institution with sophisticated record-keeping systems.

Quorum

A quorum is the number of *shares, not shareholders*, that must be present at a shareholders' meeting before the meeting may properly transact business. Unless a quorum is present, the shareholders are powerless to take action except to adjourn the meeting until a quorum can be assembled. Any other action taken is invalid. If the Articles of Incorporation do not specify what constitutes a quorum, Section 32 of the Model Act provides that a majority of the corporation's outstanding shares having voting power, represented in person or by "proxy," shall constitute a quorum for a meeting of shareholders.

It is important to name a realistic quorum, because a quorum requirement that is too difficult to attain may result in the shareholders never having a proper meeting. If there are many shareholders, perhaps a smaller percentage such as one-third of the shares with voting rights (Section 32 of the Model Act forbids a percentage smaller than one-third) may be indicated. On the other hand, if there are few shareholders they are probably more intimately involved in the corporation's management and a quorum of greater than 50% would be feasible, since the shareholders would be more likely to attend meetings. In addition, where the shareholders are also the corporation's directors and officers, a high quorum results in attendance by a broad base of shareholders with a management perspective, which could foster better coordination between management and shareholders.

Also, a high-quorum requirement helps to protect minority shareholders' interests since these shareholders could absent themselves from a meeting which was scheduled to consider actions unfavorable to them, thereby preventing the quorum needed to do business.

Vote

Section 32 of the Model Act also provides that the affirmative vote of a majority of the shares entitled to vote, represented in person or by proxy at a shareholders' meeting, shall carry a motion, unless a greater number is required by statute or by the Articles of Incorporation. The section also allows the Articles to require class voting which would supersede the majority-vote language.

Proxies. A "proxy" is an authorization from a shareholder who is absent, to another person who will be present at a shareholders' meeting, to vote the absent shareholder's stock. A proxy is not necessarily an absentee vote. The shareholder with the absentee's proxy may be given discretion to vote however he or she wishes to vote, or the absent shareholder may indicate how he or she wants the shares voted on particular issues. Section 33 of the Model Act expressly authorizes shareholder voting by proxy. The proxy must be in writing and signed by the shareholder or the shareholder's duly authorized attorney in fact. The proxy, unless it specifies otherwise, is valid for 11 months from the date of its issuance. The solicitation of proxies is governed, for the most part, by state law. For large, widely traded corporations, proxies and their solicitation are regulated by federal statutes which, in those cases, supersede local law.

In deciding whether to allow proxies, the organizers must weigh the importance they attach to personal attendance, versus the possibility that a shareholder may be unable to attend, but still wants to vote.

Informal Actions. Section 145 of the Model Act provides that any shareholders' action may be taken without a meeting, if a written consent, setting forth the action taken, is signed by *all the shareholders* entitled to vote on the matter. For the sake of convenience, the Bylaws could restate this provision so that the corporation's internal regulations clearly state that this procedure may be used. Many corporations with a small number of shareholders operate almost exclusively by unanimous written consent and rarely have actual shareholder meetings. This eliminates worries about adequacy of notice of meetings and logistical problems of assembling all the shareholders at the same time. A consent resolution, or different copies of the same resolution, may simply be passed around to all the shareholders for their signature.

Cumulative Voting. As discussed in Chapter 7, cumulative voting is a system of voting for directors whereby each share possesses as many votes as there are directors to be elected. For example, Jane Doe has 10 shares and there are three seats on the Board to be filled. With cumulative voting, Doe would have 30 votes to cast as she chooses, either all for one candidate or distributed among as many candidates as she likes. This type of voting helps minority shareholders to elect some representatives on the Board of Directors, instead of being completely outvoted by the holders of 51% of the corporation's stock. For instance, if, in our hypothetical corporation, Doe had 10 shares and Mary Smith had 15, Smith would, in the absence of cumulative voting, be able to elect all three directors. She would simply vote her 15 shares for each of her three favorite candidates. Doe would vote her 10 shares for her three candidates. Since each of Smith's candidates received 15 votes to only 10 for Doe's candidates, the Smith candidates would be elected.

With cumulative voting, each shareholder could divide his or her votes in any way he or she pleases. Doe would have 30 votes (10 shares × 3 directors) and Smith 45 (15 X 3). If Doe casts all her 30 votes for one candidate, mathematically she is assured of that candidate's election. No matter how Smith divides her votes she cannot have three candidates all having more votes than Doe's one.

In a small corporation, increased shareholder involvement in management functions may be desirable, and cumulative voting is one system for achieving this. Cumulative voting is most effective the larger the number of places to be filled on the Board. Thus one way for the effects of cumulative voting to be diluted is for only one or two directors to be scheduled for election at any one time.

Cumulative voting varies among the states. Some require it, some forbid it, and others leave it to the Articles of Incorporation with formulations such as "cumulative voting is not available unless it is provided for in the Articles of Incorporation" or "cumulative voting is required unless the Articles provide to the contrary." The provision may be restated in the Bylaws, but in those permissive states inclusion of some provision should be in the Articles. In any case, cumulative voting is available *only* in the election of directors. It is not available for *any* other purpose.

SECTION THREE—DIRECTORS

The Board of Directors is the body responsible for managing the corporation. It makes basic policy decisions for the corporation and selects the corporate officers to implement these decisions. The Board, however, must act as a whole, collectively, and not through its individual members. Thus a single director has no legal power, where there are other directors, to determine corporate policies. Of course, when there is only one director this point is moot.

Unless the Articles or Bylaws indicate otherwise, there is no requirement that the directors be residents of the state of incorporation, shareholders of the corporation, or of any particular age (Section 35 of the Model Act). Section 36 requires that there be at least one director, but Section 35 allows the management authority of the Board to be transferred, in whole or in part, by the Articles to any other person or persons. Thus, while one director is still required, the position may be stripped of power by the Articles of Incorporation. The initial director(s) must be named in the Articles of Incorporation, but these directors could hold office only until the first meeting of the shareholders, at which time they could be reelected or replaced, by vote of the shareholders, with the parties who will operate the corporation.

Powers

The Board generally has the power to manage the business and affairs of the corporation. As mentioned previously, this includes the power to make policy decisions and to choose the people who will carry out these decisions. However, with such broad powers also come extensive duties.

Directors must always use their best efforts to manage the corporation's business and earn profits for its shareholders. The standard to which directors are held in making their managerial decisions is that of the diligence, skill, and care that a reasonably prudent person would exercise in similar circumstances. Directors must act within their authority, as defined in the Articles, Bylaws, and applicable provisions of the statute, must avoid conflicts of interest with the corporation, and may not compete with its business or usurp a corporate business opportunity for their personal benefit.

If a director falls below these standards, he or she may be sued by a shareholder to recover—on behalf of the corporation—any damage caused to the corporation by the director's misconduct. Such a lawsuit is known as a "stockholder's derivative suit" because the shareholder is suing for a harm done to the corporation, not one done directly to the shareholder. If the shareholder is successful, any recovery goes to the corporation, not to the shareholder.

To protect themselves from liability for authorizing improper actions, directors should attend and participate in Board meetings and keep abreast of the corporation's affairs. Then, if the director believes that the Board has voted to approve an improper action, that director should register his or her protest on the record of the minutes of the meeting or file a written protest with the corporation's Secretary immediately after the meeting (Section 48 of the Model Act). This will confirm the director's dissenting vote and will help shield him or her from liability. This procedure may not, however, be used by a director to change, after the fact, his or her original vote in favor of an action.

Number, Tenure, and Qualifications

The Bylaws should state how many directors the corporation will have. The organizers should keep this number manageable. In a small corporation, the number of directors may be determined by the number of organizer-shareholders. In such a corporation, there could be as many directors as there are shareholders who intend to be active in the management of the corporation's affairs.

As discussed previously, the Board of Directors is elected by the corporation's shareholders (Section 36 of the Model Act). This election may be accomplished at the shareholders' annual meeting, or by the shareholders acting by unanimous written consent. Generally, directors elected at an annual meeting hold office until the next annual meeting, at which time they may, in the absence of a Bylaw provision to the contrary, run for reelection. If no new election of directors is held, the incumbent directors simply continue to serve on the Board. The Bylaws *could* limit the number of terms that a director may serve. In a small corporation, however, where the shareholders also run the business, that type of restriction is not advisable since it would disqualify the investors from management after a few years.

The organizers may want to create different *classes of directors*— distinguished by the length and termination date of their terms. If the number of directors is nine or more, the Articles of Incorporation may provide for two or three classes of directors, with "each class to be as nearly equal in number as possible." After the first election of directors, the first class would serve for one year, the second for two, and the third for three years (Section 37 of the Model Act). Then, when the first term of each class expires, the newly elected directors in that class would serve for three-year terms (or two-year terms if only two classes were established). This staggers the election of directors so that all directors are not up for election at the same time. The goal is to provide some continuity on the Board, although critics suggest that continuity is accomplished by shareholder inertia, regardless of the classification of directors. Moreover, classes of directors may be unnecessary and superfluous if provision has been made for election of directors by classified shares, or if a shareholder's agreement assures certain persons (usually the shareholders) places on the Board.

Meetings

In order to perform their managerial duties, the Board of Directors must meet or may take action by unanimous written consent. If they choose to meet, their meetings may take place either within or outside of the state of incorporation, as provided in the Bylaws or by resolution of the Board.

Although it is not required by statue, the Board may want to hold an annual meeting to review the year's business, and the Bylaws could list the date, time, and place of such a meeting. A convenient date would be the date of the shareholders' meeting, with the directors convening immediately after the shareholders have adjourned.

The Board may find it necessary to meet on a more regular basis than once a year. To provide for other meetings, the Bylaws could list the date, time, place, and so forth of "regular" meetings of the Board. For instance, "regular meetings of the Board of Directors shall be held at 8:00 P.M. on the first Tuesday of every month, at the corporation's principal office (Section 43 of the Model Act).

The organizers must decide how frequently these regular meetings should be held. This will depend on the nature of the corporation, the attention its activities demand, the willingness of the directors to gather frequently for meetings, and the feasibility of taking certain Board actions pursuant to unanimous written consent. Many corporations hold Board meetings once a month, and if the organizers feel the corporation will need periodic, in-person review, the Bylaws could provide for a monthly directors' meeting.

Instead of a Bylaws provision, a "standing resolution" could announce a regular date and time for Board meetings. A standing resolution also should alleviate notice problems since the resolution would be part of the minutes of the Board meeting which would be provided to all directors, and would set a regular meeting time far in advance. A simple resolution passed by the Board which announces only the details of its next meeting may create practical notice problems if many directors are absent from the meeting at which the resolution was passed and these directors are not made aware of the resolution.

Because there can be no guarantee that regularly scheduled meetings will coincide with unexpected problems that may require the immediate attention of the Board, the Bylaws should contain a mechanism for calling meetings to respond to unanticipated events. A provision for "special meetings" of the Board will accomplish this (Section 43 of the Model Act).

A provision for special meetings should list the persons empowered to call such meetings and the type of notice required. The Chairperson of the Board would be a logical choice to call meetings, as would be the President of the corporation, or a certain number of directors (one, two, three, etc.).

Notice, which should be defined in the Bylaws, may be personal, by telephone, telegraph, mail, or any other method the organizers feel is effective (Section 43 of the Model Act). (Note the difference between the notice for directors' meetings and the notice required for shareholders' meetings—the latter must be in *writing*.) The period of notice should be brief—a day or two—since this type of meeting may be called to respond to an emergency.

Quorum

Before the Board of Directors may take any valid actions, a certain percentage of the directors must be present at the Board meeting. Section 40 of the Model Act states that a majority of the directors shall constitute a quorum unless a *greater* number is required by the Articles of Incorporation or the Bylaws; thus the quorum may not be *less* than a majority of the directors.

The statutory provision of a majority quorum applies only if the Articles or Bylaws are silent on the subject. A majority quorum is a common choice, but in a small corporation there may be sentiment that no decisions should be made without a broader representation of the

Board present. In such case, a higher quorum (three-fifths, two-thirds, three-fourths, etc.) would be appropriate and may act as a protection for minority directors just as a high quorum for shareholders' meetings protects the interests of minority shareholders.

Manner of Acting

The Bylaws should also reflect the organizers' decision on the margin of vote required to carry a motion of a Board meeting. Again, the common choice is that the vote of a majority of directors present at a meeting with a quorum carries an issue, and this percentage is established by Section 40 of the Model Act, if the corporation does not require a greater percentage in its Articles or Bylaws.

Greater-than-majority vote requirements are a means to protect minority interests on the Board, just as greater-than-majority quorum requirements deter actions unfavorable to minority directors. In the context of greater-than-majority *vote* requirement, minority interests could be present at a Board meeting, vote on uncontroversial issues, debate others, and, if difficulties were not resolved, the minority directors could try to muster enough support to prevent the majority from achieving the margin of vote required for taking action.

Action Without a Meeting. Section 44 of the Model Act allows the Board of Directors (as well as committees) to act by unanimous written consent, in lieu of actually meeting together. Action by consent is very convenient since it avoids the logistical difficulties of assembling a quorum of directors. Instead of meeting, all the directors simply sign a consent which describes the actions they agree to take. The consent document need not be signed by all directors at the same time, nor must directors physically sign the same piece of paper, as long as they all sign copies of the same document.

Proxies. Directors may not vote by proxy. This is implicit in Section 40 of the Model Act, which speaks of the vote requirement at directors' meetings as a majority of the directors *present*. This is also supported by case law which gives the rationale that directors must exercise their personal judgment on corporate issues and that this can only be done by their presence at the meeting.

Vacancies

Section 38 of the Model Act provides that vacancies on the Board of Directors caused by resignation, removal, death, and so forth may be filled by vote of a majority of the remaining directors, even though less than a quorum. The Model Act says that the vacancy or vacancies *may* be filled by the remaining directors. This is because many cases have held that the shareholders retain an inherent right to fill vacancies on the Board regardless of the fact that the Bylaws give a similar right to directors. Similarly, where the vacancy results from an increase in the number of directors the corporation is to have, the Model Act says that the Board may fill it and, again according to the cases, so may the shareholders. Where each class of classified shares elects a representative to the Board, only the class that elected the director is eligible to vote to fill the vacancy.

Removal

Section 39 of the Model Act provides that directors may be discharged by vote of the shareholders for "cause"—that is, conduct detrimental to the best interests of the corporation—or without cause—that is, the shareholders may decide they no longer wish to retain a particular director. This latter provision could result in discharges for personal and private disputes and affords little protection to directors representing a minority of the corporation's shares. Thus the Model Act permits removal only after a meeting of shareholders called expressly for the purpose of considering removal. It is advisable for the Bylaws to provide, as many cases require in removal-for-cause situations, that the director be given written notice of the charges against him or her and an opportunity to present a defense before the shareholders vote. This clarifies the dispute and is fair to the challenged director. The Bylaws could also provide that the Board of Directors itself may remove a director from office for "cause." Some cases hold that this power does not exist unless it is stated in the Bylaws.

Resignation

Because directors may want to resign, resignation procedures should be defined. The Bylaws could state that directors may resign at any time by delivering a written resignation to the Board of Directors, Chairperson of the Board, President, Secretary, or any other party or parties that the organizers feel is appropriate. The resignation should be effective on the date stated in the resignation or on its receipt by the appropriate party.

Compensation

Section 35 of the Model Act states that directors may establish compensation for themselves for serving as directors unless the articles provide otherwise. The organizers may want to echo this provision in the Bylaws in order to clarify that directors may receive salaries. If the organizers feel directors should not be paid salaries as directors (although they could still be paid for serving as officers, for instance), the prohibition or distinction must be included in the Articles or else the statutory provision will prevail and directors will be eligible to receive salaries.

SECTION FOUR—OFFICERS

This section describes the corporation's officers and their duties. Traditionally, officers are selected, and can be removed, by the Board of Directors. They derive their powers from the Board, which delegates authority to the officers to carry out the Board's policies. Actually, the officers are probably the most powerful group in the corporation since they direct the corporation's day-to-day affairs, subject to policy directives from the Board.

The Model Act provides that each corporation must have a President, one or more Vice-Presidents, a Secretary, and a Treasurer (Section 50). The corporation may also create other offices such as Chairperson of the Board, Vice-Chairperson of the Board, Chairperson of the Executive Committee, Executive Vice-President, Senior Vice-President, Comptroller, Assistant President, Assistant Vice-President, Assistant Treasurer, and Assistant Secretary.

The Act, however, imposes no special qualifications for a person to be eligible for corporate office. Of course, the Articles or Bylaws may impose such qualifications, including whether officers need be residents of the state, of any particular age, or shareholders in the corporation.

The Model Act also states that two or more offices, except those of President and Secretary, may be held by the same person. Thus a corporation must have at least two individuals serving as its officers. Typically, the fewer the number of shareholders, the fewer the number of officers a corporation will have.

The Bylaws should specify the titles and duties of the corporation's officers. The usual choices are President, Vice-President, Secretary, and Treasurer, with a provision that the Board or the shareholders may create any other offices they feel are necessary.

Choosing officers from among the directors tightens the Board's control of the corporation and may also make the corporation more responsive to the shareholders—since shareholders elect the directors from whom the officers are selected. Thus, if the shareholders were dissatisfied with an officer's performance, they could fail to reelect him or her as a director, precluding him or her from serving as an officer. (Of course, this device would not be available if there was a shareholders' agreement which provided that the shareholders would elect certain persons to the Board.)

A small corporation probably does not need many officers because its day-to-day affairs are not likely to be complicated. If the corporation wants to reward its supporters with titles, however, it is certainly possible to create numerous Assistant Vice-Presidents, and so forth. But the organizers should consider carefully how many officers are really needed. It is not advisable to create unneeded officers since outsiders might presume that they are in positions of power and may attempt to do business with them.

The Bylaws should provide the manner by which officers are selected. Most corporations have their Board of Directors elect the officers at the Board's annual meeting. Although officers may be selected directly by the shareholders of a small corporation in a few states, Section 50 of the Model Act provides that the President, Vice-President, Secretary, and Treasurer shall be elected by the Board in a manner and at the time as provided in the Bylaws. Additional officers may be selected by other methods, however, including election by the shareholders.

The length of officers' terms should be specified, and any provisions that prohibit officers from serving any number of consecutive terms (or more than two, three, etc. consecutive terms) should also be spelled out.

If officers must meet certain qualifications, these should be expressed in the Bylaws. Must an officer be 18 years of age or older, a shareholder in the corporation, a director? Residence in the metropolitan area is another possible qualification, especially where officers' duties require day-to-day attention.

Removal

The corporation should be able to dismiss a misbehaving officer and, therefore, some provision for dismissal of officers should be included in the Bylaws. If the Bylaws fail to deal with the issue, Section 51 of the Model Act provides that an officer may be removed by the Board of Directors when, in its judgment, the best interests of the corporation will be served. The section goes on to say that such removal will not affect any contract rights the officer may have. The mere fact of appointment as an officer does not, according to the Act, *create* contract rights. If there is a contract, however, the Board must consider its terms before deciding to remove the officer.

In a closely held corporation, this removal procedure imperils the shareholder/director/officer identity. If there is any concern about one party attempting to freeze out another party by removal, the organizers could require a higher-than-majority margin by the Board when it votes on a removal.

Resignation

Provision should also be made for officers' resignations. The Bylaws could state that officers may resign at any time by delivering a written resignation to the Board of Directors, Chairperson of the Board, President, Secretary, or any other party or parties that the organizers feel is appropriate.

Vacancies

Since the Act requires that the President, Vice-President, Secretary, and Treasurer shall be elected by the directors, it seems clear that the directors are responsible for filling these offices if they become vacant. Vacancies in other positions could be filled by vote of the body that filled that office.

Chairperson of the Board

The Chairperson's duties obviously include presiding over Board meetings and could include presiding at stockholders' meetings. The section might also say that the Chairperson shall perform such other duties as assigned by the Board.

Vice-Chairperson of the Board

Generally this person performs the duties of the Chairperson in that person's absence, and other duties as may be assigned by the Board.

President

The President is the chief executive officer of the corporation and has general responsibility for managing its business and affairs. The President implements policies established by, and is responsible to, the

Board, uses his or her discretion in running the organization's day-to-day affairs, and has general supervisory duties and, in many cases, the ability to "bind" the corporation. Thus, for instance, the President may sign contracts on behalf of the corporation or obligate the corporation on a debt. What is more, the President has the power to do so even in some cases where the Board has not delegated to the President the authority to act as he or she did.

Depending on the nature of the corporation, the organizers may feel it important to set out other presidential duties, for example, discretion in choosing projects, power to hire and fire employees, and so forth. Details are a matter of choice for the organizers. If there are specific duties unique to the President's job, however, these should be expressed in the Bylaws.

Vice-President

The Vice-President generally acts for the President in his or her absence, and performs other duties assigned by the President or the Board. The Vice-President generally does not have power to bind the corporation unless he or she is delegated specific authority on a particular point.

Secretary

The Secretary is responsible for giving notice of shareholder's and directors' meetings, receiving and sending corporate correspondence, recording stockholders on the corporation's books, keeping minutes of stockholders', Board, and Executive Committee meetings, filing reports and statements as required by local law, certifying corporate documents, and performing any other duties assigned by the Board or the President.

Treasurer

The Treasurer is responsible for corporate funds and other corporate valuables. He or she keeps accounts of receipts and expenditures, oversees deposits of the corporation's money and valuables in banks designated by the corporation, renders accounts on request to the President or the Board, and frequently makes disbursements and signs checks.

Other Officers

If there are to be Assistant Vice-Presidents, Assistant Secretaries, Assistant Treasurers, and so forth, their positions and responsibilities could also be briefly listed and described in the Bylaws.

Because certain officers are responsible for certain duties does not mean that they have to perform such duties personally. They must, however, see to it that the tasks are properly performed by whomever has been delegated responsibility for actually doing the work.

Salaries

Officers may receive salaries for their services to the corporation as officers, and the Bylaws could contain a provision reaffirming this. If the organizers want to set or to prohibit salaries for officers, for instance, so that shareholder-officers are rewarded largely or solely through their portions of corporate profits received as dividends, that restriction should be included in the Bylaws.

SECTION FIVE—FINANCIAL MATTERS

The contents of this section clarify various corporate financial transactions such as contracts, loans, checks, and bank deposits.

Contracts

The Bylaws could require that all contracts on behalf of the corporation be authorized by the Board of Directors, or could specifically delegate the authority to enter into contracts to particular officers. In a small corporation, the former provision has some attraction, since all the directors would then have an opportunity to review a contract; however, delegation of authority is more convenient, and unless otherwise stated the President generally has implicit authority to execute ordinary contracts on behalf of the corporation. Extraordinary contracts remain subject to Board approval.

Loans

The Bylaws may provide that no loans shall be made, or debts incurred, in the name of the corporation unless authorized by the Board.

Since directors could potentially be liable to the corporation if these actions were taken improperly, it is appropriate that the Board first consider and approve all borrowing. It is also a safety feature for Board members who thereby have an opportunity to examine corporate activities that might be harmful to the corporation.

Checks

The organizers must decide who will manage the corporation's money. The President and the Treasurer are logical choices, but other persons could also be designated. A possible Bylaws provision would be that two persons must always sign the corporation's checks and notes, one person being the President, and the other being any one of a group including the Treasurer, Secretary, Vice-President, or Chairperson of the Board. As a practical matter, the bank where the corporate checking account is maintained will have given the corporation a "signature card" which includes a standard Board resolution establishing the number and identity of permissible signatories. The Board will then choose the signatories, fill out the signature card, and return it to the bank which will keep it on file. Those listed will be the only signatories the bank will honor unless the Board amends its resolution, fills out another signature card, and files it with the bank.

Deposits

The Bylaws may provide that the corporation's monies shall be deposited in banks selected by the Board, the President, the Treasurer, or duly authorized persons. In addition to a conveniently located bank, the corporation should consider such factors as availability of loans, banking services offered, planning assistance available, and whether the bank has experience servicing businesses of a similar size and type.

SECTION SIX—SHARE CERTIFICATE

A share certificate is a piece of paper which evidences a shareholder's interest in a corporation. It may be a simple typewritten instrument containing the vital information regarding the interest it represents, including the name of the corporation, the number of shares represented by the certificate, who owns them, the class of shares, and its par value. The corporate certificate may also be a printed or engraved document. Blank share certificates, with space for appropriate information to be filled in, may be purchased at business stationery and legal supply stores. In fact, an entire corporate kit including share certificates, sample Bylaws, common resolutions, sample minutes, and a stock transfer ledger may be ordered from many legal stationers.

Pursuant to Section 23 of the Model Act, share interests must meet the following requirements:

1. Share interests must be represented by some form of written share certificate.

2. These certificates may be signed by the corporation's President *or* Vice-President *and* Secretary *or* Assistant Secretary.

3. The certificates must contain the corporation's seal. This can be merely a label or could be a corporate stamp which is impressed on the paper. (The latter is available from many printing companies and is generally included in the corporate kit.)

4. Every certificate representing shares issued by a corporation that is authorized by its Articles to issue shares of more than one class or series must state the designations, preferences, limitations, and relative rights of the shares of each class authorized to be issued, and the variations and preferences between shares of each series within a class, or that the corporation will furnish these details.

5. Every share certificate must state that the corporation is organized "under the laws of [the jurisdiction of incorporation]."

6. The shareholder's name must appear on his or her share certificate(s).

7. The certificate must express how many and what class of shares the certificate represents.

8. Each certificate must state the par value of the shares it represents or that the shares are of no par value, whichever is appropriate.

9. Certificates may not be issued until the shares it represents have been paid for.

10. While it is not required, it is wise to include a notation on any shares subject to a shareholders' agreement the terms of that agreement or a summary of the terms.

The Bylaws could include these provisions, and may also establish other rules regarding the corporation's shares, for example, that certificates bear the address as well as name of the shareholder, or a provision that the corporation may require a deposit or bond from a share-holder who loses a certificate and wants the corporation to replace it.

Finally, this section of the Bylaws could describe the procedures for transfers of the corporation's shares, such as notation in an official stock book, proof of stock ownership prior to allowing transfer, physical presentation of the stock certificates, and so forth.

SECTION SEVEN—FISCAL YEAR

This section may state the corporation's fiscal year, or may provide that the fiscal year shall be established by resolution of the Board of Directors. A fiscal year could be the calendar year, January 1–December 31, or any other 12-month interval. If the corporation has a period of greater activity than other times (seasonal, Christmas, etc.), the fiscal year could end just after that period. This allows the annual report and annual meetings to reflect and discuss the results of this period of peak activity.

SECTION EIGHT—CORPORATE SEAL

The corporation is not required to have a formal corporate seal but if it decides to adopt a seal, the seal may be described in the Bylaws, (e.g., "The corporation's seal shall consist of a round figure with the corporation's name written around the circumference") or the Bylaws may provide that the corporation's seal shall be adopted by resolution of the Board of Directors.

SECTION NINE—NOTICE REQUIREMENTS

A general summary of the requirements for notice of various corporate meetings could be included in the Bylaws. In addition, a provision concerning waiver of notice could be included. For instance, the Bylaws could state:

> Whenever any notice is required to be given under the provisions of the law, the Articles of Incorporation, or these Bylaws, a written waiver thereof, signed by the person or persons entitled to said notice, and filed with the records of the meeting, whether before or after the time stated therein, shall be deemed to be the equivalent to such notice. In addition,

any stockholders who attend a meeting, in person, or by proxy, without protesting at the commencement of the meeting the lack of proper notice thereof to him or her, or any director who attends a meeting of the Board of Directors, or any member of any committee who attends a committee meeting, without protesting, at the commencement of the meeting, such lack of notice, shall be conclusively deemed to have waived notice of such meeting.

SECTION TEN—PROCEDURES FOR AMENDMENTS

The procedure for amending the corporation's Articles of Incorporation is prescribed by Section 59 of the Model Act. This procedure requires that

(a) The Board of Directors shall adopt a resolution setting forth the proposed amendment and directing that it be submitted to a vote at a meeting of shareholders, which may be either an annual or a special meeting.

(b) Written or printed notice setting forth the proposed amendment or a summary of the changes to be effected thereby shall be given to each shareholder of record entitled to vote at such meeting within the time and in the manner provided in this chapter for the giving of notice of meetings of shareholders. If the meeting be an annual meeting, the proposed amendment or such summary shall be included in the notice of such annual meeting.

(c) At such meeting a vote of the shareholders entitled to vote shall be taken on the proposed amendment. The proposed amendment shall be adopted upon receiving the affirmative vote of the holders of at least a majority of the outstanding shares entitled to vote, unless any class of shares is entitled to vote as a class in respect thereof, as hereinafter provided, in which event the proposed amendment shall be adopted upon receiving the affirmative vote of the holders of at least two-thirds of the outstanding shares of each class of shares entitled to vote as a class in respect thereof and of the total outstanding shares entitled to vote.

(d) Any number of amendments may be submitted to the shareholders, and voted upon by them, at one meeting.

In addition, the Bylaws should describe how they themselves may be amended or altered. Pursuant to Section 27 of the Model Act, the Bylaws may be amended by majority vote of the Board of Directors, unless that power is granted to the shareholders in the Articles of Incorporation. Vesting this responsibility in the shareholders is one way for the shareholders of a small corporation to keep a rein on the corporation's management; however, if there are many shareholders, granting the shareholders the power to amend the Bylaws may be unworkable. If the organizers decide that the Bylaws may be amended by the Board, they should specify whether an amendment requires a greater-than-majority vote, (e.g., two-thirds, three-fifths, etc.). As with other high-vote requirements discussed earlier, a greater-than-majority vote requirement for Bylaws changes would tend to preserve the existing Bylaws and the management structure they produced.

SECTION ELEVEN—COMMITTEES

The Model Act recognizes two types of committees, those exercising the authority of the Board of Directors in the management of the corporation, and those with lesser responsibilities. The former type of committee is called an Executive Committee. Provision for an Executive Committee in the Articles or Bylaws is optional; however, if the organizers envision that the Board may want to delegate some or all of its duties to a smaller (and perhaps more efficient) group of directors, the Articles or Bylaws must contain a provision allowing the Board to pass a resolution approving the delegation of power to an Executive Committee. A delegation may be particularly useful when there is only one or two organizers, but a statutory requirement of three directors. The one or two organizers must operate with others in order to comply with the three-director requirement. If the organizers do not want an outsider to interfere with running the corporation, the Articles or Bylaws could provide for the possibility of an Executive Committee which will exercise the authority of the Board in the management of the corporation. Then the Board, by majority vote, must pass a resolution that creates the Committee and delegates authority to it.

The one or two organizers/directors who want to maintain control of the corporation may then designate themselves as the members of the Executive Committee and run the corporation virtually unmolested by the other director or directors.

Any committee exercising the Board's authority *must* be *selected by* and be comprised of directors. The Article or Bylaw provision authorizing such a committee could state the following:

> The Board of Directors, by resolution adopted by a majority of the Board, may appoint an Executive Committee consisting of at least one director who shall exercise such powers and functions of the Board as provided in the resolution of the Board establishing such Committee.

If the Board delegates its authority to an Executive Committee, it is not thereby relieved of its responsibilities nor are directors who do not serve on the Committee relieved of their responsibilities and potential liabilities as directors (Section 42 of the Model Act). It may, therefore, be wise for the Board to reserve some control over the Executive Committee. For example, the Board might retain the power to dissolve the Committee at any time, the power to limit the areas in which the Committee may act, or the power to veto any Executive Committee decisions.

The Bylaws may express the manner of selection of Executive Committee members, the authority of the Committee, the term of office of members of the Committee, and any operating procedures which the organizers wish to impose on the Committee—including quorum requirements, the percentage of vote necessary to carry a motion, procedures for filling vacancies on the Committee, whether meetings by phone or action by written consent are permitted, and who will preside at Committee meetings. All or part of the foregoing may also be contained in the resolution of the Board that establishes the Committee. The procedural details could even be left to the Committee to determine once it comes into existence. However, an Executive Committee is a powerful group, and the Board or the organizers may want to define its operations specifically before it goes to work.

Common choices concerning quorum and vote requirements for Executive Committee actions are that a majority of the Committee constitutes a quorum and that a motion is carried by majority vote of the committee members present at a meeting at which a quorum is present. If the Executive Committee has been delegated all or much of the powers of the Board, however, especially where there is a large Board, there may be reason to impose a high-quorum and/or high-vote requirement, since under the majority-quorum, majority-vote procedure, the following is possible:

Twenty-one-person Board delegates its authority to a five-person Executive Committee. Three members of the Committee constitute a quorum, therefore two members voting together could carry the vote. Thus, the 21-person Board could be subject to, and potentially liable for, the decisions of two Executive Committee members.

The preceding situation could be avoided by increasing the quorum for Executive Committee meetings, the vote requirement, or both, or requiring a majority (two-third, three-fourth, etc.) vote of the *entire* committee to carry a motion. (These considerations are not relevant, however, if the *purpose* of the Executive Committee is to centralize control to prevent a certain director or directors from interfering with the organizers' management of the corporation.)

The differences between creating a committee that exercises the authority of the Board, and creating any other type of committee, are significant enough to reemphasize. If any committee is to possess the authority of the Board, the Bylaws must permit its existence, that is, say that the Board *may* create such a committee. Then if the Board later decides to implement such a committee, a majority of the entire Board must pass a resolution creating the committee. This resolution could include the power of the Board to dissolve the Committee, the right of the Board to veto Committee decisions, the power of the Committee to act *only* during intervals between meetings of the Board, the procedure for selecting members of the Executive Committee, and so forth.

Committees that do not exercise powers of the Board do not require prior authorization in the Bylaws. To create such a committee, the Board need only pass a resolution designating the committee and appointing its members. The Bylaws may, but need not, state that the Board has the authority to create this second type of committee.

These committees may be either "standing" or "ad hoc." Ad hoc committees are created in response to one-of-a-kind situations, for example, the Ad Hoc Committee on Merger with Company X. Standing committees are continuing committees created to deal with areas of continuous concern to the corporation, for example, advertising, investment, charitable contributions, and so forth. While ad hoc committees disband after dealing with the situation that motivated their creation, standing committees remain to deal with continuing issues that arise in their areas.

It is also important to remember that *only* directors may comprise a committee exercising the Board's powers, while outsiders may serve on the other types of committees. The Bylaws *could* require these other committees to be comprised only of directors, or shareholders, but such a restriction would exclude some useful experts, who, although they were not directors or stockholders, nevertheless could be very helpful to the corporation (lawyers, accountants, etc.). Since any decisions by such committees are only recommendations to the Board, there is not a delegation of policy-making authority to nondirectors.

10

CORPORATE OPERATIONS

The preceding chapters have examined many of the legal requirements and legal alternatives applicable to corporations and their principals. This chapter will deal with some of the more practical aspects of corporate existence and, where appropriate, the legal implications of those realities. The assumptions for the following discussion are that the corporation is (or the planned corporation will be) a closely held corporation and that the principals are (or will be) directly involved in management and, in many cases, with the product or service provided by the corporation.

In such cases, there is a natural tendency for the owners to treat the corporation's business and property as if they were their own. That is, they use corporate property in their personal activities; they commingle corporate and personal funds; they add money to, or take money from, the corporation without appropriate authorization or record keeping; and they fail to document important corporate decisions or activities. In fact, record keeping of any kind is often neglected.

While it is true that in many cases such conduct does not lead to dire consequences, there are several significant problems raised by it. They involve the government, fellow shareholders, and third persons dealing with the corporation.

GOVERNMENTAL RELATIONS

Problems with government take several common forms. Perhaps the most common is the failure of the corporation to file annual reports. Most states require corporations organized in that state or licensed to do business there to file an annual report with the Secretary of State (or other official). The report typically requires the corporation to inform the state of who its directors, officers, and, occasionally, major shareholders are. It may also require such information as the number of shares outstanding or the name and address of the registered agent. There is usually a small fee connected with the filing.

The form is usually mailed well in advance of its due date to the registered agent of the corporation at its registered address (both as listed with the state by the corporation). The registered agent should then, if he or she is a principal, fill out and return the form. If the agent is not a principal, he or she should forward the form to an officer of the corporation who should complete and return it. The failure to file the form generally carries with it a cash penalty and, often, after successive failures, an automatic revocation of the corporate charter. While the charter may be reinstated retroactively, there is some question of individual liability during the period of revocation.

There is also a problem concerning the proper licensing of "foreign" corporations.* Unlike individuals (or partnerships or sole proprietorships) corporations cannot travel from state to state without being subject to restrictions. Each state may legally close its doors to foreign corporations or severely restrict them. In fact, this does not occur and all states allow foreign corporations in. The procedure is for a foreign corporation to file with the state where it wants to do business a document very similar to Articles of Incorporation.

Among other things, the foreign corporation must list a registered agent and registered office in the new state. Once filed, the foreign corporation receives a certificate of authority for a foreign corporation which entitles it to do business in the foreign state. To keep that authority current, the foreign corporation must file an annual report similar to the one filed by a domestic corporation. This is in addition to filing a report with the state of incorporation. Failure to file results in penalties, including a revocation of authority to do business. A foreign corporation which never had authority, or has had its authority revoked, yet continues to do business in the foreign state, subjects itself

* Corporations incorporated in a state, but doing business in a different state are said to be foreign corporations in the second state. They are "domestic" corporations in the state of incorporation.

to civil and sometimes criminal penalties and may subject its principals to personal liability.

Another potential difficulty with the government that is raised by inadequate record keeping concerns taxation. In order to arrive at a corporation's tax liability, it is necessary to list items of income and deductible expense. If records are not adequately kept, merely determining the appropriate figures will be difficult. Of perhaps greater concern, however, is a challenge by the IRS or the state tax department to the figures used. In these situations, the disallowance of a deduction or credit will result in higher taxes, interest, and perhaps civil penalties. In extreme cases, criminal sanctions could be imposed. Therefore, it is critical for principals to keep, or instruct corporate employees to keep, good records and to document important transactions. This support is necessary to justify any challenged item.

RECORD KEEPING

Similarly, decisions and activities, financial and otherwise, must be documented to protect minority interests from overreaching by the majority. Meetings must be held; notice of these meetings must be given, as required by statute or Bylaws, or notice must be waived; minutes must reflect decisions made and should reflect the discussion leading to those decisions; and minutes and supporting documents should be kept in an orderly way and in safe and accessible places.

The value of good record keeping also comes up in buy-sell situations between shareholders. These situations may be the result of a formal shareholders' agreement or of a more informal desire of one (or more) shareholder wishing to get out of the corporation or of another shareholder(s) wishing to have a larger stake in the corporation. Either of these might arise in friendly or hostile circumstances.

In the friendly situation, negotiations may have moved along to the point of determining a formula for the price of the purchase or sale of shares, but the books, due to inadequate record keeping, do not accurately reflect the value of the corporation. In the hostile situation, it may be that the lack of record keeping is the cause of the demand to be bought out.* A minority shareholder may feel that the majority interest is running the corporation for personal benefit and in disregard of

---

* It should be noted that, in the absence of a shareholders' agreement to the contrary, a minority shareholder has no right to be bought out. Conversely, a majority shareholder is not obligated to take a minority shareholder out of his or her investment. So long as the minority shareholder is not being oppressed, a buy-out depends on the voluntary agreement of the parties.

minority concerns. In such a case, the lack of records may be designed to mask the true state of affairs of the corporation and itself could be a basis for a lawsuit by a dissatisfied minority shareholder.

PIERCING THE CORPORATE VEIL

In addition, the lack of corporate formality, including the lack of good record keeping, could in some extreme circumstances remove the corporate protection against individual liability from the principals. This process, known as "piercing the corporate veil," arises when a claimant against the corporation finds the corporation's assets insufficient to meet his or her claim. The claimant will then ask the judge in a lawsuit against the corporation and its shareholders and directors to disregard the corporation's existence and hold the principals individually liable for what appears to be a claim only against the corporation. The basis for this request is that since the principals have not treated the business as if it were a corporation, they should not have the protection of limited liability. Among the things the claimant will want to point to are the lack of corporate meetings, minutes, financial documents, and records, the use of corporate assets for personal purposes, and the commingling of corporate and personal assets.

While it is rare for a court actually to "pierce the corporate veil," the risks are sufficiently serious so that shareholders should beware. Since it is relatively simple to prevent a piercing, being forewarned is, indeed, being forearmed. All that is necessary is to comply with the state's legal requirements concerning corporate formation and operation, keep adequate records, and maintain a separation between personal and corporate activities. If there is to be some overlap in this area, be sure it is done with full disclosure to other directors/shareholders, with majority (or, if necessary, super-majority) consent and with a written record of the decision.

11

TAXES

FEDERAL INCOME TAXES

Since a corporation is recognized by the law as an individual entity apart from those who make it up, it stands to reason that a corporation will be taxed as an individual. Section 11 of the Internal Revenue Code, indeed, imposes an income tax on corporations. In many ways, the corporate tax is like that imposed on individuals but there are differences. Among the most important are the rate structure and the items that may be deducted. The Tax Reform Act of 1986 (TRA) highlights many of these differences through several changes in the law. This chapter and the next will explain some of federal tax law as it applies to corporations and their shareholders. It should be kept in mind, however, that the Internal Revenue Code is enormously complex with implications and ramifications not always readily observable, even to the practiced eye. These subtleties have been exacerbated by TRA. Therefore, while tax planning is an undertaking of great importance, it should not be undertaken without experienced, professional assistance.

To begin with the basics, Section 63 of the Internal Revenue Code defines the taxable income of a corporation as its "gross income minus the deductions allowed [by the Code]." This means that in determining how much tax a corporation has to pay, one must first determine its total income. From that amount may be subtracted allowable "deductions," that is, amounts actually spent or otherwise allowed pursuant to the Code, particularly Parts VI and VIII (Sections 161–194 and 241–250, which include deductions for interest paid, rental payments on business property, salaries paid, depreciation, bad debts, etc). Once the deductible amounts have been subtracted, you are left with "taxable income." It is against this amount that the tax rates are applied. It is here that one of the major changes wrought by the TRA appears, generally to the benefit of the small corporation.

The benefit comes from the reduction in corporate tax rates. The highest rate has been reduced from 46 to 34%, effective for tax years *after* June 30, 1987. (It should be noted that for any corporate tax year which begins before and ends after June 30, 1987, the old and new rates will be combined.)

Essentially, there are three corporate tax brackets: for taxable income up to $50,000, the rate is 15%; for taxable income in excess of $50,000 but not more than $75,000, the rate is 25%; and for taxable income over $75,000, the rate is 34%. (Some of this benefit is reduced for corporations with taxable income in excess of $100,000. For them there is a 5% surtax phased in from the $100,000 level to $335,000. At that point, the benefit of the graduated tax has been eliminated and the corporation is paying at a flat 34% for all of its taxable income.) An interesting and important sidelight to these changes is that the top corporate rate is now higher than the top individual rate, a switch from former practice. This switch will have a major impact on how controlling shareholders do their tax planning.

The way the corporate tax works may best be understood by a simple example. Assume Corporation X provides a service, for example, gardening. In its tax year, it receives $175,000 for performing its gardening services and also $10,000 interest on its bank account. Therefore, its income is $185,000. From this it may deduct (among other possible items): salaries it paid to employees—$60,000; rent for its office and its equipment—$15,000; and insurance, phone and utilities—$5,000. This total deduction of $80,000 must be subtracted from the $185,000 income leaving a taxable income of $105,000:

Income	$185,000
Deductible Expenses	− 80,000
Taxable Income	$105,000

The corporate tax rates are then applied to the taxable income of Corporation X. For the first $50,000 of taxable income, the rate is 15%—giving a tax of $7,500. The next $25,000 is taxed at 25% for a tax of $6,250. The next $30,000 is taxed at 34%—for a tax of $10,200. Finally, there is a 5% surtax on everything over $100,000 (up to

$335,000). In this case, the surtax is applied to $5,000—giving a tax of $250. The tax for each of these brackets is then added up to arrive at Corporation X's tax liability. Again, a short chart may be helpful in summarizing.

Corporation X's Income		Corporate Tax Rate	Corporation X's Tax
First	$ 50,000	15%	$ 7,500
Next	$ 25,000	25%	$ 6,250
Remaining	$ 30,000	34%	$10,200
Excess over			
$100,000	$ 5,000	5% (surtax)	$ 250
	$105,000		$24,200

It should be noted that the total tax to be paid does not correspond to any of the marginal tax brackets. In fact, the amount owed is just a bit more than 23% of the taxable income of the corporation. This is because of the "graduated" element of the tax structure. This means that corporations, like individuals, are taxed on *brackets* of income. If Corporation A had only $50,000 of taxable income, it would pay the same tax on that $50,000 as Corporation X paid on the *first* $50,000 of its $105,000 taxable income.*

Returning to our example of Corporation X, it has a tax liability of $24,200 on taxable income of $105,000. Assuming, for this example, that the taxable income is synonymous with gross profit, Corporation X had $80,800 after-tax (or net) profit ($105,000 − $24,200 = $80,800). Assume further that the corporation needed to retain some of that profit for corporate purposes and wished to distribute the rest as dividends to its shareholders. Therefore, the Board decides to keep $50,000 and to distribute $30,800 to the shareholders. Each individual shareholder receiving a portion of that distribution is required to report it, thereby subjecting it to tax as part of his or her personal income. Thus the same pool of money which was taxed as part of the corporation's gross income is taxed again as part of the shareholder's income. This is known as "double taxation" and is a drawback to incorporating. Despite this

---

* Again, it should be noted that the 5% surtax has the effect of reducing and, eventually, eliminating the "graduated" feature. Once a corporation reaches $335,000 of taxable income, the 5% additional tax on everything over $100,000 (i.e., $235,000) results in that corporation paying, as a practical matter, 34% on all its income

First	$ 50,000 at 15%	= $ 7,500
Next	$ 25,000 at 25%	= $ 6,250
Remaining	$260,000 at 34%	= $88,400
Excess Over	$100,000 at 5%	= $11,750
TOTAL TAX	$113,900	= 34%
	$335,00	

fact, many people believe that the advantages of incorporation far outweigh this disadvantage. In addition, there are ways of avoiding or minimizing the effect of double taxation and these will be explored in Chapter 12.

TAX PROCEDURES

Besides its obligation to report and pay taxes on its income, a corporation must fulfill several other requirements of the Internal Revenue Code. As a taxpayer, for instance, a corporation must obtain a taxpayer's ID number which is the corporate equivalent of a Social Security number. It is obtained by filing IRS Form SS-4. In addition, a corporation is responsible for filing a corporate income tax return every year on Form 1120. If the corporation has chosen a business year of January through December, its tax return must be filed on or before March 15 following the close of its business year. If any other business year has been chosen, the return must be filed on or before the fifteenth day of the third month following the close of that business year.

If the corporation's income tax is not filed within the prescribed time (and if no extension has been granted), a penalty tax is imposed for *each month* the return is overdue.

Estimated Tax Returns

In addition to filing an annual tax return, a corporation may be required to make periodic payments of its estimated taxes during the tax year. The IRS publishes a work sheet, Form 1120-W, "U.S. Corporation Worksheet for Computation of Estimated Income Tax," which is an aid to computing these estimated tax payments.

If the corporation must make estimated tax payments, these payments must be deposited in specially designated commercial banks or Federal Reserve Banks, accompanied by a Form 503, "Federal Tax Deposit, Corporation Income Taxes."

Reporting Dividends Paid

If the corporation pays dividends during the year it may have to file a Form 1099-DIV for each shareholder who received $10 or more in dividends. The key to this reporting requirement is whether the dividend was paid out of the corporation's "earnings and profits." Generally this means that if the dividends were derived from profits of the current tax year, or from profits accumulated from previous years, the corporation must report using Form 1099-DIV. If the dividends are not paid from the corporation's "earnings and profits," but are paid out of the corporation's capital surplus, the corporation must report these using "Corporate Report of Nontaxable Dividends Schedule A," Form 1096. These dividends are not taxable because they are *not* income. It is as if the shareholder is getting back part of his or her capital contribution. The result is a reduction of the shareholder's basis in his or her stockholding.

Employment Taxes

A significant tax obligation, and one which apparently causes small businesses constant difficulty, is the collection and payment of "employment taxes." The corporation's first step along this line is to apply for an "Employers' Identification Number," on Form SS-4. This number will then be the corporation's ID number for all its contacts with the IRS, not only those relating to employees.

If the corporation has one or more "employees," it may have to withhold their federal income taxes from their wages. An "employee" is a person who performs services and who is subject to the will and control of an employer, both as to *what* shall be done, and *how* it shall be done. If there is question whether a person is an "employee," the corporation may file a Form SS-8 for a determination of that individual's status.

There are two basic types of taxes that the corporation is responsible for in connection with its employees. The corporation must withhold a portion of each employee's wages for payment of the employee's own taxes, if the amount of his or her wages received during each payroll period exceeds the amount of the employee's "withholding allowances" for the same period. "Withholding allowances" are exemptions from what the employer would generally have to withhold from a particular salary. The exemptions are based on such factors as the employee's marital status, the number of dependents he or she has, and so forth.

In order to discover how many withholding allowances each employee is claiming, the corporation should have each employee complete a Form W-4, "Employee's Withholding Allowance Certificate," when the employee begins employment.

The corporation is also responsible for withholding Social Security taxes from every employee's wages. *Both the corporation and the employee must pay a Social Security tax on the employee's wages.*

This tax is calculated as a percentage of each employee's salary, up to a certain maximum salary figure—with the salary in excess of that figure not subject to Social Security tax. The corporation must file quarterly returns on Form 941 to report on its withholding from employees' wages and its own payments of Social Security taxes.

Generally, the corporation must deposit the income and Social Security taxes it withholds, together with the Social Security taxes it pays on behalf of each employee, with an authorized commercial bank or Federal Reserve Bank. Each deposit should be accompanied by a "Federal Tax Deposit," Form 501. How frequently the corporation must make deposits is determined by the amount of taxes owed.

On or before January 31 of each year, the corporation must also file an "Unemployment Tax Return," Form 940, and pay an unemployment tax. This is a corporate tax and may not be withheld from an employee's wages. This tax may also be payable in quarterly installments, depending on the total amount of the tax due.

These employment-related taxes are very important and, as mentioned previously, it is the corporation's responsibility to see that they are paid and that the proper sums are withheld and paid from employees' wages. If the corporation fails to collect and deposit these taxes, it subjects itself and, potentially, the corporate official or officials responsible for payment of tax obligations, to liability for the entire amount owed—including the portions that should have been withheld from *employees'* wages. If the corporation has not collected taxes properly for several years, this could amount to a huge sum. If the corporation does not pay what it owes, the IRS may seize the assets of the corporation and sell them in order to satisfy amounts due.

The IRS publishes a "Circular E, Employer's Tax Guide"; a "Business Tax Kit," Publication 454; and a "Tax Guide for Small Businesses," all of which are helpful and explain in greater detail the tax obligations and procedures discussed above.

In addition to the payment of federal taxes, many states impose income, real and personal property, and sales taxes on corporations operating within their borders. Corporate organizers and officers should check with their state's tax department or with a local attorney for information and assistance.

12

TAX OPTIONS FOR A
SMALL BUSINESS

Chapter 11 touched on the corporation's basic tax responsibilities. These responsibilities are applicable to corporations of any size. This chapter deals with a few tax problems and planning opportunities of small business corporations. After identifying the problems, the chapter will address Subchapter S Corporations, Section 1244 stock, and debt financing.

TAX DRAWBACKS OF INCORPORATION

One of the significant drawbacks of incorporation is the double tax to which shareholders may be exposed. First, the corporate income is taxed to the corporation. Next, that part of the corporate income which is distributed to shareholders as dividends is subject to tax again as income of the recipient. This has led to the development of a number of methods designed to avoid the double tax. One method was for shareholder-directors not to declare a dividend. Without a distribution, there would be no second tax. Unfortunately, there also would be no dividend income to the shareholders. In many cases this would be an undesirable characteristic for shareholders.

Congress, in an attempt to crack down on this undistributed corporate income and any accompanying *unneeded* accumulations of cash at the corporate level, passed Section 531 et seq. of the Internal Revenue Code (IRC), which penalizes such accumulations for any corporation "formed or availed of for the purpose of avoiding the income tax with respect to its shareholders . . . by permitting earnings and profits to accumulate instead of being distributed" (IRC Section 532(a)). For an accumulation to be permissible, it must be limited to what is "reasonably" needed for the business. This, of course, changes from business to business and from time to time within the same business. There is also a minimum amount that can be accumulated regardless of need. The formula for determining this amount for any business is found in IRC Section 535(c)(2).

In an effort to avoid this penalty while still avoiding a taxable distribution to shareholders, attempts were made, particularly in closely held corporations where shareholders were also employees or otherwise involved in the business, to distribute its "profits" in the form of nontaxable fringe benefit expenses. For instance, health, life, and disability insurance are obvious ways for the corporation to pick up expenses which are deductible for it but which would be *nondeductible* if paid by the shareholder-employee. Less obvious are meals, automobiles, gasoline, parking, and other similar items paid for (and deducted by) the corporation and received, tax free, by the shareholder. Again, Congress and the IRS have made attempts to eliminate or reduce the availability of some of these devices but their success to date has been limited.

A second tax drawback to the corporate form is the fact that net business losses (the excess of expenses over income) do not, as a rule, pass through directly to the shareholders. While shareholders do not wish their corporations to incur actual losses, if losses are incurred the shareholders would generally prefer to have those losses passed through to them individually in order to offset their personal incomes from other sources.

Moreover, there are some "losses" which appear only in the accountant's books rather than in the dollars and cents of business operations. A typical form of such losses is known as "depreciation." Depreciation (now also called Accelerated Cost Recovery System—ACRS) is an allowance permitted by IRC Sections 167 and 168 of a reasonable deduction for the loss, due to wear and tear (including obsolescence), of a so-called capital asset. The asset, in order to qualify for depreciation, must be used in a trade or business or be held for the production of income. Personal, nonbusiness items, are not eligible for the depreciation deduction.

While there are many ways to calculate the depreciation deduction, a simple example should suffice for the purpose of this book. Suppose

Company X bought a machine for $10,000. Assume also the machine was expected to run and be productive for five years before it needed to be replaced. Since the asset, the machine, was to last for an extended period (more than merely the tax year in which it was purchased), the tax law requires the taxpayer to deduct the cost of that machine over its productive life rather than all at once in the year of purchase. The *actual* life of the machine, however, is speculative, so various tax conventions have been developed to accommodate the need for some certainty in the tax law. Therefore, if the type of machine typically lasts for five years, the tax code allows the taxpayer to use that term as the useful life of the asset for the purpose of the depreciation deduction.

The actual amount of the depreciation deduction is determined by dividing the asset's basis (normally, its cost) by its useful life. In our example, you would divide $10,000 (the machine's cost, or basis) by 5 (the machine's useful life). This would give the taxpayer a deduction of $2,000 for each of the five years of the asset's life. The idea is that when the asset finally wears out and needs to be replaced, its cost would have been fully deducted with annual savings to the taxpayer to help replace the asset.*

In many cases, however, the asset survives for a much longer period than its prescribed useful life, or the asset's purchase was financed by a borrowing to be paid back over a period longer than the asset's statutory useful life. In some cases, primarily in the area of real property, the asset may actually *appreciate* in value over time. Nevertheless, the depreciation deduction may still be taken under one of the standard formulae permitted in the Internal Revenue Code. Therefore, in any particular year, the deduction for depreciation may not correspond to any actual expenditure or to any real loss in value suffered by the company. These "paper" losses (those found only in the accountant's records) are the type business people desire when they speak of "tax losses." Unfortunately for the typical shareholder, these losses, as others, do not pass through the corporation to the shareholders. Rather, the corporation may take the losses to offset its own income. If the losses exceed the corporate income, the excess loss may be carried over to subsequent years to offset income in those years. The carryover would be added to the losses for the year in question, and if losses still exceeded income the taxpayer would carry the excess over into the next year, and so on until the carryovers were used up (i.e., until income in a particular year exceeds losses plus any loss carryover). The shareholders, however, would not get a direct benefit from such losses.

* There are many other methods of depreciation and a wealth of complexities involved. It is important to speak to a trained tax advisor to determine how depreciation affects your business.

The effect of this process is the logical extension of the concept of a corporation as a separate entity. The corporation is a taxpayer in its own right. As such, *it*, and not its shareholders, uses the tax benefits accorded by depreciation and other write-offs. The only benefit derived by the shareholders would be the reduction or elimination of corporate income which, in turn, reduces or eliminates corporate tax obligations, leaving more after-tax money in the corporate treasury. This money can be used for some combination of corporate expansion, corporate reserves, or distribution as dividends to shareholders.

SUBCHAPTER S CORPORATIONS

There are, however, provisions in the tax law that allow corporate income or losses to pass untaxed through the corporation. Instead, the income or loss is taxed directly to the shareholder on a pro rata basis. That is, if a shareholder owns 50% of the corporation's stock, that shareholder takes 50% of the income or losses on his or her personal tax return.

For example, assume that Corporation X has taxable income of $20,000 this year. This sum would be subject to a 15% tax. Therefore X would pay $3,000. The $17,000 remaining could be distributed as dividends to X's shareholders. If X had only one shareholder, Jane Doe, who earned a salary of $20,000 per year, and X paid her a dividend of the $17,000 remaining after taxes, her total income would be $37,000 and, disregarding deductions for this example, she would be subject to approximately $10,360 in taxes (28% bracket). Thus the total tax liability in this situation is

$$\$3,000 \text{ (Corporation X)} + \$10,360 \text{ (Doe)} = \$13,360.$$

However, if Corporation X elected to be taxed as an S Corporation, there would be no $3,000 corporate tax. X's $20,000 of taxable income would "pass through" to Doe (this would be true regardless of whether the $20,000 was actually paid to her or retained by the corporation). Doe, therefore, would have an income of $40,000 for the year— $20,000 of salary, plus $20,000 "passed through" to her from the corporation. She would be subject to approximately $11,200 in taxes on that $40,000 income. The total tax in this situation is, therefore, only $11,200, $2,160 less than without the S Corporation election.

Subchapter S is comprised of IRC Sections 1361–1379. These sections allow certain types of corporations, denominated as "small business corporations," to be taxed similarly to (but not exactly like) partnerships. Thus, for the most part, there is no corporate tax to pay. The shareholders retain the liability protection offered by corporate existence, yet largely avoid two of the major drawbacks of the corporate form: double taxation and no pass-through of corporate losses.

There are several statutory requirements which do limit the number of corporations eligible for Subchapter S treatment. These requirements are found in IRC Section 1371 and include:

1. The corporation must be a domestic (U.S.) corporation.
2. It may not have more than 35 shareholders.
3. The shareholders must be (with certain limited exceptions) individuals.
4. There may not be a nonresident alien among the shareholders.
5. There may be only one class of stock.

For this purpose, only "issued" and "outstanding" stock is considered. If there is "authorized" but unissued stock of a different class, it will not disqualify the corporation from S Corporation status. Stock is considered to be of different "classes" for S Corporation purposes if the shares are not identical with respect to the rights and interest that they convey in the control, profits, and assets of the corporation. Nevertheless, shares of stock which are identical in all respects except that they have different voting rights have been held to be only one class of shares. Any distinctions in dividend payments, liquidation rights, or any other modifications of voting power, however, disqualify the corporation from S Corporation status.

These terms have greater complexity than might initially appear. For instance, while there is a requirement that shareholders be only individuals, estates and certain trusts (among them "voting trusts") are to some extent, included within the definition of "individual." Similarly, a husband and wife jointly owning shares are considered an individual and, for the purposes of the number of shareholders, only *one* individual. On the other hand, a partnership is *not* considered an individual at all and is, therefore, not an eligible shareholder.

If the corporation qualifies as a "small business corporation," it may become an "electing small business corporation" (electing to be taxed as an S Corporation) by filing Form 2553, "Election by a Small Business Corporation." This election requires the consent of *all* the corporation's shareholders, and must be made prior to the taxable year for which it is to be effective, or by the fifteenth day of the third month of that taxable year. The election is then effective for that year and all succeeding years, unless it is terminated in one of the following ways:

1. The corporation ceases to meet any of the various eligibility requirements for S Corporation status.

2. The corporation terminates its own election by filing a revocation with the IRS. Though the revocation is formally filed in the name of the corporation, it requires the signatures of all the shareholders.

3. A corporation which converted to S Corporation status from standard (Subchapter C) status has excess passive income for three successive years and has at the end of each of those years accumulated earnings and profits dating from before the conversion.

This last basis for terminating an election is applicable only to corporations which began their existence as C Corporations (which are subject to the standard corporate tax) and later converted to S Corporation status. At the time of the conversion the C Corporation might have "retained earnings," that is, earnings from various years which were not distributed to shareholders. While these earnings would have been taxed at the corporate level, they would not have been taxed to the shareholders because they were not distributed. If this is the case (i.e., C Corporation's earnings and profits remain undistributed) for three successive years *and* for each of those years S Corporation has excess net passive income* (i.e., net passive investment income in excess of 25% of the company's gross receipts) the S Corporation status will be terminated. Remember, however, that the terminating factor applies only to corporations which converted from C to S Corporations and then only in particular and controllable financial circumstances.

On the other hand, an S Corporation which is subject to this termination, in that it converted from a C Corporation and has accumulated earnings and profits at the end of each year but has excess net passive income for only two (rather than the prohibited three) successive years, does not get off with no repercussion at all. Instead, in each such year, the excess net passive income (or the corporation's taxable income if less than the excess passive income) will be taxed to the corporation at the maximum rate applicable to corporations. This, of course, is an exception to the general rule that Subchapter S Corporations pay no tax themselves.

The Tax Reform Act creates another exception to this general rule.

---

* This generally involves such items as rents, royalties, and income from securities and investments.

Again, this exception involves a corporation which converted to S status from C status. If, at the time of the conversion, the C Corporation owned assets which had appreciated in value, there existed what is known as "built-in gain." If, within 10 years of the conversion from C to S status, the corporation disposes of any assets with built-in gain, the gain will be recognized and taxed to the corporation at the highest rate applicable to corporations for that year. The rate will be applied to the lesser of the recognized built-in gain or the taxable income of the corporation as if it were a C rather than a S Corporation. The total amount of gain that can be taxed to the corporation is limited to the amount of built-in gain on the date of the conversion to S Corporation status. Thus if assets continue to appreciate in value after conversion this rule does not apply. However, all gains of preexisting assets recognized within the 10 year period are presumed to be built-in gains. It is up to the corporation to prove that the appreciation arose after conversion.

While its S Corporation election is in effect, a corporation generally is not subject to corporate income taxes. Instead, each shareholder (determined as of the last day of the corporation's tax year) includes in his or her income the amount he or she *would* have received as a dividend if the corporation had distributed all its taxable income for each tax year, pro rata, to its shareholders.

If the amount of these "constructive dividends" is actually distributed at a later date, it will not subject the shareholder to a second tax. Each shareholder computes the total amount of constructive dividends previously treated as received, then subtracts from that amount the total amount of any of the corporation's *losses* that have been passed through to him or her. The result is the shareholder's "net share of the corporation's undistributed taxable income." If the corporation then distributes dividends, the shareholder will not be taxed, *up to* the amount of the shareholder's "net share of the corporation's undistributed taxable income." Any dividends in excess of the amount of the shareholder's "net share" are fully taxable.

Just as the corporation's taxable income is "passed through" to its shareholders, so are its losses—but to a more limited extent. In fact, one of the purposes of an S Corporation is to permit small business corporations realizing losses in their initial stages of operation to pass through these losses to their shareholders to offset income the shareholders may, subject to TRA receive from other sources. Thus, with an S Corporation, each shareholder may use a portion of his or her share of the corporation's losses to his or her personal income tax return to reduce taxable income.

The "pass-through" of tax losses is not unlimited, however. A shareholder may not deduct a share of the corporation's tax loss that exceeds that shareholder's "investment" in the corporation. At a given time, a shareholder's "investment" equals the "basis" of his stock plus any debt the corporation owes the shareholder; that is, (the cost of the stock to the shareholder + the amount of "constructive dividends" the shareholder is considered to have received − the amount of dividends actually paid which have been previously taxed as "constructive dividends" − losses previously "passed through" to the shareholder) + the amount of any loan by the shareholder to the corporation, or the principal amount of any debt security held by the shareholder.

For instance, in the case of shareholder A:

Stock purchase price	$100
Corporation's debt to A	100
"Constructive dividends" attributed to A in the past	100
A's investment	$300

If A owns 50% of Corporation X's stock and X has a tax loss of $500 in 1974, A's share of the loss is $250 (50% of $500). A may use the entire $250 loss to offset other income because his or her "investment" ($300) is greater than $250. However, the utilization of the $250 loss reduces A's investment to $50 ($300 − $250 = $50). Therefore, in 1975, if the corporation loses $200, A's share of the loss would be $100 (50% of $200); however, unless A has made additional "investments" in the corporation, A may use only $50 of that loss to offset income from other sources.

Despite the advantages available to shareholders in an S Corporation, an election of that status is not appropriate in all cases. The most obvious cases to choose an S Corporation are when the corporation expects losses and where the shareholder's tax bracket is lower than the corporation's. The first situation often occurs in the early years of a business's life. Expenses in starting the business and the costs to carry it while building a clientele usually lead to an excess of expense over income. The pass-through of all of these losses is usually desirable. As the corporation becomes profitable, the shareholders can consider terminating their S Corporation election and accept standard corporate taxation.

The second situation, where the corporate tax bracket is higher than the shareholder's, occurs at the top level of taxation where in 1988 the corporation has a 34% rate and the individual has a 28% rate (with some adjustment upward). In addition, and independent of the rates, the question of double taxation would arise. If the corporation wishes to distribute its pretax earnings but cannot do it in a manner that would give rise to a deductible expense, the distributed earnings would be exposed to tax at the corporate and shareholder levels.

In this regard, there are certain disadvantages to S Corporation status. Some deductions available to C Corporations are not available to S Corporations. Among the most important is the unavailability of certain otherwise deductible fringe benefits for any shareholder who owns 2% or more of the S Corporation stock. This means that the cost of those benefits is treated as income to the shareholder. Moreover, a C Corporation which wishes to retain or otherwise reinvest some part or even all of its earnings spares its shareholders tax on the part retained or reinvested. An S Corporation may also wish to retain some or all of its earnings, but in this case the shareholder is not spared taxation. Each shareholder will be taxed on his or her pro rata share of taxable income even if he or she does not receive any of it, that is, if all of the earnings are retained by the corporation.

Another drawback of the S Corporation is the limited flexibility it has in determining its tax year. A C Corporation can choose any fiscal year that makes sense, but under TRA an S Corporation must choose the tax year used personally by its majority or principal shareholders. If there is no common year among such shareholders, the S Corporation must use a calendar year. The only exception is if the corporation can show a legitimate business purpose for the desired tax year.

These disadvantages are only some of those that might attend an election as an S Corporation. It is important for shareholders to consider these and explore other issues and their legal and financial implications. Again, the assistance of a knowledgeable professional is highly recommended.

SECTION 1244 STOCK

In most instances, when a small corporation's stock is sold or exchanged at a loss, or becomes worthless, the stock is considered a long-term capital loss. This means that the holder of the stock must offset the amount of this "capital loss" against any "long-term capital gains" he or she may have enjoyed during the year. If the individual has no long-term capital gains to set against the long-term capital loss, then the loss may be used to offset "ordinary income" but only to a limited extent.

However, it is possible for a small corporation to issue what is known as Section 1244 stock. This allows eligible stock to be given a different tax treatment. If the stock is sold, exchanged, or becomes worthless, the shareholders of Section 1244 stock may deduct their loss on this stock from their personal income from other sources up to $100,000 for a husband and wife filing a joint return, or $50,000 for other taxpayers, in the year in which the stock is sold, exchanged, or becomes worthless.

A corporation may be eligible to issue and shareholders eligible to enjoy Section 1244 stock if they meet the following tests:

1. The corporation must be a "small business corporation," that is, the aggregate amount of money and other property received by the corporation for stock, as a contribution to capital, and as paid-in (capital) surplus, does not exceed $1 million.

2. Section 1244 benefits are available only to individuals, not to corporations, trusts, and so forth, and an individual claiming a loss on 1244 stock must be the holder of an original issue of the stock, that is, an original purchaser from the corporation.

3. Only common stock, voting or nonvoting, of a domestic corporation may qualify as 1244 stock.

4. The stock must be paid for with money or property, not services to the corporation, securities, or other stock.

5. For the five years preceding the year in which the Section 1244 stock becomes worthless (or since the corporation's inception if it has not been in existence for five years), the corporation must derive more than 50% of its total gross receipts from sources other than rents, royalties, dividends, interest, proceeds from sales or exchanges of securities, or annuities.

The advantages of Section 1244 are important when a small corporation does badly or goes out of business after having done poorly. The loss on the stock for qualifying shareholders can be used to offset ordinary income rather than being treated as a capital loss.

DEBT FINANCING

"Thin incorporation" is a term used to describe a corporation which has incurred a large amount of debt in proportion to the money it has received from the issuance of its stock. A corporation would want such a financial structure so it may take a tax deduction for interest payments on the debt, particularly when the debt is owed to the shareholders, because no deduction is allowed when the corporation distributes dividends to its shareholders.

For instance, if the corporation needed to raise $10,000, it could do so in two ways: It could sell its stock for $10,000, or it could borrow some or all of the $10,000.

1. If it sells stock and the corporation made profits it could distribute those profits as dividends to its shareholders. The distribution, however, would not be deductible from its gross income so as to reduce the amount of its taxes.

2. On the other hand, when the corporation borrows and pays interest on its debts, it may deduct the amount of these interest payments from its gross income and thereby have a smaller taxable income. Of course, if the corporation is failing and not making money, the requirement to make interest payments on debt can be troublesome. Many marginal corporations go under because of burdensome debt service.

Thus, if Corporation X made a before-tax profit of $10,000 in 1987 and distributed all of it to its shareholders as dividends, X would still be subject to corporate taxes on that $10,000. If X paid $10,000 in *interest* on debts, however, it could deduct the $10,000 from its income, leaving it with *no taxable income*. It should be noted, however, that this will also eliminate profit. If the debt is owed to shareholders, this is relatively unimportant. If, however, the debt is owed to outsiders, the loss of profits due to interest payments is a serious problem to the owners.

These results may tempt organizers to create a creditor relationship with their corporation. It is possible to do this; shareholders may be creditors of their corporation. When the proportion of debt to equity exceeds 4:1, however, the IRS tends to become suspicious that the "debt" is really a disguised form of equity. In this situation, corporation/shareholder debt instruments have been known to be reclassified for tax purposes as a form of preferred stock. The IRS will look to the ratio of debt to equity, the amount of equity itself (to determine if it is adequate under the circumstances), and also whether the shareholders are "creditors" of the corporation in the same proportions as they are shareholders. While none of these factors are determinative, they contribute to an overall impression that the "debt" is really an equity investment. If the IRS comes to that conclusion, it will disallow the corporation's deductions for "interest" paid and reclassify the distribution as a dividend. Since dividends are not deductible, the amount of the distribution will be added to reported income for the year in question and taxed. This means the corporation will be subject to an increase in tax for the year in question together with interest and, perhaps, penalties for the original underpayment.

13

THE TAX REFORM ACT
OF 1986

The Tax Reform Act of 1986 made several major changes in the tax laws which will affect shareholders both as principles in their corporations and as investors. Among the most basic changes affecting shareholders as investors are the repeal of the dividend exclusion and the elimination of the favorable treatment accorded to long-term capital gains.

DIVIDENDS AND CAPITAL GAINS

Under prior law, shareholders could exclude from their ordinary income the first $100 of qualified dividends received from corporations ($200 for a married couple filing a joint return). This limited to a small degree the impact of the double tax imposed on shareholders. Of greater financial significance was the repeal of the long-term capital gains treatment.

Previously, a noncorporate taxpayer who held a capital asset (including corporate stock) for more than six months, and then disposed of it for a gain, could exclude 60% of that gain and include only the remaining 40% in his or her gross income. If several assets were disposed of, long-term gains and losses would be netted out as would short-term gains and losses. The long- and short-term results would also be net-ted, and net long-term gain received the special treatment. The effect of this was to tax long-term gain at only 40% of the rate applied to one's ordinary income. Under the new law, this special treatment has been eliminated and net long-term gain will be fully taxed at ordinary income rates.

One benefit to help counteract these changes has been the allowance of long-term capital *losses* to offset ordinary income on a dollar-for-dollar basis (up to a $3,000 per year limit) rather than the two dollars of long-term loss needed to offset each dollar of income under prior law. Net losses in excess of $3,000 may be carried forward to subsequent years.

DEPRECIATION

There have also been several changes in the depreciation (or ACRS) rules. These changes will affect, often negatively, corporations and shareholders in S Corporations. In particular, the useful life (known as the "recovery period") of many capital assets has been lengthened, thereby making depreciation slower and the annual write-offs for depreciation smaller. Among the items given longer useful lives are cars and light trucks (from 3 years under old law to 5 years under the Tax Reform Act of 1986), office equipment (from 5 to 7 years) and housing (from 19 to $27\frac{1}{2}$ or $31\frac{1}{2}$ years). Moreover, the investment tax credit was repealed retroactive to January 1986.

On the other hand, the rate at which certain items may be depreciated was increased and the allowable expensing (i.e., deducting all in one year rather than depreciating over the useful life) of an asset was increased from $5,000 to $10,000.

PASSIVE LOSSES

Among the other major changes affecting corporations and their shareholders is the limitation on the use of "passive" losses to offset income from other sources. This new category, passive activity, is one of three income categories included in the Act. The others are active income and portfolio income. Losses in a passive activity cannot, generally, be used to offset income from either of the other categories, but are limited to offsetting income from passive activities.

Passive activities may be defined by reference either to the taxpayer or to the activity. For instance, any trade or business may be deemed "passive" as to a taxpayer if that taxpayer does not "materially participate" in it. "Material participation" requires involvement in the trade or business in a regular and substantial way. There are not yet fixed rules to determine whether a taxpayer "materially participates" in a trade or business but some commonsense guidelines have been developed. For instance: Does the taxpayer have knowledge or experience in the field or is he or she merely an investor? Does the taxpayer have another major line of business? Is the taxpayer's involvement of the type normally to be expected from a principal in such a business? While none of these is dispositive of the question, each, together with others, plays a part in the determination of whether a taxpayer materially participates. It should be noted here that a limited partner, by definition, cannot materially participate in the affairs of the partnership. Thus losses from a limited partnership may not be used to offset the limited partner's income from another income category (i.e., active or portfolio). However, the test for material participation is applied to proprietors, general partners, and shareholders in an S Corporation. For a C Corporation, the test is whether one or more shareholders who, between them, own a majority of the corporate stock, materially participate. If so, the *corporation* will not be deemed to be engaged in passive activities.

The alternative referent for passive income (or loss) is the activity itself. The Tax Reform Act of 1986, for instance, deems any rental activity as passive. Thus, rental of real estate, cars, equipment, and so forth are presumed to be passive activities.

The effect of defining an activity as passive is that any losses (including depreciation) generated by the activity cannot, in general, be used to offset income from other categories (although such losses *can* be used to offset income from *other* passive activities). This, in essence, severely restricts the tax sheltering of income through the use of paper losses generated by certain types of activities (rental) or for inactive investors.

RENTAL REAL ESTATE ACTIVITIES

The law did allow a small window of relief from the passive loss rules in relation to rental real estate activities. In such cases, a person who *"actively* participates" in the rental activity may use up to $25,000 of passive losses to offset income from nonpassive sources. The benefit of this exception diminishes as the taxpayer's adjusted gross income exceeds $100,000. At that point, one dollar of the allowable deduction is lost for every two dollars of adjusted gross income. Thus the entire allowable $25,000 deduction is eliminated when the taxpayer's adjusted gross income hits $150,000.

The "active participant" requirement for allowable passive losses in real estate situations is *not* the equivalent of "material participation" for determining whether other types of activities are passive. All that is required for "active participation" is that the taxpayer does participate in some meaningful way. This does not require day-to-day involvement but does require the taxpayer to be involved in the general direction of the activity. As a bare minimum the taxpayer must hold at least a 10% interest in the activity. One who holds a smaller interest or a limited partner—regardless of the size of the interest held—are precluded from being "active participants" and taking the benefit of this exception.

To the extent actual passive losses cannot be taken by the taxpayer in any particular year, they are not lost but may be carried forward against the taxpayer's passive income in subsequent years. If the activity giving rise to the passive losses is disposed of prior to all accumulated losses having been taken, those losses may be used to reduce any gain otherwise to be recognized through such disposition.

In addition, there are a variety of other changes wrought by TRA, running from tightening and limiting the deductibility of business meals, to imposing a new alternative minimum tax on corporations, to extending the "at-risk" rules concerning the deductibility of losses to real property investments. These will all affect taxpayers significantly. Therefore tax planning and tax accounting should be a major concern to corporations and their shareholders, who should seek professional advice in this area.

14

SECURITIES

No discussion of corporations would be complete without some comment about the securities laws. Securities, which include stocks, bonds, notes, debentures, and so forth, are regulated both by the federal government and the various states. The primary federal statutes involved are the Securities Act of 1933 and the Securities Exchange Act of 1934. The main functions of each are disclosure of information to potential investors and the prevention of fraud in security transactions.

Similarly, all the states have laws regulating, in one way or another, the purchase and sale of securities. These laws are known generically as "blue sky" laws and operate independently of the federal laws. A company proposing to sell securities in several states would have to comply with the blue sky laws of each state in which the security would be sold.

This chapter will not give complete and detailed coverage of this complex field. Rather, it will give an overview of the major requirements and common exceptions to them. The primary focus of this discussion will be the federal law, both because it is a standard for much of the state legislation and because it is one body of law which is applicable throughout the nation. State law, on the other hand, may vary greatly from state to state and each state's law is applicable only to activities in that jurisdiction.

Despite this, the typical corporation will never be subject to the federal statutes. This is because the federal laws generally apply only to larger, publicly traded corporations where the securities transactions involve interstate activities.

THE 1933 ACT: REGISTRATION AND EXEMPTION

The 1933 Act had as its main purpose the disclosure to the investing public of complete and accurate information about securities and the companies issuing them. It accomplished this goal by requiring that any person (including an issuing corporation) who made any sale of any security file a registration statement disclosing a wide variety of information. The same Act provides several exemptions from the registration requirement. These exemptions concern who must register and what types of transactions are covered.

For instance, exemptions found in Section 4 of the Act remove from coverage *most* sales of securities unless conducted by an "issuer" (generally, the company creating the security and selling it). Similarly, some sales conducted by the issuer are removed from coverage. Among the main exemptions are the following:

1. *Private Placements.*   The sale of securities to not more than 35 persons who each meet certain financial and experiential tests and where there is no general advertising or widespread solicitation of purchasers.

2. *Small Offerings.*   This exemption, which is simpler to apply than the private placement exemption, concerns the value of the offering rather than the number of investors. Currently sales of not more than $5 million worth of securities need not register.

3. *Intrastate (as opposed to Interstate) Offerings.*   Where a corporation is incorporated by and doing business in only one state and sells its securities only to residents of that state, it need not register. This exemption carries strict rules concerning even an offer by the issuer to a nonresident as well as the subsequent sale of these securities by a resident to a nonresident. These rules make it difficult to use this exemption except in the most clearly local situations.

Offerings of securities falling within these exemptions need not be registered. The availability of the exemption is, however, a very difficult issue requiring the assistance of a professional advisor.

THE 1934 ACT

The 1934 Act is broader in scope than the 1933 Act. The 1934 Act has its own separate registration requirements together with a series of provisions intended to reduce manipulation, based on superior knowledge, of the securities markets and of shareholders.

The registration requirement is limited to companies listed on a national securities exchange and to unlisted companies which have more than 500 shareholders and more than $3 million in assets (this latter group typically includes companies listed in the "over-the-counter" markets, a somewhat less centralized national trading system). Here, rather than registering each new issue of securities as it is about to be sold, whole classes of securities are described in the registration statement and updated information is provided through annual reports.

The states, under specific authority from various federal laws, have been able to maintain their own regulation of securities. States have used this authority to develop their own laws prohibiting fraud in securities transactions and requiring disclosure through registration. Thus, if a company wishes to sell its securities in several states, that company must comply with the securities laws of each of those states. In doing so, the companies are said to have "blue skied" their issue of securities. As mentioned previously, state laws may vary greatly from each other and from the federal laws. Thus it is critical that any corporation contemplating selling securities in any state hire a securities lawyer in that state in order to obtain information and advice.

SAMPLE PREINCORPORATION AGREEMENT

AGREEMENT made this ____ day of _____ , 1987, between _____ , _____ , and _____ .

WHEREAS the parties hereto wish to organize a corporation upon the terms and conditions hereinafter set forth; and

WHEREAS the parties wish to establish their mutual rights and responsibilities in relation to their organizational activities;

NOW, THEREFORE in consideration of the premises and mutual covenants contained herein, it is agreed by and between the parties as follows:

FIRST: The parties will forthwith cause a corporation to be formed and organized under the laws of _____ .

SECOND: The proposed Articles of Incorporation shall be attached hereto as Exhibit A.

THIRD: Within 7 days after the issuance of the corporation's certificate of incorporation, the parties agree that the corporation's authorized stock shall be distributed, and consideration paid, as follows:

1. ____ shares of _____ (insert either common or preferred) stock shall be issued to _____ in consideration of his payment to the corporation of $_____ cash.

2. ____ shares of _____ stock shall be issued to _____

_____ in consideration of her transfer to the corporation of _____ [list property, real or personal, to be transferred].

3. . . .

4. . . .

FOURTH: The corporation shall employ _____ as its manager for a term of ____ years and at a salary of \$_____ per annum, such employment not to be terminated without cause and such salary not to be increased or decreased without the approval of ____ % of the directors.

FIFTH: The parties agree not to transfer, sell, assign, pledge, or otherwise dispose of their shares until they have first offered them for sale to the corporation, and then, should the corporation refuse such offer, to the other shareholders on a pro rata basis. The shares shall be offered at their book value and the corporation, and in the event the corporation refuses, the other shareholders shall have thirty (30) days to purchase the shares. If the corporation or other shareholders do not purchase all the offered shares, the remaining shares may be freely transferred by their owner without price restrictions.

SIXTH: The parties to this agreement promise to use their best efforts to incorporate the organization and to commence its business.

_____

_____

_____

APPLICATION FOR RESERVATION OF CORPORATE NAME

To: Secretary of State

Pursuant to the provisions of the Business Corporation Law of ____
_____ , the undersigned hereby applies for
reservation of _____* for a period of sixty (60)
days. If a foreign corporation, name of state where organized _____
_____ .

Date _____ _____
Applicant

By _____

Its _____

Address _____

* Insert corporate name to be reserved.

ARTICLES OF INCORPORATION (GENERAL)

_____

(Name of Corporation)

The undersigned, being a natural person, does hereby act as incorporator in adopting the following articles of incorporation for the purpose of organizing a stock corporation pursuant to the provisions of the _____ [name of state] Stock Corporation Act:

FIRST: The name of the corporation (hereinafter called the corporation) is _____ , Inc.

SECOND: The duration of the corporation shall be perpetual.

THIRD: The purpose for which the corporation is organized, which shall include the transaction of any or all lawful business for which corporations may be incorporated under the provisions of the _____ Stock Corporation Act, are as follows: [list, in general terms, the corporation's purposes, such as:]

To provide computer and accounting consulting services and to market and sell computer software.

To have, in furtherance of the corporate purposes, all of the powers conferred upon business corporations organized under the _____ Stock Corporation Act.

FOURTH: The total number of shares of capital stock which the corporation has authority to issue is 2000 divided into 1000 shares of Class A common stock with $.01 par value and 1000 shares of Class B common stock with $.01 par value.

The following is a description of each class of stock of the corporation with the preferences, conversion, and other rights, restrictions, voting powers, and qualifications of each class:

1. Except as hereinafter provided with respect to voting powers, the Class A common stock and the Class B common stock of the corporation shall be identical in all respects.

2. With respect to voting powers, except as otherwise required by the laws of the State of _____ , the holders of Class A common stock shall possess all voting powers for all purposes including, by way of illustration and not of limitation, the election of directors, and holders of Class B common stock shall have no voting power whatsoever, and no holder of Class B common stock shall vote on or otherwise participate in any proceedings in which actions shall be taken by the corporation or the stockholders thereof or be entitled to notification as to any meeting of the Board of Directors or the stockholders.

FIFTH: No holder of any of the shares of any class of the corporation shall be entitled as of right to subscribe for, purchase, or otherwise acquire any shares of any class of the corporation which the corporation proposes to issue or any rights or options which the corporation proposes to grant for the purchase of shares of any class of the corporation or for the purchase of any shares, bonds, securities, or obligations of the corporation which are convertible into or exchangeable for, or which carry any rights, to subscribe for, purchase, or otherwise acquire shares of any class of the corporation; and any and all of such shares, bonds, securities, or obligations of the corporation, whether now or hereafter authorized or created, may be issued, or may be reissued or transferred if the same have been reacquired and have treasury status, and any and all of such rights and options may be granted by the Board of Directors to such persons, firms, corporations, and associations, and for such lawful consideration, and on such terms, as the Board of Directors in its discretion may determine, without first offering the same, or any thereof, to any said holder.

SIXTH: 1. The corporation shall, to the fullest extent permitted by the provisions of the _____ Stock Corporation Act, as the same may be amended and supplemented, indemnify any and all persons whom it shall have power to indemnify under said provisions from and against any and all of the expenses, liabilities, or other matters referred to in or covered by said provisions, and the indemnification provided for herein shall not be deemed exclusive of any other rights to which those indemnified may be entitled under any Bylaw, vote of stockholders, or disinterested directors, or otherwise, both as to action in his or her official capacity and as to action while holding such office, and shall continue as to a person who has ceased to be a director, officer, employee, or agent and shall inure to the benefit of the heirs, executors, and administrators of such a person.

2. The stated capital of the corporation may be reduced by the Board of Directors, without the assent of the stockholders.

SEVENTH: The post office address of the initial registered office of the corporation in the State of _____ is _____ , _____ , _____ . The name of the county or city in the State of _____ in which the said registered office of the corporation is located is the county or city of _____ .

The name of the initial registered agent of the corporation at such address is _____ . His [her] business office is identical with the initial registered office of the corporation as set forth above.

EIGHTH: The number of directors constituting the initial Board of Directors of the corporation is one (1).

The names and the addresses of the persons who are to serve as members of the initial Board of Directors of the corporation are as follows:

Name	Address
_____	_____
_____	_____
_____	_____

NINTH: The provisions for the regulation of the internal affairs of the corporation shall be as set forth in the bylaws.

Signed on _____ .

_____
Incorporator

ARTICLES OF INCORPORATION (CALIFORNIA) OF

_____
(Name of corporation)

ONE: The name of this corporation is _____ .

TWO: The purpose of the corporation is to engage in any lawful act or activity for which a corporation may be organized under the General Corporation Law of California other than the banking business, the trust company business, or the practice of a profession permitted to be incorporated by the California Corporations Code.

THREE: The name and address in this state of the corporation's initial agent for service of process is _____ , _____ , California, _____ .

FOUR: This coporation is authorized to issue _____ shares.

DATED: _____

_____
, Incorporator

I declare that I am the person who executed the above articles of incorporation, and that this instrument is my act and deed.

_____
, Incorporator

CERTIFICATE OF INCORPORATION (DELAWARE) OF

_____

(Name of corporation)
A CLOSE CORPORATION

FIRST. The name of this corporation is _____ .

SECOND. Its registered office in the State of Delaware is to be located at _____
_____ County of
_____ . The registered agent in charge thereof
is _____ ,
address same as above.

THIRD. The nature of the business and the objects and purposes proposed to be transacted, promoted, and carried on are to engage in any lawful act or activity for which corporations may be organized under the General Corporation Law of Delaware.

FOURTH. The amount of total authorized capital stock of the corporation is divided into _____ shares of _no par value_.

FIFTH. The name and mailing address of the incorporator is as follows: _____ .

SIXTH. The powers of the incorporators are to terminate upon filing of the certificate of incorporation, and the name and mailing addresses of the persons who are to serve as directors until their successors are elected are as follows:

Name   Address

_____   _____

_____   _____

_____   _____

SEVENTH. All of the corporation's issued stock, exclusive of treasury shares, shall be held of record by not more than thirty (30) persons.

EIGHTH. All of the issued stock of all classes shall be subject to the following restriction on transfer permitted by Section 202 of the General Corporation Law.

Each stockholder shall offer to the corporation or to other stockholders of the corporation a thirty (30) day "first refusal" option to purchase his or her stock should he or she elect to sell his or her stock.

NINTH. The corporation shall make no offering of any of its stock of any class which would constitute a "public offering" within the meaning of the Securities Act of 1933, as it may be amended from time to time.

I, THE UNDERSIGNED, for the purpose of forming a corporation under the laws of the State of Delaware do make, file, and record this certificate, and do certify that the facts herein stated are true; and I have accordingly hereunto set my hand.

DATED AT: _____

_____

ARTICLES OF INCORPORATION
(WASHINGTON, D.C.)

To: The Recorder of Deeds, D.C.
      Washington, D.C.

We, the undersigned natural persons of the age of twenty-one (21) years or more, acting as incorporators of a corporation under Title 29, Chapter 3 of the Code of Laws of the District of Columbia, adopt the following Articles of Incorporation for such corporation:

FIRST: The name of the corporation is _____ .

SECOND: The period of its duration is perpetual.

THIRD: The purpose or purposes for which the corporation is organized are _____ ;

To engage in and carry on any other purposes which may conveniently and consistently be conducted in conjunction with any of the purposes of the corporation;

To employ such persons as it deems necessary and proper to carry out these purposes;

To lease personal and real property, as it deems necessary, to carry on these purposes;

To acquire all or any part of the good will, rights, property, and business of any person, firm, association, or corporation heretofore and hereafter engaged in any activity similar to or in furtherance of any purposes which the corporation has the power to conduct, and to hold, utilize, enjoy, and in any manner dispose of the whole or any part of the rights, property, and business so acquired, and to assume in connection therewith any liabilities of any such person, firm, association, or corporation;

To apply for, obtain, purchase, or otherwise acquire any patents, copyrights, licenses, trademarks, trade names, rights, processes, formulas, and the like, which are or may seem capable of being used for any of the purposes of the corporation, and to use, exercise, develop, grant licenses and franchises in respect of, sell, and otherwise turn to account, the same;

To carry out all or any part of the foregoing objects as principal, factor, agent, contractor, or otherwise, either alone or through or in conjunction with any person, firm, association, or corporation, and in carrying on its purposes and for the purpose of attaining or furthering any of its objects and purposes, to make and perform any contracts and to do any acts and things, and to exercise any powers suitable, convenient or proper for the accomplishment of any of the objects and purposes herein enumerated or incidental to the powers herein specified, or which at any time may appear conducive to or expedient for the accomplishment of any such objects and purposes;

To carry out all or any part of the aforesaid objects and purposes, and to conduct its activities in all or any part of its branches, in any or all states, territories, districts, and possessions of the United States of America and in foreign countries, and to maintain offices and agencies in the aforesaid jurisdictions;

The foregoing objects and purposes shall, except when otherwise expressed, be in no way limited or restricted by reference to or inference from the terms of any other clause of this or any other article of these articles of incorporation or any amendment thereto, and shall each be regarded as independent, and construed as powers as well as objects and purposes.

The Corporation shall be authorized to exercise and enjoy all of the powers, rights, and privileges granted to or conferred upon corporations of similar character by the General Laws of the District of Columbia now or hereafter in force, and the enumeration of the foregoing powers shall not be deemed to exclude any powers, rights, or privileges so granted or conferred.

FOURTH: The aggregate number of shares which the corporation is authorized to issue is one class of 1000 at $.01 par value.

FIFTH: The preferences, qualifications, limitations, restrictions, and special or relative rights in respect to the shares of each class are set forth in the bylaws.

SIXTH: The corporation will not commence business until at least one thousand dollars ($1,000) has been received by it as consideration for the issuance of shares.

SEVENTH: The provisions for the regulation of the internal affairs of the corporation are set forth in the bylaws.

EIGHTH: The address, including street and number, of the initial registered office of the corporation is _____ and the name of the initial registered agent at such address is _____ _____ . The address, including street and number, if any, where it conducts its principal business is _____ _____ .

NINTH: The number of directors constituting the initial board of directors of the corporation is _____ ( ) and the names and addresses, including street and number, if any, of the persons who are to serve as directors until the first annual meeting of shareholders or until their successors are elected and shall qualify are as follows:

Name   Address

_____   _____

_____   _____

_____   _____

TENTH: The name and address, including street and number, if any, of each incorporator is as follows:

Name   Address

_____   _____

_____   _____

_____   _____

DATE: _____

ARTICLES OF INCORPORATION (MARYLAND)

A Maryland Close Corporation,
Organized Pursuant to Title 4 of the
Corporations and Associations Article of the
Annotated Code of Maryland

FIRST: I, _____ , whose post office address is _____ , being at least eighteen (18) years of age, hereby form a corporation under and by virtue of the General Laws of the State of Maryland.

SECOND: The name of the corporation (which is hereafter call the "Corporation") is _____ .

THIRD: The Corporation shall be a close corporation as authorized by Title 4 of the Corporations and Associates Article of the Annotated Code of Maryland, as amended.

FOURTH: The purposes for which the Corporation is formed are:
1. _____

_____ ; and to engage in any other lawful purpose and business; and

2. To have all power and do anything permitted by Section 2-103 of the Corporations and Associations Article of the Annotated Code of Maryland.

FIFTH: The post office address of the principal office of the Corporation in this State is _____

_____ .

The name and post office address of the Resident Agent of the Corporation in this State are _____

_____ .

Said Resident Agent is an individual actually residing in this State.

SIXTH: The total number of shares of capital stock which the Corporation has authority to issue is _____(___) shares of common stock, without par value.

SEVENTH: The number of directors shall be (1), which number may be increased or decreased pursuant to the By-Laws of the Corporation. The name of the director, who shall act until the first annual meeting or until his or her successor is duly chosen and qualified is:

_____ .

[It should be noted that Maryland permits a close corporation to have no Board of Directors. All power would thus reside with the shareholders. If the organizers of a close corporation choose this option, they should substitute the following for the Seventh Paragraph above]

EIGHTH: The corporation elects to have no Board of Directors. Until the election to have no Board of Directors becomes effective, there shall be one (1) director, whose name is _____ .

IN WITNESS WHEREOF, I have signed these Articles of Incorporation this ____ day of _____ , 19__ , and I acknowledge the same to be my act.

_____

CERTIFICATE OF INCORPORATION (NEW YORK)

(Name of Corporation)

Under Section 402 of the Business Corporation Law IT IS HEREBY CERTIFIED THAT:

1. The name of the corporation is: _____

2. The purpose or purposes for which the corporation is formed are as follows, to wit:

To buy sell, repair, recondition, import, export, and deal in photographic equipment and supplies, parts, and accessories of every kind. To own, operate, manage, and do everything normally associated with conducting the business of a camera and photography business.

To engage in any lawful act or activity for which corporations may be formed under the Business Corporation Law. The corporation is not formed to engage in any act or activity requiring the consent or approval of any state official, department, board, agency, or other body without such consent or approval first being obtained.

To own, operate, manage, acquire, and deal in property, real and personal, which may be necessary to the conduct of the business.

The corporation shall have all of the powers enumerated in Section 202 of the Business Corporation Law, subject to any limitation provided in the business Corporation Law or any other statute in the State of New York.

3. The county in which the office of the corporation is to be located in the State of New York is:

4. The aggregate number of shares which the corporation shall have authority to issue is 200 shares, no par value.

5. The Secretary of State is designated as agent of the corporation upon whom process against it may be served. The post office address to which the Secretary of State shall mail a copy of any process against the corporation served upon him or her is: _____

_____

IN WITNESS WHEREOF, the undersigned incorporator, being at least eighteen (18) years of age, has executed and signed this Certificate of Incorporation this _____ day of June, 19__ .

STATE OF NEW YORK)   _____
)ss.
COUNTY OF ALBANY)

On this __ day of June, 19__ , before me personally came _____
_____ to me known to be the individual described in and who executed the foregoing instrument, and he or she duly acknowledged to me that he or she executed the same.

                              _____
                                        Notary
My Commission Expires: _____ .

ARTICLES OF INCORPORATION (WISCONSIN)

Form 2 - Sec. State 1973

ARTICLES OF INCORPORATION

Executed by the undersigned for the purpose of forming a Wisconsin corporation under the "Wisconsin Business Corporation Law", Chapter 180 of the Wisconsin Statutes:

Article 1.   The name of the corporation is

Article 2.   The period of existence shall be

Article 3.   The purposes shall be

Article 4.   The number of shares which it shall have authority to issue, itemized by classes, par value of shares, shares without par value, and series, if any, within a class, is:

Class	Series (if any)	Number of Shares	Par value per share or statement that shares are without par value

Article 5.   The preferences, limitations, designation, and relative rights of each class or series of stock, are

Article 6.   Address of initial registered office is
The complete address, including street and number, if assigned, and the ZIP Code, must be stated.

Article 7.   Name of initial registered agent at such address is

Article 8. The number of directors constituting the board of directors shall be fixed by by-law.

OR

Article 8. The number of directors constituting the board of directors shall be _____.

Strike out the Article 8 you do not use.

Article 9. The names of the initial directors are:

Use of Article 9 is optional

Article 10. (Other provisions)

Article 11. These articles may be amended in the manner authorized by law at the time of amendment..

Article 12.   The name(s) and address(es) of incorporator(s) are:

NAME   ADDRESS
                    (number, street, city and ZIP Code)

_____   _____

_____   _____

_____   _____

_____   _____

Executed in duplicate on the _____day of _____, 19___

                              _____

                              _____

                              _____

                              _____

==

STATE OF WISCONSIN

County of

Personally came before me this _____day of _____A.D.19____

the above named_____

_____

to me known to be the person(s) who executed the foregoing instrument,

and acknowledged the same.

                    _____
                              Notary Public

          My Commission expires_____

==

            This document was drafted by

          _____
                    (Name of Person)

              Please print or type

==

STOCK CERTIFICATE

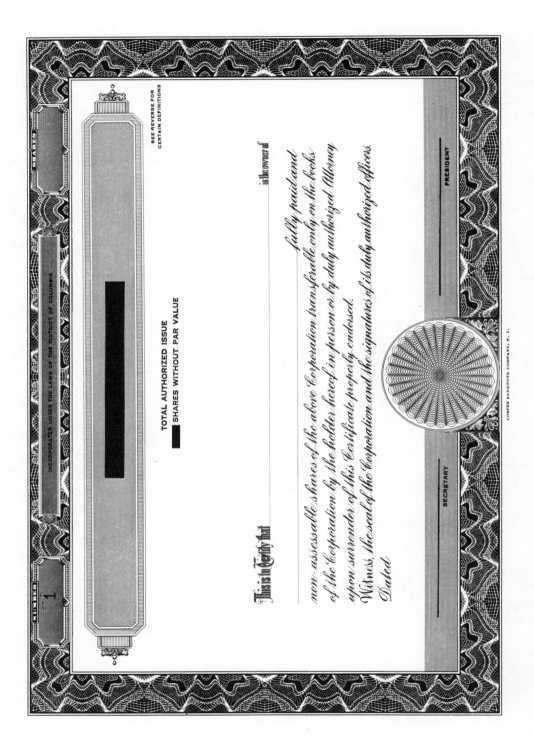

146

The following abbreviations, when used in the inscription on the face of this certificate, shall be construed as though they were written out in full according to applicable laws or regulations:

TEN COM — as tenants in common

TEN ENT — as tenants by the entireties

JT TEN — as joint tenants with right of survivorship and not as tenants in common

UNIF GIFT MIN ACT — .... Custodian ....
                                    (Cust)   (Minor)
under Uniform Gifts to Minors

Act ....
                (State)

Additional abbreviations may also be used though not in the above list.

*For value received*_____ *hereby sell, assign, and transfer unto*

PLEASE INSERT SOCIAL SECURITY OR OTHER
IDENTIFYING NUMBER OF ASSIGNEE

(PLEASE PRINT OR TYPEWRITE NAME AND ADDRESS INCLUDING POSTAL ZIP CODE OF ASSIGNEE)

_____ *Shares*

represented by the within Certificate, and do hereby irrevocably constitute and appoint

_____ *Attorney*

to transfer the said Shares on the books of the within named Corporation with full power of substitution in the premises.

Dated _____ *19*___

In presence of

_____   _____

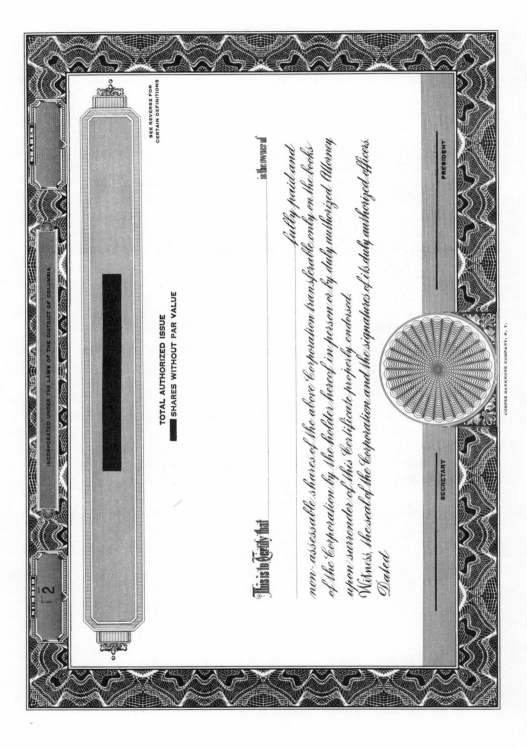

148

The following abbreviations, when used in the inscription on the face of this certificate, shall be construed as though they were written out in full according to applicable laws or regulations:

TEN COM — as tenants in common
TEN ENT — as tenants by the entireties
JT TEN — as joint tenants with right of survivorship and not as tenants in common

UNIF GIFT MIN ACT — .... Custodian ....
                  (Cust)   (Minor)
under Uniform Gifts to Minors
Act ....
          (State)

Additional abbreviations may also be used though not in the above list.

For value received_____ hereby sell, assign, and transfer unto

PLEASE INSERT SOCIAL SECURITY OR OTHER
IDENTIFYING NUMBER OF ASSIGNEE

(PLEASE PRINT OR TYPEWRITE NAME AND ADDRESS INCLUDING POSTAL ZIP CODE OF ASSIGNEE)

_____ *Shares*

represented by the within Certificate, and do hereby irrevocably constitute and appoint

_____ *Attorney*
to transfer the said Shares on the books of the within named Corporation with full power of substitution in the premises.
Dated_____ 19___

    In presence of

_____   _____

BYLAWS

ARTICLE I

Offices

SECTION 1. *Registered Office.* The registered office of the Corporation within the [State of corporation] shall be at _____
_____ .

SECTION 2. *Other Offices.* The corporation may also have an office or offices other than said registered office at such place or places, either within or without the State, as the Board of Directors shall from time to time determine or the business of the corporation may require.

ARTICLE II

Meetings of Stockholders

SECTION 1. *Place of Meetings.* All meetings of the stockholders for the election of directors or for any other purpose shall be held on [date] at _____ o'clock _.м., at such place as may be fixed from time to time by the Board of Directors, or at such other place, either within or without the State, as shall be designated from time to time by the Board of Directors.

SECTION 2. *Annual Meeting.* The annual meeting of stockholders, commencing with the year 1987, shall be held on the second Tuesday of March, if not a legal holiday, and if a legal holiday, then on the next succeeding day not a legal holiday, at 10:00 A.M., or at such other date and time as shall be designated from time to time by the Board of Directors. At such annual meeting, the stockholders shall elect, by a plurality vote, a Board of Directors and transact such other business as may properly be brought before the meeting.

SECTION 3. *Special Meetings.* Special meetings of stockholders, unless otherwise prescribed by statute, may be called at any time by the Board of Directors or the Chairperson of the Board, if one shall have been elected, or the President, and shall be called by the Secretary upon the request in writing of a stockholder or stockholders holding of record at least 20% of the voting power of the issued and outstanding shares of stock of the Corporation entitled to vote at such meeting.

SECTION 4. *Notice of Meetings.* Written notice of each annual and special meeting of stockholders stating the date, place, and hour of the meeting, and, in the case of a special meeting, the purpose or purposes for which the meeting is called, shall be given to each stockholder of record entitled to vote thereat not less than ten (10) nor more than fifty (50) days before the date of the meeting. Business transacted at any special meeting of stockholders shall be limited to the purposes stated in the notice. Notice shall be given personally or by mail and, if by mail, shall be sent in a postage prepaid envelope, addressed to the stockholder at his or her address as it appears on the records of the Corporation. Notice by mail shall be deemed given at the time when the same shall be deposited in the United States mail, postage prepaid. Notice of any meeting shall not be required to be given to any person who attends such meeting, except when such person attends the meeting in person or by proxy for the express purpose of objecting, at the beginning of the meeting, to the transaction of any business because the meeting is not lawfully called or convened, or who, either before or after the meeting, shall submit a signed written waiver of notice, in person or by proxy. Neither the business to be transacted at, nor the purpose of, an annual or special meeting of stockholders need be specified in any written waiver of notice.

SECTION 5. *List of Stockholders.* The officer who has charge of the stock ledger of the Corporation shall prepare and make, at least ten (10) days before each meeting of stockholders, a complete list of the stockholders entitled to vote at the meeting, arranged in alphabetical order, showing the address of and the number of shares registered in the name of each stockholder. Such list shall be open to the examination of any stockholder, for any purpose germane to the meeting, during ordinary business hours, for a period of at least ten (10) days prior to the meeting, either at a place within the city, town or village where the meeting is to be held, which place shall be specified, in the notice of meeting, or if not specified, at the place where the meeting is to be held. The list shall be produced and kept at the time and place of the meeting during the whole time thereof, and may be inspected by any stockholder who is present.

SECTION 6. *Quorum, Adjournments.* The holders of a majority of the voting power of the issued and outstanding stock of the Corporation entitled to vote thereat, present in person or represented by proxy, shall constitute a quorum for the transaction of business at all meetings of stockholders, except as otherwise provided by statute or by the Articles of Incorporation. If, however, such a quorum shall not be present or represented at any meeting of stockholders, the stockholders entitled to vote thereat, present in person or represented by proxy, shall have power to adjourn the meeting from time to time, without notice other than announcement at the meeting, until a quorum shall be present or represented. At such adjourned meeting at which a quorum shall be present or represented, any business may be transacted which might have been transacted at the meeting as originally called. If the adjournment is for more than thirty (30) days, or, if after adjournment a new record date is set, a notice of the adjourned meeting shall be given to each stockholder of record entitled to vote at the meeting.

SECTION 7. *Organization.* At each meeting of stockholders the Chairperson of the Board, if one shall have been elected, or, in the Chairperson's absence or if one has not been elected, the President, shall act as chairperson of the meeting. The Secretary, or in his or her absence or inability to act, the person whom the chair of the meeting shall appoint, shall act as secretary of the meeting and keep the minutes thereof.

SECTION 8. *Order of Business.* The order of business at all meetings of the stockholders shall be as determined by the chair of the meeting.

SECTION 9. *Voting.* Except as otherwise provided by statute or the Articles of Incorporation, each stockholder of the Corporation shall be entitled at each meeting of stockholders to one vote for each share of capital stock of the Corporation standing in his or her name on the record of stockholders of the Corporation:

(a) on the date fixed pursuant to the provisions of Section 7 of Article V of these bylaws as the record date for the determination of the stockholders who shall be entitled to notice of and to vote at such meeting; or

(b) if no such record date shall have been so fixed, then at the close of business on the day next preceding the day on which notice thereof shall be given, or, if notice is waived, at the close of business on the date next preceding the day on which the meeting is held.

Each stockholder entitled to vote at any meeting of stockholders may authorize another person or persons to act for him or her by a proxy signed by such stockholder or his or her attorney-in-fact, but no proxy shall be voted after three (3) years from its date, unless the proxy provides for a longer period. Any such proxy shall be delivered to the secretary of the meeting at or prior to the time designated in the order of business for so delivering such proxies. When a quorum is present at any meeting, the vote of the holders of a majority of the voting power of the issued and outstanding stock of the Corporation entitled to vote thereon, present in person or represented by proxy, shall decide any question brought before such meeting, unless the question is one upon which by express provision of statute or of the Articles of Incorporation or of these bylaws, a different vote is required, in which case such express provision shall govern and control the decision of such question. Unless required by statute, or determined by the chair of the meeting to be advisable, the vote on any question need not be by ballot. On a vote by ballot, each ballot shall be signed by the stockholder voting, or by his proxy, if there be such proxy, and shall state the number of shares voted.

SECTION 10. *Inspectors.* The Board of Directors may, in advance of any meeting of stockholders, appoint one or more inspectors to act at such meeting or any adjournment thereof. If any of the inspectors so appointed shall fail to appear or act, the chair of the meeting shall, or if inspectors shall not have been appointed, the chair of the meeting may, appoint one or more inspectors. Each inspector, before entering upon the discharge of his or her duties, shall take and sign an oath faithfully to execute the duties of inspector at such meeting with strict impartiality and according to the best of his or her ability. The inspectors shall determine the number of shares of capital stock of the Corporation outstanding and the voting power of each, the number of shares represented at the meeting, the existence of a quorum, the validity and effect of proxies, and shall receive votes, ballots, or consents, hear and determine the results, and do such acts as are proper to conduct the election or vote with fairness to all stockholders. On request of the chair of the meeting, the inspectors shall make a report in writing of any challenge, request, or matter determined by them and shall execute a certificate of any fact found by them. No director or candidate for the office of director shall act as an inspector of an election of directors. Inspectors need not be stockholders.

SECTION 11. *Action by Consent.* Whenever the vote of stockholders at a meeting thereof is required or permitted to be taken for or in connection with any corporate action, by a statute or provision of the Articles of Incorporation or of these bylaws, the meeting and vote of stockholders may be dispensed with, and the action taken without such meeting and vote, if a consent in writing, setting forth the action so taken, shall be signed by the holders of all the outstanding stock entitled to vote thereon.

ARTICLE III

Board of Directors

SECTION 1. *General Powers.* The business and affairs of the Corporation shall be managed by or under the direction of the Board of Directors. The Board of Directors may exercise all such authority and powers of the Corporation and do all such lawful acts and things as are not by statute or the Articles of Incorporation directed or required to be exercised or done by the stockholders.

SECTION 2. *Number, Qualifications, Election, and Term of Office.* The number of directors constituting the initial Board of Directors shall be _____ ( ) . Thereafter, the number of directors may be fixed, from time to time, by the affirmative vote of a majority of the entire Board of Directors or by action of the stockholders of the Corporation. Any decrease in the number of directors shall be effective at the time of the next succeeding annual meeting of stockholders unless there shall be vacancies in the Board of Directors, in which case such decrease may become effective at any time prior to the next succeeding annual meeting to the extent of the number of such vacancies. Directors need not be stockholders. Each director shall hold office until his or her successor shall have been elected and qualified, or until his or her death, resignation, or removal as hereinafter provided in these bylaws.

SECTION 3. *Place of Meetings.*   Meetings of the Board of Directors shall be held at such place or places, within or without the State, as the Board of Directors may from time to time determine or as shall be specified in the notice of any such meeting.

SECTION 4. *First Meeting.*   The Board of Directors shall meet for the purpose of organization, the election of officers and the transaction of other business, as soon as practicable after each annual meeting of stockholders, on the same day and at the same place where such annual meeting shall be held. Notice of such meeting need not be given. Such meeting may be held at any other time or place (within or without the State) which shall be specified in a notice thereof given as hereinafter provided in Section 7 of this Article III.

SECTION 5. *Regular Meetings.*   Regular meetings of the Board of Directors shall be held at such time and place as the Board of Directors may fix. If any day fixed for a regular meeting shall be a legal holiday at the place where the meeting is to be held, then the meeting which would otherwise be held on that day shall be held at the same hour on the next succeeding business day. Notice of regular meetings of the Board of Directors need not be given except as otherwise required by statute or these bylaws.

SECTION 6. *Special Meetings.*   Special meetings of the Board of Directors may be called by the Chairperson of the Board, if one shall have been elected, or by two or more directors of the Corporation, or by the President.

SECTION 7. *Notice of Meetings.*   Notice of each special meeting of the Board of Directors (and of each regular meeting for which notice shall be required) shall be given by the Secretary as hereinafter provided in this Section 7, in which notice shall be stated the time and place of the meeting. Except as otherwise required by these bylaws, such notice need not state the purpose of such meeting. Notice of each such meeting shall be mailed, postage prepaid, to each director, addressed to his or her residence or usual place of business, by first-class mail, at least five (5) days before the day on which such meeting is to be held, or shall be sent addressed to him or her at such place by telegraph, cable, telex, telecopier, or other similar means, or be delivered personally or be given by telephone or other similar means, at least twenty-four (24) hours before the time at which such meeting is to be held. Notice of any such meeting need not be given to any director who shall, either before or after the meeting, submit a signed waiver of notice or who shall attend such meeting, except when he or she shall attend for the express purpose of objecting, at the beginning of the meeting, to the transaction of any business because the meeting is not lawfully called or convened.

SECTION 8. *Quorum and Manner of Acting.* A majority of the Board of Directors then in office shall constitute a quorum for the transaction of business at any meeting of the Board of Directors, and, except as otherwise expressly required by statute or the Articles of Incorporation or these bylaws, the act of a majority of the directors present at any meeting at which a quorum is present shall be the act of the Board of Directors. In the absence of a quorum at any meeting of the Board of Directors, a majority of the directors present thereat may adjourn such meeting to another time and place. Notice of the time and place of any such adjourned meeting shall be given to the directors unless such time and place were announced, at the meeting at which the adjournment was taken, to the other directors. At any adjourned meeting at which a quorum is present, any business may be transacted which might have been transacted at the meeting as originally called. The directors shall act only as a Board and the individual directors shall have no power as such.

SECTION 9. *Organization.* At each meeting of the Board of Directors, the Chairperson of the Board, if one shall have been elected, or, in the absence of the Chairperson of the Board or if one shall not have been elected, the President (or, in his or her absence, another director chosen by a majority of the directors present) shall act as Chair of the meeting and preside thereat. The Secretary (or, in his or her absence, any person appointed by the chair) shall act as secretary of the meeting and keep the minutes thereof.

SECTION 10. *Resignations.* Any director of the Corporation may resign at any time by giving written notice of his or her resignation to the Corporation. Any such resignation shall take effect at the time specified therein or, if the time when it shall become effective shall not be specified therein, immediately upon its receipt. Unless otherwise specified therein, the acceptance of such resignation shall not be necessary to make it effective.

SECTION 11. *Vacancies.* Any vacancy in the Board of Directors, whether arising from death, resignation, removal (with or without cause), an increase in the number of directors, or any other cause, may be filled by the vote of a majority of the directors then in office, though less than a quorum, or by the sole remaining director, or by the stockholders at the next annual meeting thereof or at a special meeting thereof. Each director so elected shall hold office until his or her successor shall have been elected and qualified.

SECTION 12. *Removal of Directors.* Any director may be removed, either with or without cause, at any time by the holders of a majority of the voting power of the issued and outstanding capital stock of the Corporation entitled to vote at an election of directors. Any director may be removed for cause by the Board of Directors.

SECTION 13. *Compensation.* The Board of Directors shall have authority to fix the compensation, including fees and reimbursement of expenses, of directors for services to the Corporation.

SECTION 14. *Committees.* The Board of Directors may, by resolution passed by a majority of the entire Board of Directors, designate one or more committees, including an Executive Committee, each committee to consist of one or more of the directors of the Corporation. The Board of Directors may designate one or more directors as alternate members of any committee, who may replace any absent or disqualified member at any meeting of the committee. Except to the extent restricted by statute or the Articles of Incorporation, each such committee, to the extent provided in the resolution creating it, shall have and may exercise all the powers and authority of the Board of Directors and may authorize the seal of the Corporation to be affixed to all papers which require it. Each such committee shall serve at the pleasure of the Board of Directors and have such name as may be determined from time to time by resolution adopted by the Board of Directors. Each committee shall keep regular minutes of its meetings and report the same to the Board of Directors.

SECTION 15. *Action by Consent.* Unless restricted by the Articles of Incorporation, any action required or permitted to be taken by the Board of Directors or any committee thereof may be taken without a meeting if all members of the Board of Directors or such committee, as the case may be, consent thereto in writing, and the writing or writings are filed with the minutes of the proceedings of the Board of Directors or such committee, as the case may be.

ARTICLE IV

Officers

SECTION 1. *Number and Qualifications.* The officers of the Corporation shall be elected by the Board of Directors [or by the stockholders] and shall include the President, one or more Vice-Presidents, the Secretary, and the Treasurer. If the Board of Directors wishes, it may also elect as an officer of the Corporation a Chairperson of the Board, and may elect other officers (including one or more Assistant Treasurers and one or more Assistant Secretaries) as may be necessary or desireable for the business of the Corporation. Any two or more offices may be held by the same person except the offices of President and Secretary. Each officer shall hold office until his or her successor shall have been duly elected and shall have qualified, or until his or her death, resignation, or removal, as hereinafter provided in these bylaws.

SECTION 2. *Resignations.* Any officers of the Corporation may resign at any time by giving written notice of his or her resignation to the Corporation. Any such resignation shall take effect at the time specified therein or, if the time when it shall become effective shall not be specified, immediately upon receipt. Unless otherwise specified therein, the acceptance of any such resignation shall not be necessary to make it effective.

SECTION 3. *Removal.* Any officer of the corporation may be removed, either with or without cause, at any time by the Board of Directors at any meeting thereof.

SECTION 4. *Chairperson of the Board.* The Chairperson of the Board, if one shall have been elected, shall be a member of the Board, an officer of the Corporation, and, if present, shall preside at each meeting of the Board of Directors or of the stockholders. He or she shall advise and counsel with the President, and, in his or her absence, with other executives of the Corporation, and shall perform such other duties as may from time to time be assigned by the Board of Directors.

SECTION 5. *The President.* The President shall be the chief executive officer of the Corporation. He or she shall, in the absence of the Chairperson of the Board or if a Chairperson shall not have been elected, preside at each meeting of the Board of Directors or the stockholders. He or she shall perform all duties incident to the office of the

President and chief executive officer and such other duties as may from time to time be assigned by the Board of Directors.

SECTION 6. *Vice-President.* Each Vice-President shall perform all such duties as from time to time may be assigned to him or her by the Board of Directors or the President. At the request of the President, or in his or her absence or in the event of his or her inability or refusal to act, the Vice-President, or if there shall be more than one, the Vice-Presidents in the order determined by the Board of Directors (or if there be no such determination, the Vice-Presidents in the order of their election), shall perform the duties of the President, and, when so acting, shall have the powers of and be subject to the restrictions placed upon the President in respect of the performance of such duties.

SECTION 7. *Treasurer.* The Treasurer shall

a. Have charge and custody of, and be responsible for, all the funds and securities of the Corporation;

b. Keep full and accurate accounts of receipts and disbursements in books belonging to the Corporation;

c. Deposit all moneys and other valuables to the credit of the Corporation in such depositories as may be designated by the Board of Directors or pursuant to its direction;

d. Receive, and give receipts for, moneys due and payable to the Corporation from any source whatsoever;

e. Disburse the funds of the Corporation and supervise the investments of its funds, taking proper vouchers therefore;

f. Render to the Board of Directors, whenever the Board of Directors may require, an account of the financial condition of the Corporation; and

g. In general, perform all duties incident to the office of Treasurer and such other duties as from time to time may be assigned by the Board of Directors.

SECTION 8. *Secretary.* The Secretary shall

a. Keep or cause to be kept, in one or more books provided for that purpose, the minutes of all meetings of the Board of Directors, the committees of the Board of Directors, and the stockholders;

b. See that all notices are duly given in accordance with the provisions of these bylaws and as required by law;

c. Be custodian of the records and the seal of the Corporation and affix and attest the seal to all certificates for shares of the Corporation (unless the seal of the Corporation on such certificates shall be a facsimile, as hereinafter provided) and affix and attest the seal to all other documents to be executed on behalf of the Corporation under its seal;

d. See that the books, reports, statements, certificates and other documents and records required by law to be kept and filed are properly kept and filed; and

e. In general, perform all duties incident to the office of Secretary and such other duties as from time to time may be assigned by the Board of Directors.

SECTION 9. *The Assistant Treasurer.*   The Assistant Treasurer, or if there shall be more than one, the Assistant Treasurers in the order determined by the Board of Directors (or if there be no such determination, then in the order of their election) shall, in the absence of the Treasurer or in the event of his or her inability or refusal to act, perform the duties and exercise the powers of the Treasurer and shall perform such other duties as from time to time may be assigned by the Board of Directors.

SECTION 10. *The Assistant Secretary.*   The Assistant Secretary, or if there be more than one, the Assistant Secretaries in the order determined by the Board of Directors (or if there be no such determination, then in the order of their election) shall, in the absence of the Secretary or in the event of his or her inability or refusal to act, perform the duties and exercise the powers of the Secretary and shall perform such other duties as from time to time may be assigned by the Board of Directors.

SECTION 11. *Officers' Bonds or Other Security.*   If required by the Board of Directors, any officer of the Corporation shall give a bond or other security for the faithful performance of his or her duties, in such amount and with such surety as the Board of Directors may require.

SECTION 12. *Compensation.*   The compensation of the Officers of the Corporation for their services as such officers shall be fixed from time to time by the Board of Directors. An officer of the Corporation shall not be prevented from receiving compensation by reason of the fact that he or she is also a director of the Corporation.

ARTICLE V

Stock Certificates and Their Transfer

SECTION 1. *Stock Certificates.*   Every holder of stock in the corporation shall be entitled to have a certificate, signed by or in the name of the Corporation, by the President or a Vice-President and by the Secretary or an Assistant Secretary of the Corporation, certifying the number of shares owned by him or her in the Corporation. If the Corporation shall be authorized to issue more than one class of stock or more than one series of any class, the designations, preferences, and relative, participating, optional, or other special rights of each class of stock or series thereof, and the qualifications, limitations, or restriction of such preferences and/or rights shall be set forth in full or summarized on the face or back of the certificate which the Corporation shall issue to represent such class or series of stock, provided that, except as otherwise provided in the Business Corporation Law of _____ _____ , in lieu of the foregoing requirements, there may be set forth on the face or back of the certificate which the Corporation shall issue to represent such class or series of stock, a statement that the Corporation will furnish without charge to each stockholder who so requests the designations, preferences, and relative, participating, optional, or other special rights of each class of stock or series thereof and the qualifications, limitations, or restrictions of such preferences and/or rights.

SECTION 2. *Facsimile Signatures.*   Any or all of the signatures on a certificate may be a facsimile. In case any officer, transfer agent, or registrar who has signed or whose facsimile signature has been placed upon a certificate shall have ceased to be such officer, transfer agent, or registrar before such certificate is issued, it may be issued by the Corporation with the same effect as if he or she were such officer, transfer agent, or registrar at the date of issue.

SECTION 3. *Lost Certificates.*   The Board of Directors may direct a new certificate or certificates to be issued in place of any certificate or certificates theretofore issued by the Corporation alleged to have been lost, stolen, or destroyed. When authorizing such issue of a new certificate or certificates, the Board of Directors may, in its discretion and as a condition precedent to the issuance thereof, require the owner of such lost, stolen, or destroyed certificate or certificates, or his or her legal representative, to give the Corporation a bond, in such sum as it may direct, sufficient to indemnify it against any claim that may be made against the corporation on account of the alleged loss, theft, or destruction of any certificate or the issuance of such new certificate.

SECTION 4. *Transfers of Stock.*   Upon surrender to the Corporation or the transfer agent of the Corporation of a certificate for shares duly endorsed or accompanied by proper evidence of succession, assignment, or authority to transfer, it shall be the duty of the Corporation to issue a new certificate to the person entitled thereto, cancel the old certificate, and record the transaction upon its records, provided, however, that the Corporation shall be entitled to recognize and enforce any lawful restriction on transfer. Whenever any transfer of stock shall be made for collateral security, and not absolutely, it shall be so expressed in the entry of transfer if, when the certificates are presented to the Corporation for transfer, both the transferor and the transferee request the Corporation to do so.

SECTION 5. *Transfer Agents and Registrars.*   The Board of Directors may appoint, or authorize any officer or officers to appoint, one or more transfer agents and one or more registrars.

SECTION 6. *Regulations.*   The Board of Directors may make such additional rules and regulations, not inconsistent with these bylaws, as it may deem expedient concerning the issue, transfer, and registration of certificates for shares of stock of the Corporation.

SECTION 7. *Fixing Record Date.*   In order that the Corporation may determine the stockholders entitled to notice of or to vote at any meeting of stockholders or any adjournment thereof, or to express consent to corporate action in writing without a meeting, or entitled to receive payment of any dividend or other distribution or allotment of any rights, or entitled to exercise any rights in respect of any change, conversion, or exchange of stock, or for the purpose of any other lawful action, the Board of Directors may fix, in advance, a record date, which shall not be more than fifty (50) nor fewer than ten (10) days before the date of such meeting, nor more than sixty (60) days prior to any other action. A determination of stockholders of record entitled to notice of or to vote at a meeting of stockholders shall apply to any adjournment of the meeting, provided, however, that the Board of Directors may fix a new record date for the adjourned meeting.

SECTION 8. *Registered Stockholders.*   The Corporation shall be entitled to recognize the exclusive right of a person registered on its records as the owner of shares of stock to receive dividends and to vote as such owner, shall be entitled to hold liable for calls and assessments a person registered on its records as the owner of shares of stock, and shall not be bound to recognize any equitable or other claim to or interest in such share or shares or stock on the part of any other person, whether or not it shall have express or other notice thereof, except as otherwise provided by the laws of _____ .

ARTICLE VI

Indemnification of Directors and Officers

SECTION 1. *General.* The Corporation shall indemnify any person who was or is a party or is threatened to be made a party to any threatened, pending, or completed action, suit, or proceeding, whether civil, criminal, administrative, or investigative (other than an action by or in the right of the Corporation) by reason of the fact that he or she is or was a director, officer, employee, or agent of the Corporation, or is or was serving at the request of the Corporation as a director, officer, employee, or agent of another corporation, partnership, joint venture, trust, or other enterprise, against expenses (including attorneys' fees), judgments, fines, and amounts paid in settlement actually and reasonably incurred by him or her in connection with such action, suit, or proceeding if such person acted in good faith and in a manner reasonably believed to be in or not opposed to the best interests of the Corporation, and, with respect to any criminal action or proceeding, had no reasonable cause to believe the conduct was unlawful. The termination of any action, suit, or proceeding by judgment, order, settlement, conviction, or upon a plea of nolo contendere or its equivalent, shall not, of itself, create a presumption that the person did not act in good faith and in a manner which he or she reasonably believed to be in or not opposed to the best interests of the Corporation, and, with respect to any criminal action or proceeding, had reasonable cause to believe that the conduct was unlawful.

SECTION 2. *Derivative Actions.* The Corporation shall indemnify any person who was or is a party or is threatened to be made a party to any threatened, pending, or completed action or suit by or in the right of the Corporation to procure a judgment in its favor by reason of the fact that he or she is or was a director, officer, employee or agent of the Corporation, or is or was serving at the request of the Corporation as director, officer, employee, or agent of another corporation, partnership, joint venture, trust, or other enterprise against expenses (including attorneys' fees) actually and reasonably incurred by him or her in connection with the defense or settlement of such action or suit if he or she acted in good faith and in a manner he or she reasonably believed to be in or not opposed to the best interests of the Corporation. No indemnification shall be made in respect of any claim, issue, or matter as to which such person shall have been adjudged to be liable for negligence or misconduct in the performance of his or her duty to the Corporation unless and only to the extent that the court in which such action or suit was brought shall determine upon application that, despite the adjudication of liability but in view of all the circumstances of the case, such person is fairly and reasonably entitled to indemnity for such expenses which the court shall deem proper.

SECTION 3. *Indemnification in Certain Cases.* To the extent that a director, officer, employee, or agent of the Corporation has been successful on the merits or otherwise in defense of any action, suit, or proceeding referred to in Sections 1 and 2 of this Article VI, or in defense of any claim, issue, or matter therein, he or she shall be indemnified against expenses (including attorneys' fees) actually and reasonably incurred in connection therewith.

SECTION 4. *Procedure.* Any indemnification under Section 1 and 2 of this Article VI (unless ordered by a court) shall be made by the Corporation only as authorized in the specific case upon a determination that indemnification of the director, officer, employee, or agent is proper in the circumstances because he or she has met the applicable standard of conduct set forth in such Section 1 and 2. Such determination shall be made: (a) by the Board of Directors by a majority vote of a quorum consisting of directors who were not parties to such action, suit, or proceeding; or (b) if such a quorum is not obtainable, or, even if obtainable and a quorum of disinterested directors so directs, by independent legal counsel in a written opinion; or (c) by the stockholders.

SECTION 5. *Advances for Expenses.* Expenses incurred in defending a civil or criminal action, suit, or proceeding may be paid by the Corporation in advance of the final disposition of such action, suit, or proceeding as authorized by the Board of Directors in the specific case, upon receipt of an undertaking by or on behalf of the director, officer, employee, or agent to repay such amount, unless it shall ultimately be determined that he or she is entitled to be indemnified by the Corporation as authorized in this Article VI.

SECTION 6. *Rights Not Exclusive.* The indemnification provided by this Article VI shall not be deemed exclusive of any other rights to which those seeking indemnification may be entitled under any law, bylaw, agreement, vote of stockholders, or disinterested directors, or otherwise, both as to action in his or her official capacity and as to action in another capacity while holding such office, and shall continue as to a person who has ceased to be a director, officer, employee, or agent and shall inure to the benefit of the heirs, executors, and administrators of such a person.

SECTION 7. *Insurance.* The Corporation shall have power to purchase and maintain insurance on behalf of any person who is or was a director, officer, employee or agent of the Corporation, or is or was serving at the request of the Corporation as a director, officer, employee, or agent of another corporation, partnership, joint venture, trust, or other enterprise, against any liability asserted against him or her and incurred by him or her in any capacity, or arising out of his or her status as such, whether or not the Corporation would have the power to indemnify him or her against such liability under the provisions of this Article VI.

SECTION 8. *Definition of Corporation.* For the purposes of this Article VI, references to "the Corporation" include all constituent corporations absorbed in a consolidation or merger as well as the resulting or surviving corporation, so that any person who is or was a director, officer, employee, or agent of such a constituent corporation as a director, officer, employee, or agent of another corporation, partnership, joint venture, trust, or other enterprise shall stand in the same position under the provisions of this Article VI with respect to the resulting or surviving corporation as he or she would if he or she had served the resulting or surviving corporation in the same capacity.

ARTICLE VII

General Provisions

SECTION 1. *Dividends.* Subject to statute and the Articles of Incorporation, dividends upon the shares of stock of the Corporation may be declared by the Board of Directors. Dividends may be paid in cash, in property, or in shares of stock of the Corporation, unless otherwise provided by statute or the Articles of Incorporation.

SECTION 2. *Reserves.* Before payment of any dividend, there may be set aside out of any funds of the Corporation available for dividends such sum or sums as the Board of Directors may, from time to time, in its absolute discretion, think proper as a reserve or reserves to meet contingencies, or for equalizing dividends, or for repairing or maintaining any property of the Corporation, or for such other purpose as the Board of Directors may think conducive to the interest of the Corporation. The Board of Directors may modify or abolish any such reserves in the manner in which the reserves were created.

SECTION 3. *Seal.*   The seal of the Corporation shall be in such form as shall be approved by the Board of Directors.

SECTION 4. *Fiscal Year.*   The fiscal year of the Corporation shall be fixed, and once fixed, may thereafter be changed by resolution of the Board of Directors.

SECTION 5. *Checks, Notes, Drafts, and So Forth.*   All checks, notes, drafts, or other order for the payment of money of the Corporation shall be signed, endorsed, or accepted in the name of the Corporation by such officer, officers, person, or persons as from time to time may be designated by the Board of Directors or by an officer or officers authorized by the Board of Directors to make such designation.

SECTION 6. *Execution of Contracts, Deeds, and So Forth.*   The Board of Directors may authorize any officer or officers, agent or agents, in the name and on behalf of the Corporation, to enter into or execute and deliver any and all deeds, bonds, mortgages, contracts, and other obligations or instruments, and such authority may be general or confined to specific instances.

SECTION 7. *Voting of Stock in Other Corporations.*   Unless otherwise provided by resolution of the Board of Directors, the Chairperson of the Board or the President, from time to time, may (or may appoint one or more attorneys or agents to) cast the votes which the Corporation may be entitled to cast as a shareholder or otherwise in any other corporation, any of whose shares or securities may be held by the Corporation, at meetings of the holders of the shares or other securities of such other corporation, or to consent in writing to any action by any such other corporation. In the event one or more attorneys or agents are appointed, the Chairperson of the Board or the President may instruct the person or persons so appointed as to the manner of casting such votes or giving such consent. The Chairperson of the Board or the President may, or may instruct the attorneys or agents appointed to, execute or cause to be executed in the name and on behalf of the Corporation and under its seal or otherwise, such written proxies, consents, waivers, or other instruments as may be necessary or proper in the premises.

ARTICLE VIII

Amendments

These bylaws may be amended or repealed or new bylaws adopted (a) by action of the stockholders entitled to vote thereon at any annual or special meeting of stockholder, or (b) by action of the Board of Directors. Any bylaw made by the Board of Directors may be amended or repealed by the stockholders.

MINUTES OF ORGANIZATION MEETING OF BOARD OF DIRECTORS

The organization meeting of the Board of Directors of the _____ Corporation was held on the date, time, and at the place set forth in the written Waiver of Notice signed by all the Directors, fixing the time and place, and attached to the minutes of this meeting.

The following directors were present:

_____

_____

_____

being all the members of the Board of Directors.

The meeting was called to order by _____ .

It was moved, seconded, and unanimously carried, that _____ _____ act as Temporary Chairperson, and that _____ _____ act as Temporary Secretary.

The Chairperson reported that the Articles of Incorporation were filed in the Office of the Secretary of State and that the incorporation was effective as of the date of filing. The Secretary was then instructed to insert the duplicate original of the Articles of Incorporation together with the Certificate of Incorporation in the corporate minute book.

The Secretary then presented a form of bylaws governing the business affairs of the Corporation. After review, upon motion duly made, seconded and unanimously carried, it was

> RESOLVED, that the form of bylaws submitted to this meeting be, and it hereby is, approved, and adopted as the bylaws of this Corporation and that the Secretary is hereby instructed to insert the bylaws in the Corporate minute book immediately following the Articles of Incorporation and the Certificate of Incorporation.

The meeting proceeded to the election of officers. Upon nominations duly made and seconded, the following were elected and qualified:

President   _____
Vice-President   _____
Secretary   _____
Treasurer   _____

The President of the Corporation thereupon assumed the Chair and the Secretary of the corporation assumed the duties of secretary of the meeting.

There was presented to the meeting a specimen of a proposed certificate to represent the shares of the Corporation. Upon motion duly made, seconded, and unanimously carried, it was

> RESOLVED, that the specimen form of certificate be, and the same hereby is, approved and adopted as the certificate to represent the shares of this Corporation; and further

> RESOLVED, that the specimen certificate so presented to the meeting be annexed to the minutes thereof.

The Secretary submitted to the meeting a seal proposed for use as the corporate seal of the corporation. Upon motion duly made, seconded, and unanimously carried, it was

> RESOLVED, that the form of seal submitted to this meeting be, and it hereby is, approved and adopted as and for the Corporate seal of this corporation.

The banking arrangements of the Corporation were then discussed. After discussion, on motion duly made, seconded, and carried, a proposed Secretarial Certificate to be furnished by the Secretary of the Corporation to [name of banking institution] was unanimously approved, and the resolutions set forth in such Secretarial Certificate were unanimously adopted. A conformed copy of such Secretarial Certificate was ordered annexed to the minutes of the meeting.

The Chairperson presented to the meeting a certain written offer addressed to the Corporation by _____ , dated _____ _____ , 19___ , pertaining to the issuance of the shares of the Corporation. A discussion followed. Upon motion duly made, seconded, and unanimously carried, it was

RESOLVED, that the written offer dated _____ , pertaining to the issuance of shares by _____ _____ be, and the same hereby is in all respects, approved for and on behalf of the Corporation; and further

RESOLVED, that a copy of such written offer be annexed to the minutes of this meeting; and further

RESOLVED, that the Corporation issue and deliver to _____ _____ upon receipt of the consideration therefor pursuant to the terms of the aforesaid proposal, a certificate representing _____ shares of the Corporation, _____ par value per share; and further

RESOLVED, that the shares so issued shall be fully paid and nonassessable, and that the value of the aforesaid consideration and the stated capital with respect to such shares shall be _____ and further

RESOLVED, that the officers of the Corporation be, and they hereby are, authorized, empowered, and directed to take any and all steps, and to execute and deliver any and all instruments in connection with consummating the transaction contemplated by the aforesaid proposal and in connection with carrying the foregoing resolutions into effect.

There being no further business to come before the meeting, upon motion duly made, seconded, and unanimously carried, the same was adjourned.

_____
                                    Secretary

ATTEST:
Board of Directors

_____   _____

OFFER TO PURCHASE SHARES

_____

[Date]

To the Board of Directors of

_____

The undersigned hereby offers to purchase _____

[Number]

shares of _____ stock at purchase price of $_____ per

[class]

share for a total payment of $_____ .

_____

[Name of Purchaser]

BOARD RESOLUTION ACCEPTING OFFER TO PURCHASE SHARES

The Chairperson presented to the meeting a written offer from
_____ , dated
_____ , 19_____ , to purchase _____ shares of
the _____ stock of this corporation.
Upon motion duly made, seconded, and unanimously carried, it was

RESOLVED, that the written offer from _____
_____ , dated
_____ , 19_____ , and attached hereto, to purchase
_____ shares of the _____
                                    [class]
stock of this corporation is hereby accepted on behalf of the Corporation; and further

RESOLVED, that upon receipt of the consideration therefore, the Secretary is directed to issue to _____ , a certificate representing
_____ shares of the _____ stock of this Corporation; and further
                              [class]
RESOLVED, that the shares so issued shall be treated as fully paid and non-assessable.

ATTEST:

_____   _____
Secretary   President

WAIVER OF NOTICE OF ANNUAL MEETING OF SHAREHOLDERS

The undersigned, being all of the shareholders of the _____ Corporation, hereby agree that the annual meeting of shareholders of the corporation be held on the [date], at [time] and at [address] designated in this waiver. We hereby waive all notice whatsoever of such meeting and of any adjournment or adjournments thereof.

We further agree that any and all lawful business may be transacted at such meeting or at any adjournment or adjournments thereof as may be deemed appropriate as determined by any shareholder present thereat and that any such business transacted at such meeting or at any adjournment or adjournments thereof shall be of the same force and effect as if such meeting or adjourned meeting were held after notice.

Dated: _____

_____
Shareholder

_____
Shareholder

_____
Shareholder

PROXY FOR ANNUAL MEETING OF SHAREHOLDERS

KNOW ALL PERSONS BY THESE PRESENTS, that I am the owner of _____ shares of the _____ stock of _____ Corporation, and I hereby appoint and constitute my true and lawful attorney and proxy with full power of substitution and revocation to attend and represent me at the annual meeting of shareholders of the corporation to be held on _____ , 19____ . _____ _____ may vote my shares on any question, proposition, or resolution, or any other matter which may come before the meeting or any adjournment thereof upon which I would be entitled to vote if personally present.

This proxy shall be void if I personally attend said meeting.

IN WITNESS WHEREOF, I have executed this proxy on the day of _____ , 19____ .

_____
Shareholder

MINUTES OF FIRST MEETING
OF SHAREHOLDERS

The first meeting of shareholders of the _____ Corporation was held on the date, time, and at the place set forth in the written Waiver of Notice signed by the shareholders, fixing such time and place, and attached to the minutes of this meeting.

The meeting was called to order by the President, heretofore elected by the Board of Directors, and the following shareholders, being all of the shareholders of the Corporation, were present:

_____

_____

_____

There was presented to the meeting the following:

1. Certificate of Incorporation
2. Articles of Incorporation
3. Copy of bylaws of the corporation, duly adopted by the directors
4. Minutes of organization meeting of directors
5. Corporate certificate book
6. Corporate certificate record book

Upon motion duly made, seconded, and unanimously carried, it was

> RESOLVED, that the items listed above have been examined by all shareholders, and are all approved and adopted, and that all acts taken and decisions reached, as set forth in such documents, be, and they hereby are, ratified and approved by the shareholders of the corporation.

There being no further business to come before the meeting, upon motion duly made, seconded, and unanimously carried, the same was adjourned.

_____
Secretary

ATTEST:

_____

_____

_____

SHAREHOLDERS' AGREEMENT

AGREEMENT made this _____ day of _____ , 19_____ , between [name of corporation], having its principal office at _____ , [State] , and [shareholder's name], of [shareholder's address], and [shareholder's name], of [shareholder's address], and [shareholder's name], [shareholder's address].

WHEREAS, the parties desire to promote their mutual interests and the interests of the Corporation by making provision to avoid future differences,

NOW, THEREFORE, it is mutually agreed as follows:

1. Each of the undersigned shareholders agrees that so long as he or she shall remain a shareholder in [name of corporation], he or she will vote his or her respective shares of stock in the corporation for each of the following named persons as a director, so long as that person remains a shareholder of the Corporation:

1. _____
2. _____
3. _____

Any of the foregoing directors who ceases to be a shareholder in the Corporation shall submit to the Corporation his or her resignation as a director when he or she transfer his or her shares.

2. For the best interest of [name of corporation], the undersigned shareholders agree to have each of the following persons appointed and elected as an officer of [name of corporation], as long as he or she remains a shareholder and performs faithfully, efficiently, and competently for the Corporation.

President _____

Vice-President _____

Secretary _____

Treasurer _____

Any of the foregoing officers who ceases to be a shareholder in the Corporation shall submit to the Corporation his or her resignation as an officer when he or she transfers his or her shares.

3. Each of the undersigned persons agrees that he or she will devote his or her best efforts to develop the best interests of the Corporation.

4.(a) The undersigned shareholders agree that if any action be taken at a meeting of the shareholders or directors of the Corporation by a vote of less than _____% of the shareholders or directors, as the case may be, the dissenting shareholder may require the other shareholders or directors within _____ days either to (1) rescind the action dissented from, or (2) purchase the shares owned by the dissenter at a price per share computed on a pro rata basis according to Section 4(d) of this agreement. The individual shareholders party to this agreement agree that should their vote in favor of the action be dissented from, they will either (1) rescind it, or (2) purchase the dissenter's shares within _____ days.

(b) The undersigned shareholders agree that they will not transfer, assign, sell, pledge, hypothecate, or otherwise dispose of the shares of stock owned by any of them, or the certificates of stock representing their interests, unless such shares of stock shall have been first offered to the Corporation at a price per share computed on a pro rata basis according to the provisions of Section 4(d) of this agreement. Such offer shall be made in writing and shall remain open for the Corporation's acceptance for a period of _____ days. In the event the Corporation wishes to accept the offer, it must agree in writing to purchase the entire amount of stock offered and shall at that time make a down payment of _____% of the purchase price. The balance of the purchase price shall be paid as provided in section 4(e) of this agreement. If the Corporation should not choose to purchase the shares within _____ days, they shall then be offered to the remaining stockholder's on a pro rata basis. Such offer shall be made in writing and shall remain open for a period of _____ days. In the event the stockholders wish to accept the offer, they must agree in writing to purchase any or all of their pro rata portion of shares, and make a down payment in the amount of _____ % of the purchase price. The balance of the purchase price shall be paid as provided in Section 4(e) of this agreement. If any shareholder should elect not to purchase his or her pro rata portion, or should purchase less than the full amount, the remainder shall be offered to the other shareholders on a pro rata basis. The amount of stock that remains unpurchased after this offering to the shareholders shall be freely transferable and no longer subject to the provisions and limitations of this agreement. This agreement shall not bar a transfer, assignment, bequest, or sale of shares of stock by one of the undersigned shareholders to a member of his or her immediate family, who shall, however, take his or her stock subject to all the limitations of this agreement as if he or she were a party to it.

(c) The parties to this agreement agree that upon the death of [name of shareholders], _____ , or _____ , the executors, administrators, or legal representatives of the deceased shall, within _____ days after qualification as such, sell to [name of corporation], and the corporation agrees to buy, all the shares of stock in (name of corporation), owned by the deceased at the time of his or her death. It is the wish of the parties to this agreement that within the period specified above after the death of the shareholder, his or her family shall terminate all interest in the corporation, and all members of the family to whom any shares of stock have been or shall be transferred shall sell to the corporation all shares of its stock owned by them, within _____ days. The price per share shall be computed on a pro rata basis according to the provisions of Section 4(d) of this agreement.

(d) The parties to this agreement agree that as of the date hereof one share of stock in the corporation shall be worth $_____ . It is the intention of the parties to review this figure _____ times a year, on _____[date]_____ , and that the last agreed-upon figure prior to a transfer described in Sections 4(a), (b), or (c) shall be conclusive as to the value of the stock for such purposes.

(e) The purchase price shall be paid as follows: _____% in cash within _____ days after the qualification of the legal representatives of the deceased shareholder. _____% of the unpaid balance shall be paid within the succeeding _____ days, and _____% of the still remaining unpaid balance within _____ days. Interest at the rate of _____% shall be calculated on the outstanding unpaid balance. The corporation reserves the right to prepay the whole or any part of the amount owed without the imposition of a premium or penalty therefore.

5. The parties hereto agree that they will take no action or dispose of

their stock in such a way as to cause the termination of the corporation's ability to be taxed as an electing small business corporation under Subchapter S of the Internal Revenue Code of 1954.

6. Each stock certificate of the corporation shall contain the following information:

> Transfer or pledge of these shares is restricted under a shareholders' agreement dated _____ , 19___ . A copy of the agreement, which affects other rights of the holder of these shares, is on file at the office of the corporation at [address of corporate offices].

7. Should any dispute arise between any one or more of the parties to this agreement as to their rights under any provisions of this agreement, the parties hereby agree to refer such dispute to the American Arbitration Association, whose decision on the questions shall be binding on the parties and shall be without appeal.

8. The corporation is authorized to enter into this agreement by a resolution adopted by the shareholders and directors, dated _____ _____ , 19___ .

9. This agreement or any of its provisions may be changed only by the mutual consent of the parties hereto, and unless so changed it remains binding upon all the parties, their heirs, executors, administrators, legal representatives, and assigns, who shall execute and deliver all necessary documents required to carry out the terms of this agreement.

IN WITNESS WHEREOF, the individual parties hereto set their hands and seals, and the corporation has caused this agreement to be signed by its duly authorized officers and the corporate seal affixed.

NAME OF CORPORATION

BY: _____
            President

[Names of shareholders] _____

_____

_____

ATTEST:

_____
        Secretary

VOTING TRUST AGREEMENT

An agreement made this _____ day of _____ , 19_____ , between stockholders of [name of corporation], a corporation organized under the laws of _____ , whose names are hereunto subscribed and all other stockholders of the said company who shall join in and become parties to this agreement as hereinafter provided, all of which stockholders are hereinafter called subscribers, and _____ , who is hereinafter called the trustee(s):

Whereas, the subscribers are respectively owners of shares of common stock in the corporation and the amounts set out opposite their signatures hereto;

And whereas, with a view to the safe and competent management of the corporation, in the interest of all the stockholders thereof, the subscribers are desirous of creating a trust in the following manner;

Now, it is hereby agreed and declared as follows:

1. The subscribers shall forthwith endorse, assign, and deliver to the trustee(s) the certificates representing the shares of stock owned by them respectively, and shall do all things necessary for the transfer of their respective shares to the trustee(s) on the books of the corporation.

2. Every other stockholder in the corporation may become a party to this agreement by signing it and assigning and delivering the certificate(s) of his or her shares to the trustee(s).

3. The trustee(s) shall hold the shares of stock transferred to them, under the terms and conditions hereinafter set forth.

4. The trustee(s) shall surrender to the proper officer of the corporation the certificates of the subscribers, and shall receive for them new certificates issued to them as trustee(s) under this agreement.

5. The trustee(s) shall issue to each of the subscribers a trust certificate for the number of shares transferred by the subscriber to the trustees. Each trust certificate shall state that it is issued under this agreement, and shall set forth each subscriber's proportional interest in the trust. The trustee(s) shall keep a list of the shares of stock transferred to them, and shall keep a record of all trust certificates issued or transferred on their books, which records shall contain the names and addresses of the trust certificate holders and the number of shares represented by each trust certificate. Such list and record shall be open at all reasonable times to the inspection of the trust certificate holders.

6. It shall be the duty of the trustee(s), and they, or a majority of them, shall have the power to represent the holders of such trust certificates and the stock transferred to the trustee(s) as aforesaid, and vote upon such stock, as in the judgment of the trustee(s), or of a majority of them, may be for the best interest of the corporation, in the election of directors and upon any and all matters and questions which may be brought before them, as fully as any stockholder might do.

7. The trustee(s) shall collect and receive all dividends that may accrue upon the shares of stock subject to this trust, and shall pay the same to the trust certificate holders in proportion to the number of shares respectively represented by their trust certificates.

8. The trustee(s) shall be entitled to be fully indemnified out of the dividends coming into their hands for all costs, changes, expenses, and other liabilities properly incurred by them in the exercise of any power conferred upon them by this agreement; and the subscribers hereby covenant with the trustee(s) that in the event of the monies and securities in their hands being insufficient for that purpose, the subscribers and each of them will, in proportion to the amounts of their respective shares and interests, indemnify the trustee(s) of and from all loss or damage which they may sustain or be put to, by reason of anything they may lawfully do in the execution of this trust.

9. In the event that the holder of any trust certificate shall desire to sell or pledge his or her beneficial interest in the shares of stock represented thereby, he or she shall first give to the trustee(s) notice in writing of such desire, and the trustee(s) shall have the right to purchase the trust certificates at the book value of the stock represented by such certificates at the time of such purchase. If the trustee(s) shall exercise such option to purchase, they shall hold the beneficial interest

thereof for the benefit of all the remaining trust certificate holders who shall, upon _____ days' notice given by the trustee(s) before exercising such option, contribute their respective proportionate share of the purchase money to be paid by the trustee(s). In the event that the trustee(s) shall not exercise such option to purchase the subscriber's interest, and only in that event, the holder of such trust certificate shall have the right to sell the same to such person and for such price as he or she sees fit.

10. In the event of any trustee dying, resigning, refusing, or becoming unable to act, the surviving or other trustee(s), if any, shall appoint a trustee or trustees to fill the vacancy or vacancies, and any person so appointed shall thereupon be vested with all the duties, powers, and authority of a trustee as if originally named herein.

11. This trust shall continue for _____ years from the date hereof, and shall then terminate, provided, however, that the beneficial owners of _____% of the shares of stock subject to this agreement may at any time terminate this trust by resolution adopted at a meeting of the trust certificate holders called by any one of them, upon notice of _____ days, stating the purpose of such meeting, in writing, mailed to the trust certificate holders at their respective addresses as they appear in the records of the trustee(s). Upon the termination of the trust the trustee(s) shall, upon the surrender of the trust certificates by the respective holders thereof, assign and transfer to them the number of shares of stock thereby represented.

IN WITNESS WHEREOF, the individual parties hereto set their hands and seals, and the corporation has caused this agreement to be signed by its duly authorized officers.

ATTEST: NAME OF CORPORATION

_____   By: _____
Secretary   President

                                 Name of Shareholders _____

                                 _____

                                 _____

                                 Name of Trustee(s) _____

                                 _____

                                 _____

COMPARISON CHART—MODEL ACT AND STATE STATUTES

The following chart compares selected sections of the Model Business Corporation Act with similar provisions in state statutes. The chart is intended as a general guide and not as a substitute for research and/or professional advice. The sections compared are those of more general significance where there are differences with the Model Act. Sections were left out of the chart because of their more esoteric nature or their close similarity with the Model Act. Always check your state's law for precise information.

COMPARISON CHART: MODEL ACT SECTIONS

State	2	3	6	7	9	14	15	25	29	31	34	36	38	43	44	45	48	50	52	54	58	59	85 86 87	92 93	106	115	144	146
Alabama	C	C	C	I	I	E	A	I	B	C	B	B	C	C	I	J	J	B	A	A	A	N	J	A	I			J
Alaska	C	C	C	I	I	C	A	I	B	C	B	B	I	I	I	I	B	L	A	A	B	I	C	I	C			J
Arizona	C	C	I	C	I	E	A	C	G	I	D	C	B	A	C	B	I	B	L	A	A	A	N	A	C			J
Arkansas	C	A	C	I	C	A	C	G	B	C	D	B	K	C	A	B	I	A	L	C	B	M	A	O	C			J
California	C	A	C	I	D	E	A	C	G	C	B	B	K	A	C	A	B	I	A	L	A	A	A	O	C			J
Colorado	C	A	C	C	D	C	A	I	G	B	C	B	B	A	C	C	B	I	B	L	C	A	C	O	I			I
Connecticut	C	A	C	C	D	E	A	I	G	G	C	H	K	A	C	B	A	C	A	A	A	M	N	C	C			J
Delaware	C	A	C	C	D	E	A	C	G	G	D	H	K	A	C	A	C	A	C	A	A	A	N	A	C			J
Florida	C	C	C	C	D	E	A	C	G	G	D	H	K	A	C	A	C	A	A	L	A	A	N	A	O		P	J
Georgia	C	A	C	C	D	C	A	C	G	G	D	B	K	J	C	A	C	A	A	L	A	A	N	C	C		P	J
Hawaii	C	A	C	J	D	E	A	C	G	G	D	H	K	A	J	A	C	A	A	L	A	A	M	N	I	O	P	J
Idaho	C	A	I	D	D	E	A	C	G	J	D	H	K	A	J	A	C	A	L	A	A	M	N	O	O	P	J
Illinois	C	A	C	D	C	A	C	C	G	G	D	B	K	C	C	A	C	I	A	L	A	C	C	C	C	I		J
Indiana	C	A	A	I	D	E	A	C	G	G	D	B	K	I	C	A	C	C	A	L	A	A	M	N	A	O	C	J
Iowa	C	A	A	C	D	C	A	I	G	G	D	B	K	C	J	A	C	C	B	L	A	C	C	I	I	I		I
Kansas	C	A	A	A	I	E	A	C	G	G	D	B	K	C	J	A	C	A	A	M	A	A	N	A	O	J		J
Kentucky	C	A	A	D	E	A	C	G	G	D	H	K	C	C	A	C	A	C	A	A	M	A	O	A	O	P		J
Louisiana	C	A	A	D	E	A	C	G	G	D	H	K	C	C	A	C	A	C	A	A	M	A	N	A	O	P		J
Maine	C	A	A	C	E	A	C	G	J	D	H	K	C	J	A	C	A	C	A	A	M	A	O	P		J
Maryland	C	A	A	I	C	E	A	C	G	J	D	H	K	C	C	A	B	C	A	A	A	M	N	A	O	P		J
Massachusetts	C	A	A	A	C	E	A	C	G	C	B	K	C	C	A	B	C	A	A	M	N	C	O	C				J
Michigan	C	A	A	A	D	E	A	C	G	D	H	K	C	C	A	C	A	C	A	A	M	A	O	C				J
Minnesota	C	A	A	A	D	E	A	C	G	J	D	H	K	C	C	A	C	A	C	A	A	M	A	O	C			J
Mississippi	C	A	C	I	I	C	A	I	B	D	H	K	C	C	I	B	A	B	C	I	A	I	I	C	C	I		I
Missouri	C	A	C	I	D	C	A	G	B	C	H	K	C	C	A	C	C	L	A	A	C	A	C	C	I			J
Montana	C	A	C	I	E	A	I	G	B	C	B	K	C	A	I	A	C	I	C	L	A	A	C	I	C	I		J
Nebraska	C	A	C	I	I	E	A	C	G	B	C	B	K	C	C	I	B	A	C	L	A	A	C	C	I			J
Nevada	C	A	A	I	D	E	A	C	G	J	C	H	K	C	C	A	C	A	C	L	A	A	M	N	C	O	I	J

State	Provisions
New Hampshire	C A A D E A C G J C H J C A A L A A M N A C J J
New Jersey	C A A I D E A C G B C H K C C A A C C L A I N C O A J
New Mexico	C A C I E I I C G B C K C C C I C L I A M I O I I
New York	C A C I D E A C G B C H K C C A A C C L A A M N C A J
North Carolina	C C C I C A C I B C H K C C A A B C C L A A M A C I J
North Dakota	C C A I I C A C I B C K C C C B C L I A I I C I I
Ohio	C A C A D E A C G B C H K C C A A B A L A A M N A O C J
Oklahoma	C A C A D E A C I B C H K C C A C C L A C N C C C J
Oregon	C I A I I C A I G B C K C B C I C B L I A C C I C J
Pennsylvania	C C C I D E A C G B C H K C C C A A M C C A M C J J
Rhode Island	C C C A C E A C G B C H K C C A C A J C A A N I A J
South Carolina	C C C A C C G B D H K C C C A I C C A A I A C I J
South Dakota	C A A I I C A I I B C K C B A A C C L A A C C C I J
Tennessee	C A I C D A C G B C H K A J I B C C L A A M C C C J
Texas	C A C C D C I I B C K A I B C L A C C C C C J
Utah	C A A A I E A A I I B C K A J I B I C L A M C I I J
Vermont	C A C A D E A C G B C H K C C A C A L A A C N C J J
Washington	C A C A D E A I I B C K A C A C I B L C A C I I I J
West Virginia	C A C I D E I C G I C B K C A C A A L A A C C C J
Wisconsin	C C C I D E A C G B C K C C A J I B A C L A A E I C C J
Wyoming	C I C I I I A C G B C K C C C I A C L I A C I A I J
Washington D.C.	C C C D C A C G B C B K A C C B I

A Many technical differences (check state laws).
B Uses older version of Model Act (1962, 1969).
C Essentially the same as Model Act with some technical differences.
D Sets specific time limit on duration.
E May have officer or agents.
F Power lies in director or shareholder to appeal, adopt, or amend.
G Requires prior notice by specified number of days in advance.
H Require at least one director.

I Identical to Model Act.
J No state provision.
K Vacancy may be filled by Board.
L Minimum dollar amount—before start of operation ($1000).
M Must provide notice to creditor of intent to dissolve.
N Has one-step provision for dissolution.
O May serve process on registered agent.
P No provision for waiver by directors.

APPLICATION FOR EMPLOYER IDENTIFICATION NUMBER, FORM SS-4

For clear copy on both parts, please type or print with ball point pen and press firmly.

Form **SS-4**
(Rev. November 1985)

Department of the Treasury
Internal Revenue Service

Application for Employer Identification Number

(For use by employers and others. Please read
the separate instructions before completing this form.)

For Paperwork Reduction Act Notice, see separate instructions.

OMB No. 1545-0003

Expires 8-31-88

1 Name (True name. See instructions.)

2 Social security no., if sole proprietor

3 Ending month of accounting year

4 Trade name of business if different from item 1

5 General partner's name, if partnership; principal officer's name, if corporation; or grantor's name, if trust

6 Address of principal place of business (Number and street)

7 Mailing address, if different

8 City, state, and ZIP code

9 City, state, and ZIP code

10 Type of organization ☐ Individual ☐ Trust ☐ Partnership ☐ Plan administrator ☐ Governmental ☐ Nonprofit organization ☐ Corporation ☐ Other (specify)

11 County of principal business location

12 Reason for applying ☐ Started new business ☐ Purchased going business ☐ Other (specify)

13 Acquisition or starting date (Mo., day, year). See instructions.

14 Nature of principal activity (See instructions.)

15 First date wages or annuities were paid or will be paid (Mo., day, year).

16 Peak number of employees expected in the next 12 months (If none, enter "0") ▶ | Nonagricultural | Agricultural | Household

17 Does the applicant operate more than one place of business? ☐ Yes ☐ No

18 Most of the products or services are sold to whom? ☐ Business establishments (wholesale) ☐ General public (retail) ☐ Other (specify) ☐ N/A

19 If nature of business is manufacturing, state principal product and raw material used.

20 Has the applicant ever applied for an identification number for this or any other business? ☐ Yes ☐ No

If "Yes," enter name and trade name. Also enter approx. date, city, and state where the application was filed and previous number if known. ▶

Under penalties of perjury, I declare that I have examined this application, and to the best of my knowledge and belief it is true, correct, and complete.

Signature and Title ▶

Date ▶

Telephone number (include area code)

Please leave blank ▶	Geo.	Ind.	Class	Size	Reas. for appl.	**Part I**

INSTRUCTIONS FOR FORM SS-4

Instructions

Who must file.—Every person who has not previously obtained an identification number and who (a) pays wages to one or more employees, or (b) is required to have an identification number for use on any return, statement, or other document, even though not an employer, must file a Form SS–4.

Trusts, estates, corporations, partnerships, nonprofit organizations (such as churches, clubs, etc.), and similar non-individual persons must use employer identification numbers even if they have no employees.

Individuals who file Schedules C or F (Form 1040) must also use employer identification numbers if they are required to file excise, alcohol, tobacco, firearms, or employment tax returns.

Only one application for an identification number should be filed, regardless of the number of establishments operated. This is true even though the business is conducted under one or more business or trade names. Each corporation of an affiliated group must be treated separately, and each must file a separate application. If a business is sold or transferred and the new owner does not have an identification number, the new owner cannot use the identification number assigned to the previous owner, and must file an application on Form SS–4 for a new identification number.

Where to file.—

If your principal business, office or agency, or legal residence in the case of an individual, is located in:	File with the Internal Revenue Service Center at:	
New Jersey, New York City and counties of Nassau, Rockland, Suffolk, and Westchester	Holtsville, NY	00501
New York (all other counties), Connecticut, Maine, Massachusetts, New Hampshire, Rhode Island, Vermont	Andover, MA	05501
District of Columbia, Delaware, Maryland, Pennsylvania	Philadelphia, PA	19255
Alabama, Florida, Georgia, Mississippi, South Carolina	Atlanta, GA	31101
Michigan, Ohio	Cincinnati, OH	45999
Arkansas, Kansas, Louisiana, New Mexico, Oklahoma, Texas	Austin, TX	73301
Alaska, Arizona, Colorado, Idaho, Minnesota, Montana, Nebraska, Nevada, North Dakota, Oregon, South Dakota, Utah, Washington, Wyoming	Ogden, UT	84201
Illinois, Iowa, Missouri, Wisconsin	Kansas City, MO	64999
California, Hawaii	Fresno, CA	93888
Indiana, Kentucky, North Carolina, Tennessee, Virginia, West Virginia	Memphis, TN	37501

If you have no legal residence, principal place of business, or principal office or agency in any Internal Revenue district, file your return with the Internal Revenue Service Center, Philadelphia, PA 19255.

When to file.—(a) Those who pay wages must file on or before the seventh day after the date on which business begins. (b) Others must file in sufficient time for the identification number to be included in return, statement, or other document.

Specific Instructions

Items 1, 2, and 3.—Enter in item 1 the true name of the applicant and enter in item 2 the trade name, if any, adopted for business purposes. For example, if John W. Jones, an individual owner, operates a restaurant under the trade name of "Busy Bee Restaurant," "John W. Jones" should be entered in item 1 and "Busy Bee Restaurant" in item 2. Enter the social security

(Continued on page 4)

Page 2

ELECTION BY A SMALL BUSINESS CORPORATION, FORM 2553

Form **2553**
(Rev. February 1986)

Department of the Treasury
Internal Revenue Service

Election by a Small Business Corporation

(Under section 1362 of the Internal Revenue Code)

▶ **For Paperwork Reduction Act Notice, see page 1 of instructions.**
▶ **See separate instructions.**

OMB No. 1545-0146

Expires 1-31-89

Note: *This election, to be treated as an "S corporation," can be approved only if all the tests in Instruction B are met.*

Part I · Election Information

Name of corporation (see instructions)	Employer identification number (see instructions)	Principal business activity and principal product or service (see instructions)
Number and street		Election is to be effective for tax year beginning (month, day, year)
City or town, state and ZIP code		Number of shares issued and outstanding (see instructions)

Is the corporation the outgrowth or continuation of any form of predecessor? . . . . ☐ Yes ☐ No

If "Yes," state name of predecessor, type of organization, and period of its existence ▶ ....

Date and place of incorporation

A If this election takes effect for the first tax year the corporation exists, enter the earliest of the following: (1) date the corporation first had shareholders, (2) date the corporation first had assets, or (3) date the corporation began doing business. ▶

B Selected tax year: Annual return will be filed for tax year ending (month and day) ▶ ....

See instructions before entering your tax year. If the tax year ends any date other than December 31, you must complete Part II or Part IV on back. You may want to complete Part III to make a back-up request.

C Name of each shareholder, person having a community property interest in the corporation's stock, and each tenant in common, joint tenant, and tenant by the entirety. (A husband and wife (and their estates) are counted as one shareholder in determining the number of shareholders without regard to the manner in which the stock is owned.)	D Shareholders' Consent Statement. We, the undersigned shareholders, consent to the corporation's election to be treated as an "S corporation" under section 1362(a). (Shareholders sign and date below.)*	E Stock owned		F Social security number (employer identification number for estates or trust)	G Tax year ends (month and day)
		Number of shares	Dates acquired		

*For this election to be valid, the consent of each shareholder, person having a community property interest in the corporation's stock, and each tenant in common, joint tenant, and tenant by the entirety must either appear above or be attached to this form. (See instructions for Column D, if continuation sheet or a separate consent statement is needed.)

Under penalties of perjury, I declare that I have examined this election, including accompanying schedules, and statements, and to the best of my knowledge and belief, it is true, correct, and complete.

Signature and Title of Officer ▶   **Date** ▶

See Parts II, III, and IV on back.

Form **2553** (Rev. 2-86)

Part II **Selection of Tax Year Under Revenue Procedure 83-25**

H Check the applicable box below to indicate whether the corporation is:

☐ Adopting the tax year entered in item B, Part I.

☐ Retaining the tax year entered in item B, Part I.

☐ Changing to the tax year entered in item B, Part I.

I Check the applicable box below to indicate the representation statement the corporation is making as required under section 7.01 (item 4) of Revenue Procedure 83-25, 1983-1 C.B. 689.

☐ Under penalties of perjury, I represent that shareholders holding more than half of the shares of the stock (as of the first day of the tax year to which the request relates) of the corporation have the same tax year or are concurrently changing to the tax year that the corporation adopts, retains, or changes to per item B, Part I.

☐ Under penalties of perjury, I represent that shareholders holding more than half of the shares of the stock (as of the first day of the tax year to which the request relates) of the corporation have a tax year or are concurrently changing to a tax year that, although different from the tax year the corporation is adopting, retaining, or changing to per item B, Part I, results in a deferment of income to each of these shareholders of three months or less.

☐ Under penalties of perjury, I represent that the corporation is adopting, retaining, or changing to a tax year that coincides with its natural business year as verified by its satisfaction of the requirements of section 4.042(a), (b), (c), and (d) of Revenue Procedure 83-25.

J Check here ☐ if the tax year entered in item B, Part I, is requested under the provisions of section 8 of Revenue Procedure 83-25. Attach to Form 2553 a statement and other necessary information pursuant to the ruling request requirements of Revenue Procedure 85-1. The statement must include the business purpose for the desired tax year. See instructions.

Part III **Back-Up Request by Certain Corporations Initially Selecting a Fiscal Year (See Instructions.)**

Check here ☐ if the corporation agrees to adopt or to change to a tax year ending December 31 if necessary for IRS to accept this election for S corporation status (temporary regulations section 18.1378-1(b)(2)(ii)(A)). This back-up request does not apply if the fiscal tax year request is approved by IRS or if the election to be an S corporation is not accepted.

Part IV **Request by Corporation for Tax Year Determination by IRS (See Instructions.)**

Check here ☐ if the corporation requests the IRS to determine the permitted tax year for the corporation based on information submitted in Part I (and attached schedules). This request is made under provisions of temporary regulations section 18.1378-1(d).

☆ U.S.G.P.O.: 1986-491-473/20122

INSTRUCTIONS FOR FORM 2553

Department of the Treasury
Internal Revenue Service

Instructions for Form 2553

(Revised February 1986)

Election by a Small Business Corporation

(Section references are to the Internal Revenue Code, unless otherwise specified.)

Paperwork Reduction Act Notice.—We ask for this information to carry out the Internal Revenue laws of the United States. We need it to insure that you are complying with these laws and to allow us to figure and collect the right amount of tax. You are required to give us this information.

A. Purpose.—To elect to be treated as an "S Corporation," a corporation must file Form 2553. The election permits the income of the S corporation to be taxed to the shareholders of the corporation except as provided in Subchapter S and section 58(d). (See section 1363.)

B. Who May Elect.—Your corporation may make the election only if it meets the following tests:

1. It is a domestic corporation.

2. It has no more than 35 shareholders. A husband and wife (and their estates) are treated as one shareholder for this requirement. All other persons are treated as separate shareholders.

3. It has only individuals, estates, or certain trusts as shareholders.

4. It has no nonresident alien shareholders.

5. It has only one class of stock. See sections 1361(c)(4) and (5) for additional details.

6. It is not an ineligible corporation as defined in section 1361(b)(2). See section 6(c) of Public Law 97-354 for additional details.

7. It has a calendar tax year or other permitted tax year as explained in instruction G.

8. Each shareholder consents as explained in the instructions for Column D.

See sections 1361, 1362 and 1378 for additional information on the above tests.

C. Where to File.—File this election with the Internal Revenue Service Center where the corporation will file **Form 1120S**, U.S. Income Tax Return for an S Corporation. See the Instructions for Form 1120S for Service Center addresses.

You should keep a copy of Form 2553 for the corporation's files.

D. When to Make the Election.—Complete Form 2553 and file it either: (1) at any time during that portion of the first tax year the election is to take effect which occurs before the 16th day of the third month of that tax year (or at any time during that year, if that year does not extend beyond the period described above) or (2) in the tax year before the first tax year it is to take effect. An election made by a small business corporation after the 15th day of the third month but before the end of the tax year is treated as made for the next year. For example, if a calendar tax year corporation makes the election in April 1985, it is effective for the corporation's 1986 calendar tax year.

For purposes of this election, a newly formed corporation's tax year starts when it has shareholders, acquires assets, or begins doing business, whichever happens first.

E. Acceptance or Non-acceptance of Election.—IRS will notify you if your election is accepted and when it will take effect. You should generally receive determination on your election within 60 days after you have filed Form 2553. Do not file Form 1120S until you are notified that your election is accepted. If you are now required to file **Form 1120**, U.S. Corporation Income Tax Return, or any other applicable tax return, continue filing it until your election takes effect.

You will also be notified if your election is not accepted.

Care should be exercised to ensure the election is received by Internal Revenue Service. If you are not notified of acceptance or non-acceptance of your election within 3 months of date of filing (date mailed), you should take follow-up action by corresponding with the service center where the election was filed. If filing of Form 2553 is questioned, an acceptable proof of filing is: (1) Certified receipt (timely filed); (2) Form 2553 with accepted stamp; (3) Form 2553 with stamped IRS received date; or (4) IRS letter stating that Form 2553 had been accepted.

F. End of Election.—Once the election is made, it stays in effect for all years until it is terminated. During the 5 years after the election has been terminated, the corporation can make another election on Form 2553 only if the Commissioner consents. See section 1362(g). However, the 5-year waiting period does not apply to terminations made under Subchapter S rules in effect for tax years beginning before January 1, 1983. See sections 1362(d), (e), and (f) for rules regarding termination of election.

G. Permitted Tax Year.—Section 1378 provides that no corporation may make an election to be an S corporation for any tax year unless the tax year is a permitted tax year. A permitted tax year is a tax year ending December 31 or any other tax year for which the corporation establishes a business purpose to the satisfaction of IRS. See section 1378(c) if a 50 percent shift in ownership occurs in an existing S corporation after its election is made.

H. Investment Credit Property.—Although the corporation has elected to be an S corporation under section 1362, the tax imposed by section 47 in the case of early disposition of investment credit property will be imposed on the corporation for credits allowed for tax years for which the corporation was not an S corporation. The election will not be treated as a disposition of the property by the corporation. See section 1371(d).

Specific Instructions

Part I.—Part I must be completed by all corporations.

Name and Address of Corporation.—If the corporation's mailing address is the same as someone else's such as a shareholder's, please enter this person's name below the corporation's name.

Employer Identification Number.—If you have applied for an employer identification number (EIN) but have not received it, enter "applied for." If the corporation does not have an EIN, you should apply for one on **Form SS-4**, Application for Employer Identification Number, available from most IRS or Social Security Administration offices. Send Form SS-4 to the IRS Service Center where Form 1120S will be filed.

Principal Business Activity and Principal Product or Service.—Use the Codes for Principal Business Activity contained in the Instructions for Form 1120S. Your principal business activity is the one that accounts for the largest percentage of total receipts. Total receipts are gross receipts plus all other income.

Also state the principal product or service. For example, if the principal business activity is "grain mill products," the principal product or service may be "cereal preparation."

Number of Shares Issued and Outstanding.—Enter only one figure. This figure will be the number of shares of stock that have been issued to shareholders and have not been reacquired by the corporation. This is the number of shares all shareholders own, as reported in column E, Part I.

Item B.—The selected tax year must be a permitted tax year as defined in instruction G.

A newly formed corporation may automatically adopt a tax year ending December 31.

Generally, an existing corporation may automatically change to a tax year ending December 31, if all of its principal shareholders have tax years ending December 31, or if all of its principal shareholders are concurrently changing to such tax year. If a corporation is automatically changing to a tax year ending December 31, it is not necessary for the corporation to file **Form 1128**, Application for Change in Accounting Period. A shareholder may not change his or her tax year without securing prior approval from IRS. For purposes of the automatic change, a principal shareholder is a shareholder who owns 5% or more of the issued and outstanding stock of the corporation. See temporary regulations section 18.1378-1 for additional details.

If a corporation wants to change to a tax year ending December 31, but does not qualify for an automatic change as explained above, it may want to complete Part IV and indicate in an attached statement that it wants to change to a tax year ending December 31.

If a corporation selects a tax year ending other than December 31, it must complete Part II or IV in addition to Part I.

Column D.—Shareholders' Consent Statement.—Each person who is a shareholder at the time the election is made must consent to the election. If the election is made during the corporation's first tax year for which it is effective, any person who held stock at any time during that portion of that year which occurs before the time the election is made must consent to the election although the person may have sold or transferred his or her stock before the election is made. Each shareholder consents by signing in column D or signing a separate consent statement, described below.

The election by a small business corporation is considered made for the following tax year if one or more of the persons who held stock at any time during that portion of that year which occurs before the time the election is made did not consent to the election. See section 1362(b)(2).

If a husband and wife have a community interest in the stock or in the income from it, both must consent. Each tenant in common, joint tenant, and tenant by the entirety also must consent.

A minor's consent is made by the minor or the legal guardian. If no legal guardian has been appointed, the natural guardian makes the consent (even if a custodian holds the minor's stock under a law patterned after the Uniform Gifts to Minors Act).

Continuation Sheet or Separate Consent Statement.—If you need a continuation sheet or use a separate consent statement, attach it to Form 2553. The separate consent statement must contain the name, address, and employer identification number of the corporation and the shareholder information requested in columns C through G of Part I.

If you wish, you may combine all the shareholders' consents in one statement.

Column E.—Enter the number of shares of stock each shareholder owns and the dates the stock was acquired. If the election is made during the corporation's first tax year for which it is effective, do not list the shares of stock for those shareholders who sold or transferred all of their stock before the election was made but who still must consent to the election for it to be effective for the tax year.

Column G.—Enter the month and day that each shareholder's tax year ends. If a shareholder is changing his or her tax year, enter the tax year the shareholder is changing to. If the election is made during the corporation's first tax year for which it is effective, you do not have to enter the tax year of shareholders who sold or transferred all of their stock before the election was made but who still must consent to the election for it to be effective for the tax year.

Signature.—Form 2553 must be signed by the president, treasurer, assistant treasurer, chief accounting officer, or other corporate officer (such as tax officer) authorized to sign.

Part II.—Items H and I of Part II are to be completed by a corporation that selects a tax year ending other than December 31, and that qualifies under section 4.02, 4.03, or 4.04 of Revenue Procedure 83-25, 1983-1 C.B. 689. Items H and I are completed in place of the additional statement asked for in section 7.01 of the procedure. Sections 4.02, 4.03, and 4.04 provide for expeditious approval of certain corporations' requests to adopt, retain, or change to a tax year ending other than December 31. The representation statements in Part II of Form 2553 highlight the three types of requests provided for in the revenue procedure. A corporation adopting, retaining, or changing its accounting period under the procedure must comply with or satisfy all conditions of the procedure.

The revenue procedure applies only to the tax years of corporations which are electing S corporation status by filing Form 2553. A corporation is permitted to adopt, retain, or change its tax year only once under the procedure. It is not necessary for the corporation to file Form 1128 when adopting or changing its tax year under the procedure.

Items H and J of Part II are to be completed by a corporation that is making a request as specified in section 8 of the procedure. Section 8 provides that if a corporation wants to adopt, retain, or change to a tax year not specified under section 4.02, 4.03, or 4.04 of the procedure or certain paragraphs of temporary regulations section 18.1378-1, it should attach a statement to Form 2553 pursuant to the ruling request requirements of Revenue Procedure 85-1, 1985-1 C.B. 404. (Changes to this revenue procedure are usually incorporated annually into a new revenue procedure as the first revenue procedure of the year.) The statement must show the business purpose for the desired tax year.

Approval of tax year selections made under section 4.02, 4.03, or 4.04 of Revenue Procedure 83-25 are generally automatic; however, a request under section 8 is not automatic. If a request is made under section 8, the corporation may want to make the back-up request under Part III. See section 8 of the procedure for details.

Part III.—Check the box in Part III to make the back-up request provided by temporary regulations section 18.1378-1(b)(2)(ii)(A). This section provides that corporations requesting to retain (or adopt) a tax year ending other than December 31, may make a back-up request to adopt or change to a tax year ending December 31, in case the initial request for a fiscal year is denied. In order to make the back-up request, a corporation requesting to retain its tax year ending other than December 31, must qualify for an automatic change of its tax year under temporary regulations section 18.1378-1(b)(1).

Part IV.—Check the box in Part IV to request the IRS to determine your permitted tax year under the provisions of temporary regulations section 18.1378-1(d). If you check the box in Part IV, enter "See Part IV" in the space in item B, Part I, for month and year.

You may attach a schedule to Form 2553 showing any additional information you want the IRS to consider in making the determination. IRS will notify you of the permitted tax year determination. The tax year determination by IRS is final.

APPLICATION FOR AUTOMATIC EXTENSION OF TIME TO FILE CORPORATION INCOME TAX RETURN, FORM 7004

Form **7004**

(Rev. October 1986)

Department of the Treasury
Internal Revenue Service

Application for Automatic Extension of Time
To File Corporation Income Tax Return

OMB No. 1545-0233
Expires 9-30-89

Name of corporation	Employer identification number

Number and street

City or town, state, and ZIP code

Check type of return to be filed:

☐ Form 1120   ☐ Form 1120-FSC   ☐ Form 990-C   ☐ Other (specify)..

☐ Form 1120-A   ☐ Form 1120S   ☐ Form 990-T

☐ Form 1120F   (Check here ▶ ☐ if you do not have an office or place of business in the U.S.)

1a I request an automatic 6-month extension of time until ...., 19 ...., to file the income tax return of the corporation named above for calendar year 19 ...., or tax year ending ...., 19 ....

b If this tax year is for less than 12 months, check reason:

☐ Initial return   ☐ Final return   ☐ Change in accounting period approved   ☐ Consolidated return to be filed

2 Does this application also cover subsidiaries to be included in a consolidated return? . . . . ☐ Yes ☐ No
If "Yes," complete the following:

Name and address of each member of the affiliated group	Employer identification number	Tax period

3 Tentative tax (see instructions)		
4 **Credits: a** Overpayment from prior year allowed as a credit		
b Estimated tax payments (deposits) for the tax year		
c Less refund of estimated tax for the tax year applied for on Form 4466		
d Credit from regulated investment companies and credit for overpaid windfall profit tax . .		
e Credit for Federal tax on gasoline and special fuels		
5 Total—Add lines 4a through 4e.		
6 **Balance due**—Subtract line 5 from line 3. This amount should be deposited with a Federal Tax Deposit (FTD) Coupon		

Signature.—Under penalties of perjury, I declare that I have been authorized by the above-named corporation to make this application and, to the best of my knowledge and belief, the statements made are true, correct, and complete.

_____   _____   _____

(Signature of officer or agent)   (Title)   (Date)

Form **7004** (Rev. 10-86)

General Instructions

(Section references are to the Internal Revenue Code, unless otherwise noted.)

A. Paperwork Reduction Act Notice.—We ask for this information to carry out the Internal Revenue laws of the United States. We need it to ensure that taxpayers are complying with these laws and to allow us to figure and collect the right amount of tax. You are required to give us this information.

B. Purpose of Form.—Form 7004 should be used by a corporation to request an automatic 6-month extension of time to file its income tax return.

The extension will be allowed if Form 7004 is filed properly by the due date and if the balance due on line 6 is deposited with a **Form 8109**, Federal Tax Deposit Coupon.

Foreign corporations without an office or place of business in the U.S. may pay the tax by check or money order, made payable to the Internal Revenue Service.

Note: On all payments, write the corporation's employer identification number, the type of tax, and the tax year to which the payment applies.

Foreign corporations with an office or place of business in the U.S. and other corporations qualifying for an automatic 3-month extension under Regulations section 1.6081-2(a) should not file Form 7004 unless they are unable to file their returns within the 3-month extended period. In these situations, Form 7004 should be filed by the 15th day of the 3d month following the close of the tax year to obtain a 6-month extension.

Form 7004 does not extend the time for payment of tax.

C. When and Where To File.—File Form 7004 by the due date of the return with the Internal Revenue Service Center where the corporation will file the return.

D. Penalty for Not Paying Tax.—Section 6651 provides a penalty for not paying tax (other than estimated income tax) when due.

The late payment penalty is ½% a month or part of a month unless you have reasonable cause for not paying on time. If you believe you have reasonable cause, attach an explanation to your return.

Beginning January 1, 1987, the late payment penalty will be increased to 1% per month when a taxpayer fails to respond to an IRS notice of levy or demand for payment of tax due. See section 6651 for more information.

If you are allowed an extension of time to file, you will not be charged a late payment penalty if: the tax shown on line 3 (or the amount of tax paid by the regular due date of the return) is at least 90% of the tax shown on line 31 of Form 1120, or the comparable line on other returns; and you pay the balance due shown on the return by the extended due date.

E. Termination of Extension.—The IRS may terminate the automatic extension at any time by mailing a notice of termination to the corporation or to the person who requested the extension. The notice will be mailed at least 10 days before the termination date given in the notice.

Specific Instructions

Line 2—Affiliated Group Members.—Enter the name and address, employer identification number, and tax period for each member of the affiliated group. Generally, all members of an affiliated group must have the same tax period. See Regulations section 1.1502-76 for details.

Line 3—Tentative tax.—Enter the tentative amount of income tax for the year, reduced by any nonrefundable credits against the tax. This will usually be the tax shown on Form 1120, line 31, or the comparable line from other returns.

Line 6—Balance due.—This is the amount of tax you are required to deposit. Foreign corporations with an office or place of business in the United States and domestic corporations must deposit all income tax payments with an FTD coupon.

However, if the corporation expects to have a net operating loss carryback, the corporation may reduce the amount to be deposited to the extent of the overpayment resulting from the carryback, providing all other prior year tax liabilities have been fully paid and a **Form 1138**, Extension of Time for Payment of Taxes by a Corporation Expecting a Net Operating Loss Carryback, accompanies Form 7004. See Rev. Rul. 82-47, 1982-1 C.B. 201 for details.

Interest will be charged on any part of the final tax due not shown on line 6. The interest is figured from the original due date of the return to the date of payment.

Signature.—The person authorized by the corporation to sign the return should sign the Form 7004. This person may be:

(1) An officer of the corporation

(2) A duly authorized agent holding a power of attorney.

(3) A person currently enrolled to practice before the Internal Revenue Service.

(4) An attorney or certified public accountant qualified to practice before the IRS.

26

U.S. CORPORATION INCOME TAX RETURN, FORM 1120

U.S. Corporation Income Tax Return

Form 1120

Department of the Treasury
Internal Revenue Service

For calendar 1986 or tax year beginning _____ , 1986, ending _____ , 19 ____

▶ **For Paperwork Reduction Act Notice, see page 1 of the instructions.**

OMB No. 1545-0123

1986

Check if a—

A Consolidated return ☐
B Personal Holding Co. ☐
C Business Code No. (See the list in the instructions)

Use IRS label. Otherwise please print or type.

Name

Number and street

City or town, state, and ZIP code

D Employer identification number

E Date incorporated

F Total assets (see Specific Instructions)

	Dollars	Cents

G Check box if there has been a change in address from the previous year . . . . ▶ ☐ $

Income

1a	Gross receipts or sales _____ **b** Less returns and allowances _____ Balance ▶	1c
2	Cost of goods sold and/or operations (Schedule A)	2
3	Gross profit (line 1c less line 2)	3
4	Dividends (Schedule C)	4
5	Interest	5
6	Gross rents	6
7	Gross royalties	7
8	Capital gain net income (attach separate Schedule D)	8
9	Net gain or (loss) from Form 4797, line 17, Part II (attach Form 4797) . . .	9
10	Other income (see instructions—attach schedule)	10
11	TOTAL income—Add lines 3 through 10 and enter here . . . . ▶	11

Deductions

12	Compensation of officers (Schedule E)	12
13a	Salaries and wages _____ **b** Less jobs credit _____ Balance ▶	13c
14	Repairs	14
15	Bad debts (Schedule F if reserve method is used)	15
16	Rents	16
17	Taxes	17
18	Interest	18
19	Contributions (**see instructions for 10% limitation**)	19
20	Depreciation (attach Form 4562) **20**	
21	Less depreciation claimed in Schedule A and elsewhere on return . **21a**	21b
22	Depletion	22
23	Advertising	23
24	Pension, profit-sharing, etc., plans	24
25	Employee benefit programs	25
26	Other deductions (attach schedule)	26
27	TOTAL deductions—Add lines 12 through 26 and enter here . . . . . ▶	27
28	Taxable income before net operating loss deduction and special deductions (line 11 less line 27) .	28
29	**Less: a** Net operating loss deduction (see instructions) **29a**	
	b Special deductions (Schedule C) **29b**	29c

Tax and Payments

30	Taxable income (line 28 less line 29c)	30
31	TOTAL TAX (Schedule J)	31
32	**Payments: a** 1985 overpayment credited to 1986	
b	1986 estimated tax payments	
c	Less 1986 refund applied for on Form 4466 . ( )	
d	Tax deposited with Form 7004	
e	Credit from regulated investment companies (attach Form 2439) .	
f	Credit for Federal tax on gasoline and special fuels (attach Form 4136) .	32
33	Enter any **PENALTY** for underpayment of estimated tax—check ▶ ☐ if Form 2220 is attached .	33
34	**TAX DUE**—If the total of lines 31 and 33 is larger than line 32, enter AMOUNT OWED	34
35	**OVERPAYMENT**—If line 32 is larger than the total of lines 31 and 33, enter AMOUNT OVERPAID	35
36	Enter amount of line 35 you want: **Credited to 1987 estimated tax** ▶ Refunded ▶	36

Please Sign Here

Under penalties of perjury, I declare that I have examined this return, including accompanying schedules and statements, and to the best of my knowledge and belief, it is true, correct, and complete. Declaration of preparer (other than taxpayer) is based on all information of which preparer has any knowledge.

▶ _____   _____   ▶ _____
Signature of officer   Date   Title

Paid Preparer's Use Only

Preparer's signature ▶	Date	Check if self-employed ☐	Preparer's social security number
Firm's name (or yours, if self-employed) and address ▶		E.I. No. ▶	
		ZIP code ▶	

Schedule A — Cost of Goods Sold and/or Operations (See instructions for line 2, page 1)

1 Inventory at beginning of year.	1	
2 Purchases	2	
3 Cost of labor	3	
4 Other costs (attach schedule).	4	
5 Total—Add lines 1 through 4.	5	
6 Inventory at end of year.	6	
7 Cost of goods sold and/or operations—Line 5 less line 6. Enter here and on line 2, page 1	7	

8 a Check all methods used for valuing closing inventory:

 (i) ☐ Cost   (ii) ☐ Lower of cost or market as described in Regulations section 1.471-4 (see instructions)

 (iii) ☐ Writedown of ''subnormal'' goods as described in Regulations section 1.471-2(c) (see instructions)

 (iv) ☐ Other (Specify method used and attach explanation) ▶ ------------------------------------

 b Check if the LIFO inventory method was adopted this tax year for any goods (if checked, attach Form 970) . . . . . ☐

 c If the LIFO inventory method was used for this tax year, enter percentage (or amounts) of

 closing inventory computed under LIFO . . . . | 8c |

 d If you are engaged in manufacturing, did you value your inventory using the full absorption method (Regulations section 1.471-11)? . . . . ☐ Yes ☐ No

 e Was there any change in determining quantities, cost, or valuations between opening and closing inventory? . . . ☐ Yes ☐ No

 If ''Yes,'' attach explanation.

Schedule C — Dividends and Special Deductions (See Schedule C instructions)

	(a) Dividends received	(b) %	(c) Special deductions: multiply (a) X (b)
1 Domestic corporations subject to section 243(a) deduction (other than debt-financed stock).		see instructions	
2 Debt-financed stock of domestic and foreign corporations (section 246A)		see instructions	
3 Certain preferred stock of public utilities		see instructions	
4 Foreign corporations and certain FSCs subject to section 245 deduction		see instructions	
5 Wholly-owned foreign subsidiaries and FSCs subject to 100% deduction (sections 245(b) and (c))		100	
6 Total—Add lines 1 through 5. See instructions for limitation	/////		
7 Affiliated groups subject to the 100% deduction (section 243(a)(3))		100	
8 Other dividends from foreign corporations not included in lines 4 and 5		/////	/////
9 Income from controlled foreign corporations under subpart F (attach Forms 5471)		/////	/////
10 Foreign dividend gross-up (section 78)		/////	/////
11 IC–DISC or former DISC dividends not included in lines 1 and/or 2 (section 246(d))		/////	/////
12 Other dividends		/////	/////
13 Deduction for dividends paid on certain preferred stock of public utilities (see instructions)	/////		
14 Total dividends—Add lines 1 through 12. Enter here and on line 4, page 1 ▶			/////
15 Total deductions—Add lines 6, 7, and 13. Enter here and on line 29b, page 1 . . . . ▶			

Schedule E — Compensation of Officers (See instructions for line 12, page 1)

Complete Schedule E only if total receipts (line 1a, plus lines 4 through 10, of page 1, Form 1120) are $150,000 or more.

(a) Name of officer	(b) Social security number	(c) Percent of time devoted to business	Percent of corporation stock owned		(f) Amount of compensation
			(d) Common	(e) Preferred	
		%	%	%	
		%	%	%	
		%	%	%	
		%	%	%	
		%	%	%	
		%	%	%	
		%	%	%	

Total compensation of officers—Enter here and on line 12, page 1 . . . .

Schedule F — Bad Debts—Reserve Method (See instructions for line 15, page 1)

(a) Year	(b) Trade notes and accounts receivable outstanding at end of year	(c) Sales on account	Amount added to reserve		(f) Amount charged against reserve	(g) Reserve for bad debts at end of year
			(d) Current year's provision	(e) Recoveries		
1981						
1982						
1983						
1984						
1985						
1986						

Schedule J   **Tax Computation** (See instructions) (Fiscal year corporations see page 12 of instructions before completing Schedule J)

1   Check if you are a member of a controlled group (see sections 1561 and 1563) . . . . ▶ ☐

2a If line 1 is checked, see instructions. Enter your portion of each $25,000 taxable income bracket amount:

   (i) $ _____ *(ii)* $ _____ *(iii)* $ _____ *(iv)* $ _____

   b If your tax year includes July 1, 1987, see instructions and enter share of tax bracket amounts

   (i) _____ *(ii)* _____

3   Income tax (see instructions to figure the tax; enter this tax or alternative tax, whichever is less). Check if alternative tax is used ▶ ☐ **3**

4a   Foreign tax credit (attach Form 1118) . . . . | **4a** |

 b   Possessions tax credit (attach Form 5735) . . . . | **b** |

 c   Orphan drug credit (attach Form 6765) . . . . | **c** |

 d   Credit for fuel produced from a nonconventional source (see instructions) . . . . | **d** |

 e   General business credit. Enter here and check which forms are attached ☐ Form 3800 ☐ Form 3468 ☐ Form 5884 ☐ Form 6478 ☐ Form 8007 ☐ Form 6765 ☐ Form 8586 . | **e** |

5   Total—Add lines 4a through 4e **5**

6   Line 3 less line 5 . . . . **6**

7   Personal holding company tax (attach Schedule PH (Form 1120)) **7**

8   Tax from recomputing prior-year investment credit (attach Form 4255) **8**

9   Minimum tax on tax preference items (see instructions—attach Form 4626) **9**

10 Total tax—Add lines 6 through 9. Enter here and on line 31, page 1 . . . . **10**

Additional Information (See instruction F)	Yes	No
H Did the corporation claim a deduction for expenses connected with:		
(1) Entertainment facility (boat, resort, ranch, etc.)?		
(2) Living accommodations (except employees on business)? . .		
(3) Employees attending conventions or meetings outside the North American area? (See section 274(h).)		
(4) Employees' families at conventions or meetings?		
If "Yes," were any of these conventions or meetings outside the North American area? (See section 274(h).) . . .		
(5) Employee or family vacations not reported on Form W-2? . .		
I (1) Did the corporation at the end of the tax year own, directly or indirectly, 50% or more of the voting stock of a domestic corporation? (For rules of attribution, see section 267(c).) . .		

If "Yes," attach a schedule showing: (a) name, address, and identifying number; (b) percentage owned; (c) taxable income or (loss) before NOL and special deductions (e.g., If a Form 1120: from Form 1120, line 28, page 1) of such corporation for the tax year ending with or within your tax year; (d) highest amount owed by the corporation to such corporation during the year; and (e) highest amount owed to the corporation by such corporation during the year.

(2) Did any individual, partnership, corporation, estate, or trust at the end of the tax year own, directly or indirectly, 50% or more of the corporation's voting stock? (For rules of attribution, see section 267(c).) If "Yes," complete (a) through (e) . . . .

(a) Attach a schedule showing name, address, and identifying number.

(b) Enter percentage owned ▶ _____

(c) Was the owner of such voting stock a person other than a U.S. person? (See instructions.) **Note:** *If "Yes," the corporation may have to file Form 5472.* . . . . .
If "Yes," enter owner's country ▶ _____

(d) Enter highest amount owed by the corporation to such owner during the year ▶ _____

(e) Enter highest amount owed to the corporation by such owner during the year ▶ _____

Note: *For purposes of I(1) and I(2), "highest amount owed" includes loans and accounts receivable/payable.*

	Yes	No
J Refer to the list in the instructions and state the principal:		

Business activity ▶ _____

Product or service ▶ _____

K Was the corporation a U.S. shareholder of any controlled foreign corporation? (See sections 951 and 957.) . . . . . .
If "Yes," attach Form 5471 for each such corporation.

L At any time during the tax year, did the corporation have an interest in or a signature or other authority over a financial account in a foreign country (such as a bank account, securities account, or other financial account)? . . . .
(See instruction F and filing requirements for form TD F 90-22.1.)
If "Yes," enter name of foreign country ▶ _____

M Was the corporation the grantor of, or transferor to, a foreign trust which existed during the current tax year, whether or not the corporation has any beneficial interest in it? . . . . . .
If "Yes," the corporation may have to file Forms 3520, 3520-A, or 926.

N During this tax year, did the corporation pay dividends (other than stock dividends and distributions in exchange for stock) in excess of the corporation's current and accumulated earnings and profits? (See sections 301 and 316.) . . . .
If "Yes," file Form 5452. If this is a consolidated return, answer here for parent corporation and on Form 851, Affiliations Schedule, for each subsidiary.

O During this tax year did the corporation maintain any part of its accounting/tax records on a computerized system? . . . . .

P Check method of accounting:
(1) ☐ Cash
(2) ☐ Accrual
(3) ☐ Other (specify) ▶ _____

Q Check this box if the corporation issued publicly offered debt instruments with original issue discount . . . . . ☐
If so, the corporation may have to file Form 8281.

Schedule L | Balance Sheets

Assets	Beginning of tax year		End of tax year	
	(a)	(b)	(c)	(d)
1 Cash				
2 Trade notes and accounts receivable				
a Less allowance for bad debts				
3 Inventories				
4 Federal and state government obligations				
5 Other current assets (attach schedule)				
6 Loans to stockholders				
7 Mortgage and real estate loans				
8 Other investments (attach schedule)				
9 Buildings and other depreciable assets				
a Less accumulated depreciation				
10 Depletable assets				
a Less accumulated depletion				
11 Land (net of any amortization)				
12 Intangible assets (amortizable only)				
a Less accumulated amortization				
13 Other assets (attach schedule)				
14 Total assets				
Liabilities and Stockholders' Equity				
15 Accounts payable				
16 Mortgages, notes, bonds payable in less than 1 year				
17 Other current liabilities (attach schedule)				
18 Loans from stockholders				
19 Mortgages, notes, bonds payable in 1 year or more				
20 Other liabilities (attach schedule)				
21 Capital stock: a Preferred stock				
b Common stock				
22 Paid-in or capital surplus				
23 Retained earnings—Appropriated (attach schedule)				
24 Retained earnings—Unappropriated				
25 Less cost of treasury stock		( )		( )
26 Total liabilities and stockholders' equity				

Schedule M-1 | Reconciliation of Income per Books With Income per Return

Do not complete this schedule if the total assets on line 14, column (d), of Schedule L are less than $25,000.

1 Net income per books		7 Income recorded on books this year not included in this return (itemize)	
2 Federal income tax		a Tax-exempt interest $ _ _ _ _ _ _ _ _ _ _ _ _	
3 Excess of capital losses over capital gains			
4 Income subject to tax not recorded on books this year (itemize) _ _ _ _ _ _ _ _ _ _ _ _ _ _ _			
		8 Deductions in this tax return not charged against book income this year (itemize)	
5 Expenses recorded on books this year not deducted in this return (itemize)		a Depreciation $ _ _ _ _ _ _ _ _ _	
a Depreciation $ _ _ _ _ _ _ _ _ _ _ _		b Contributions carryover $ _ _ _ _ _ _ _ _	
b Contributions carryover $ _ _ _ _ _ _ _ _ _			
		9 Total of lines 7 and 8	
6 Total of lines 1 through 5		10 Income (line 28, page 1)—line 6 less line 9	

Schedule M-2 | Analysis of Unappropriated Retained Earnings per Books (line 24, Schedule L)

Do not complete this schedule if the total assets on line 14, column (d), of Schedule L are less than $25,000.

1 Balance at beginning of year		5 Distributions: a Cash	
2 Net income per books		b Stock	
3 Other increases (itemize) _ _ _ _ _ _ _ _ _ _		c Property	
		6 Other decreases (itemize) _ _ _ _ _ _ _ _ _	
		7 Total of lines 5 and 6	
4 Total of lines 1, 2, and 3		8 Balance at end of year (line 4 less line 7)	

U.S. CORPORATION SHORT-FORM INCOME TAX RETURN, FORM 1120-A

Form 1120-A

U.S. Corporation Short-Form Income Tax Return

To see if you qualify to file Form 1120-A, see instructions.

1235

OMB No. 1545-0890

Department of the Treasury
Internal Revenue Service

For calendar 1986 or tax year beginning _____, 1986, ending _____, 19 ___
▶ Fiscal Year Corporations See Instructions Before Computing Tax.

1986

See Instructions for list of principal business:

A Activity

B Product or service

C Code

Use IRS label. Otherwise, please type or machine print

Name

Number and street

City or town, state, and ZIP code

D Employer identification number (EIN)

E Date incorporated

F Total assets (see Specific Instructions)

	Dollars	Cents
$		

G Check method of accounting: **(1)** ☐ Cash **(2)** ☐ Accrual **(3)** ☐ Other (specify) ▶

H Check box if there has been a change in address from the previous year ▶

Income

1a Gross receipts or sales _____ **b** Less returns and allowances _____ Balance ▶		**1c**	
2 Cost of goods sold and/or operations (see instructions).		**2**	
3 Gross profit (line 1c less line 2)		**3**	
4 Domestic corporation dividends subject to the Section 243(a)(1) deduction		**4**	
5 Interest		**5**	
6 Gross rents		**6**	
7 Gross royalties		**7**	
8 Capital gain net income (attach separate Schedule D (Form 1120))		**8**	
9 Net gain or (loss) from Form 4797, line 17, Part II (attach Form 4797)		**9**	
10 Other income (see instructions)		**10**	
11 TOTAL income—Add lines 3 through 10		**11**	

Deductions

12 Compensation of officers (see instructions).		**12**	
13a Salaries and wages _____ **b** Less jobs credit _____ Balance ▶		**13c**	
14 Repairs		**14**	
15 Bad debts (if reserve method is used, answer Question K on page 2)		**15**	
16 Rents		**16**	
17 Taxes		**17**	
18 Interest		**18**	
19 Contributions (**see instructions for 10% limitation**)		**19**	
20 Depreciation (attach Form 4562)	**20**	**//////**	
21 Less depreciation claimed elsewhere on return	**21a**	**21b**	
22 Other deductions (attach schedule)		**22**	
23 TOTAL deductions—Add lines 12 through 22		**23**	
24 Taxable income before net operating loss deduction and special deductions (line 11 less line 23)		**24**	
25 **Less: a** Net operating loss deduction (see instructions)	**25a**	**//////**	
b Special deductions (see instructions)	**25b**	**25c**	

Tax and Payments

26 Taxable income (line 24 less line 25c)		**26**	
27 TOTAL TAX (from Part I, line 6 on page 2)		**27**	
28 **Payments:**			
a 1985 overpayment allowed as a credit			
b 1986 estimated tax payments			
c Less 1986 refund applied for on Form 4466	( )		
d Tax deposited with Form 7004			
e Credit from regulated investment companies (attach Form 2439)			
f Credit for Federal tax on gasoline and special fuels (attach Form 4136)		**28**	
29 Enter any **PENALTY** for underpayment of estimated tax—Check ▶ ☐ if Form 2220 is attached		**29**	
30 **TAX DUE**—If the total of lines 27 and 29 is larger than line 28, enter AMOUNT OWED		**30**	
31 **OVERPAYMENT**—If line 28 is larger than the total of lines 27 and 29, enter AMOUNT OVERPAID		**31**	
32 Enter amount of line 31 you want: **Credited to 1987 estimated tax** ▶ _____ **Refunded** ▶		**32**	

Please Sign Here

Under penalties of perjury, I declare that I have examined this return, including accompanying schedules and statements, and to the best of my knowledge and belief, it is true, correct, and complete. Declaration of preparer (other than taxpayer) is based on all information of which preparer has any knowledge.

▶ _____ Signature of officer

Date

▶ _____ Title

Paid Preparer's Use Only

Preparer's signature ▶	Date	Check if self-employed ▶ ☐	Preparer's social security number
Firm's name (or yours, if self-employed) and address ▶		E.I. No. ▶	
		ZIP code ▶	

For Paperwork Reduction Act Notice, see page 1 of the instructions.

Form **1120-A** (1986)

Form 1120-A (1986)   **Part I   Tax Computation (See Instructions)** Page **2**   Enter EIN ▶

1 Income tax (See instructions to figure the tax. Enter lesser of this tax or alternative tax.) Check if alternative tax was used ▶ ☐	**1**	
2 Credits. Check if from ☐ Form 3800 ☐ Form 3468 ☐ Form 5884 ☐ Form 6478 ☐ Form 8007 ☐ Form 6765 ☐ Form 8586	**2**	
3 Line 1 less line 2	**3**	
4 Tax from recomputing prior-year investment credit (attach Form 4255)	**4**	
5 Minimum tax on tax preference items (see instructions—attach Form 4626) . . .	**5**	
6 Total tax—Add lines 3 through 5. Enter here and on line 27, page 1	**6**	

Additional Information (See instruction F)

I Was a deduction taken for expenses connected with:

  (1) An entertainment facility (boat, resort, ranch, etc.)? Yes ☐   No ☐

  (2) Employees' families at conventions or meetings?   Yes ☐   No ☐

J Did any individual, partnership, estate, or trust at the end of the tax year own, directly or indirectly, 50% or more of the corporation's voting stock? (For rules of attribution, see section 267(c).) If "Yes," complete (1) and (2) . . . . Yes ☐   No ☐

  (1) Attach a schedule showing name, address, and identifying number.

  (2) Enter "highest amount owed;" include loans and accounts receivable/payable:

    (a) Enter highest amount owed by the corporation to such owner during the year ▶ . . . .

    (b) Enter highest amount owed to the corporation by such owner during the year ▶ . . . .

K If the reserve method is used for bad debts, complete (1) and (2) for the current year:

  (1) Amount added to the reserve account:

    (a) Current year's provision ▶

    (b) Recoveries ▶ . . . .

  (2) Amount charged against the reserve account ▶

L If an amount for cost of goods sold and/or operations is entered on line 2, page 1, complete (1) and (2):

  (1) Purchases ▶ . . . .

  (2) Other costs (attach schedule) ▶ . .

M At any time during the tax year, did you have an interest in or a signature or other authority over a financial account in a foreign country (such as a bank account, securities account, or other financial account)? (See instruction F for filing requirements for Form TD F 90-22.1.) . . . . Yes ☐   No ☐

If "Yes," write in the name of the foreign country

▶

N During this tax year was any part of your accounting/tax records maintained on a computerized system? . . . . Yes ☐   No ☐

O Enter amount of cash distributions and the book value of property (other than cash) distributions made in this tax year ▶

Part II   Balance Sheets

		(a) Beginning of tax year		(b) End of tax year	
Assets	**1** Cash				
	2 Trade notes and accounts receivable				
	a Less: allowance for bad debts	(	)	(	)
	3 Inventories				
	4 Federal and State government obligations . .				
	5 Other current assets (attach schedule) . . .				
	6 Loans to stockholders				
	7 Mortgage and real estate loans				
	8 Depreciable, depletable, and intangible assets .				
	a Less: accumulated depreciation, depletion, and amortization . .	(	)	(	)
	9 Land (net of any amortization)				
	10 Other assets (attach schedule)				
	11 Total assets				
Liabilities and Stockholders' Equity	**12** Accounts payable				
	13 Other current liabilities (attach schedule) . .				
	14 Loans from stockholders				
	15 Mortgages, notes, bonds payable				
	16 Other liabilities (attach schedule)				
	17 Capital stock (Preferred and Common stock) .				
	18 Paid-in or capital surplus				
	19 Retained earnings				
	20 Less cost of treasury stock	(	)	(	)
	21 Total liabilities and stockholders' equity . .				

Part III   Reconciliation of Income Per Books With Income Per Return (See Instructions)

1 Enter net income per books			**5** Income recorded on books this year not included in this return (itemize)			
2 Federal income tax						
3 Income subject to tax not recorded on books this year (itemize) _____			**6** Deductions in this tax return not charged against book income this year (itemize) _____			
4 Expenses recorded on books this year not deducted in this return (itemize)			**7** Income (line 24, page 1). Enter the sum of lines 1, 2, 3, and 4 less the sum of lines 5 and 6			

U.S. INCOME TAX RETURN
FOR an S CORPORATION,
FORM 1120S

Form 1120S

U.S. Income Tax Return for an S Corporation

Form **1120S**
Department of the Treasury
Internal Revenue Service

For the calendar year 1986 or tax year beginning _____, 1986, ending _____, 19 ____

▶ For Paperwork Reduction Act Notice, see page 1 of the instructions.

OMB No. 1545-0130

1986

A Date of election as an S corporation

Use IRS label. Otherwise, please print or type.

Name

Number and street

City or town, state, and ZIP code

B Business Code No. (see Specific Instructions)

C Employer identification number

D Date incorporated

E Total assets (see Specific Instructions)

Dollars | Cents

$

F. Check applicable boxes: (1) ☐ Final return (2) ☐ Change in address (3) ☐ Amended return

1986-87 fiscal year corporations see Specific Instructions before completing page 1.

Income

1a Gross receipts or sales _____ **b** Less returns and allowances _____ Balance ▶	**1c**	
2 Cost of goods sold and/or operations (Schedule A, line 7)	**2**	
3 Gross profit (subtract line 2 from line 1c)	**3**	
4 Taxable interest and nonqualifying dividends	**4**	
5 Gross rents	**5**	
6 Gross royalties	**6**	
7 Net gain or (loss) from Form 4797, line 17, Part II	**7**	
8 Other income (see instructions—attach schedule)	**8**	
9 TOTAL income (loss)—Combine lines 3 through 8 and enter here ▶	**9**	

Deductions

10 Compensation of officers	**10**	
11a Salaries and wages _____ **b** Less jobs credit _____ Balance ▶	**11c**	
12 Repairs	**12**	
13 Bad debts (see instructions)	**13**	
14 Rents	**14**	
15 Taxes	**15**	
16a Total deductible interest expense not claimed elsewhere on return (see instructions) **16a**		
b Interest expense required to be passed through to shareholders on Schedule K-1, lines 9, 13a(2), and 13a(3) **16b**		
c Subtract line 16b from line 16a	**16c**	
17a Depreciation from Form 4562 (attach Form 4562) **17a**		
b Depreciation claimed on Schedule A and elsewhere on return **17b**		
c Subtract line 17b from line 17a	**17c**	
18 Depletion (**Do not deduct oil and gas depletion.** See instructions)	**18**	
19 Advertising	**19**	
20 Pension, profit-sharing, etc. plans	**20**	
21 Employee benefit programs	**21**	
22 Other deductions (attach schedule)	**22**	
23 TOTAL deductions—Add lines 10 through 22 and enter here ▶	**23**	
24 Ordinary income (loss)—Subtract line 23 from line 9	**24**	

Tax and Payments

25 Tax:		
a Excess net passive income tax (attach schedule) **25a**		
b Tax from Schedule D (Form 1120S), Part IV **25b**		
c Add lines 25a and 25b	**25c**	
26 Payments:		
a Tax deposited with Form 7004 **26a**		
b Credit for Federal tax on gasoline and special fuels (attach Form 4136) **26b**		
c Add lines 26a and 26b	**26c**	
27 **TAX DUE** (subtract line 26c from line 25c). See instructions for Paying the Tax ▶	**27**	
28 **OVERPAYMENT** (subtract line 25c from line 26c) ▶	**28**	

Please Sign Here

Under penalties of perjury, I declare that I have examined this return, including accompanying schedules and statements, and to the best of my knowledge and belief, it is true, correct, and complete. Declaration of preparer (other than taxpayer) is based on all information of which preparer has any knowledge.

▶ _____   Signature of officer   Date   ▶ _____   Title

Paid Preparer's Use Only

Preparer's signature ▶   Date   Check if self-employed ▶ ☐   Preparer's social security number

Firm's name (or yours, if self-employed) and address ▶   E.I. No. ▶   ZIP code ▶

Form **1120S** (1986)

Schedule A   **Cost of Goods Sold and/or Operations** (See instructions for Schedule A)

1 Inventory at beginning of year	**1**		
2 Purchases	**2**		
3 Cost of labor	**3**		
4 Other costs (attach schedule)	**4**		
5 Total—Add lines 1 through 4	**5**		
6 Inventory at end of year	**6**		
7 Cost of goods sold and/or operations—Subtract line 6 from line 5. Enter here and on line 2, page 1 . .	**7**		

8a Check all methods used for valuing closing inventory:

   (i) ☐ Cost

   (ii) ☐ Lower of cost or market as described in Regulations section 1.471-4 (see instructions)

   (iii) ☐ Writedown of "subnormal" goods as described in Regulations section 1.471-2(c) (see instructions)

   (iv) ☐ Other (Specify method used and attach explanation) ▶ _____

  b Check this box if the LIFO inventory method was adopted this tax year for any goods (if checked, attach Form 970) . . . . ☐

  c If the LIFO inventory method was used for this tax year, enter percentage (or amounts) of closing

    inventory computed under LIFO . . . . | **8c** |

  d If you are engaged in manufacturing, did you value your inventory using the full absorption method (Regulations

    section 1.471-11)? . . . . ☐ Yes   ☐ No

  e Was there any change in determining quantities, cost, or valuations between opening and closing inventory? . . . . . ☐ Yes   ☐ No

    If "Yes," attach explanation.

Additional Information Required

	Yes	No
G Did you at the end of the tax year own, directly or indirectly, 50% or more of the voting stock of a domestic corporation? (For rules of attribution, see section 267(c).)		
If "Yes," attach a schedule showing:		
(1) Name, address, and employer identification number;		
(2) Percentage owned;		
(3) Highest amount owed by you to such corporation during the year; and		
(4) Highest amount owed to you by such corporation during the year.		
(Note: *For purposes of G(3) and G(4), "highest amount owed" includes loans and accounts receivable/payable.)*		
H Refer to the listing of Business Activity Codes at the end of the Instructions for Form 1120S and state your principal: Business activity ▶ _____ ; Product or service ▶ _____		
I Were you a member of a controlled group subject to the provisions of section 1561?		
J Did you claim a deduction for expenses connected with:		
(1) Entertainment facilities (boat, resort, ranch, etc.)?		
(2) Living accommodations (except for employees on business)?		
(3) Employees attending conventions or meetings outside the North American area? (See section 274(h).)		
(4) Employees' families at conventions or meetings?		
If "Yes," were any of these conventions or meetings outside the North American area? (See section 274(h).)		
(5) Employee or family vacations not reported on Form W-2?		
K At any time during the tax year, did you have an interest in or a signature or other authority over a financial account in a foreign country (such as a bank account, securities account, or other financial account)? (See instructions for exceptions and filing requirements for form TD F 90-22.1.)		
If "Yes," write the name of the foreign country ▶ _____		
L Were you the grantor of, or transferor to, a foreign trust which existed during the current tax year, whether or not you have any beneficial interest in it? If "Yes," you may have to file Forms 3520, 3520-A, or 926		
M During this tax year did you maintain any part of your accounting/tax records on a computerized system?		
N Check method of accounting: **(1)** ☐ Cash **(2)** ☐ Accrual **(3)** ☐ Other (specify) ▶ _____		
O Check this box if the S corporation has filed or is required to file Form 8264, Application for Registration of a Tax Shelter . . . . ▶ ☐		
P Check this box if the corporation issued publicly offered debt instruments with original issue discount . . . . . ▶ ☐ If so, the corporation may have to file Form 8281.		

Schedule K	Shareholders' Share of Income, Credits, Deductions, etc. (See Instructions.)		
	(a) Distributive share items		**(b) Total amount**

Income (Losses) and Deductions

1a	Ordinary income (loss) (page 1, line 24) *	1a	
b	Income (loss) from rental real estate activity(ies) (FY corporations only) . . .	1b	
c	Income (loss) from other rental activity(ies) (FY corporations only)	1c	
d	Portfolio income not reported elsewhere on Schedule K (FY corporations only) . .	1d	
2	Dividends qualifying for the exclusion	2	
3	Net short-term capital gain (loss) (Schedule D (Form 1120S)) *	3	
4	Net long-term capital gain (loss) (Schedule D (Form 1120S)) *	4	
5	Net gain (loss) under section 1231 (other than due to casualty or theft) * . .	5	
6	Other income (loss) (attach schedule)	6	
7	Charitable contributions	7	
8	Section 179 expense deduction (FY corporations attach schedule)	8	
9	Other deductions (attach schedule)	9	

Credits

10a	Jobs credit *	10a	
b	Low-income housing credit (FY corporations only)	10b	
c	Qualified rehabilitation expenditures related to rental real estate activity(ies) (FY corporations only) (attach schedule)	////	////
d	Other credits related to rental real estate activity(ies) other than on line 10b and 10c (FY corporations only) (attach schedule)	10d	
11	Other credits (attach schedule) *	11	

Tax Preference and Adjustment Items

12a	Accelerated depreciation on nonrecovery real property or 15, 18, or 19-year real property placed in service before 1-1-87	12a	
b	Accelerated depreciation on leased personal property or leased recovery property, other than 15, 18, or 19-year real property, placed in service before 1-1-87	12b	
c	Accelerated depreciation on property placed in service after 12-31-86 (FY corporations only) . .	12c	
d	Depletion (other than oil and gas)	12d	
e	(1) Gross income from oil, gas, or geothermal properties	12e(1)	
	(2) Gross deductions allocable to oil, gas, or geothermal properties . . .	12e(2)	
f	(1) Qualified investment income included on page 1, Form 1120S	12f(1)	
	(2) Qualified investment expenses included on page 1, Form 1120S	12f(2)	
g	Other items (attach schedule)	12g	

Investment Interest

13a	Interest expense on: (1) Investment debts incurred before 12-17-69	13a(1)	
	(2) Investment debts incurred before 9-11-75 but after 12-16-69	13a(2)	
	(3) Investment debts incurred after 9-10-75	13a(3)	
b	(1) Investment income included on page 1, Form 1120S	13b(1)	
	(2) Investment expenses included on page 1, Form 1120S	13b(2)	
c	(1) Income from "net lease property"	13c(1)	
	(2) Expenses from "net lease property"	13c(2)	
d	Excess of net long-term capital gain over net short-term capital loss from investment property . .	13d	

Foreign Taxes

14a	Type of income _____	////	////
b	Name of foreign country or U.S. possession _____		
c	Total gross income from sources outside the U.S. (attach schedule)	14c	
d	Total applicable deductions and losses (attach schedule)	14d	
e	Total foreign taxes (check one): ▶ ☐ Paid ☐ Accrued	14e	
f	Reduction in taxes available for credit (attach schedule)	14f	
g	Other (attach schedule)	14g	

Other Items

15	Total property distributions (including cash) other than dividend distributions reported on line 17	15	////
16	Other items and amounts not included in lines 1 through 15 that are required to be reported separately to shareholders (attach schedule).	////	////
17	Total dividend distributions paid from accumulated earnings and profits contained in other retained earnings (line 26 of Schedule L)	17	

* Calendar year filers are not required to complete lines 1a, 10a, and 11. Completion of these lines is optional because the amounts which would appear in column (b) appear elsewhere on Form 1120S or on other IRS forms or schedules which are attached to Form 1120S. See Specific Instructions for Schedules K and K-1.

Schedule L Balance Sheets	Beginning of tax year		End of tax year	
Assets	(a)	(b)	(c)	(d)
1 Cash.				
2 Trade notes and accounts receivable				
a Less allowance for bad debts				
3 Inventories.				
4 Federal and state government obligations				
5 Other current assets (attach schedule)				
6 Loans to shareholders				
7 Mortgage and real estate loans				
8 Other investments (attach schedule)				
9 Buildings and other depreciable assets				
a Less accumulated depreciation				
10 Depletable assets				
a Less accumulated depletion				
11 Land (net of any amortization)				
12 Intangible assets (amortizable only)				
a Less accumulated amortization				
13 Other assets (attach schedule)				
14 Total assets				
Liabilities and Shareholders' Equity				
15 Accounts payable				
16 Mortgages, notes, bonds payable in less than 1 year				
17 Other current liabilities (attach schedule)				
18 Loans from shareholders				
19 Mortgages, notes, bonds payable in 1 year or more				
20 Other liabilities (attach schedule)				
21 Capital stock				
22 Paid-in or capital surplus				
23 Accumulated adjustments account				
24 Other adjustments account				
25 Shareholders' undistributed taxable income previously taxed				
26 Other retained earnings (see instructions)				
Check this box if the corporation has subchapter C earnings and profits at the close of the tax year ▶ ☐ (see instructions)				
27 Total retained earnings per books—Combine amounts on lines 23 through 26, columns (a) and (c) (see instructions)				
28 Less cost of treasury stock	(	)	(	)
29 Total liabilities and shareholders' equity				

Schedule M   Analysis of Accumulated Adjustments Account, Other Adjustments Account, and Shareholders' Undistributed Taxable Income Previously Taxed (If Schedule L, column (c), amounts for lines 23, 24, or 25 are not the same as corresponding amounts on line 9 of Schedule M, attach a schedule explaining any differences. See instructions.)

	Accumulated adjustments account	Other adjustments account	Shareholders' undistributed taxable income previously taxed
1 Balance at beginning of year			
2 Ordinary income from page 1, line 24			
3 Other additions			
4 Total of lines 1, 2, and 3			
5 Distributions other than dividend distributions			
6 Loss from page 1, line 24			
7 Other reductions			
8 Add lines 5, 6, and 7			
9 Balance at end of tax year—Subtract line 8 from line 4			

U.S. PARTNERSHIP RETURN OF INCOME, FORM 1065

Form **1065**

Department of the Treasury
Internal Revenue Service

U.S. Partnership Return of Income

▶ **For Paperwork Reduction Act Notice, see Form 1065 Instructions.**

For calendar year 1986, or fiscal year beginning _____ , 1986, and ending _____ , 19 ___

OMB No. 1545-0099

1986

A Principal business activity	Use IRS label. Otherwise, please print or type.	Name	D Employer identification number
B Principal product or service		Number and street (or P.O. Box number if mail is not delivered to street address)	E Date business started
C Business code number		City or town, state, and ZIP code	F Enter total assets at end of tax year $

G Check accounting method: **(1)** ☐ Cash **(2)** ☐ Accrual **(3)** ☐ Other

H Check applicable boxes: **(1)** ☐ Final return **(2)** ☐ Change in address
 (3) ☐ Amended return

		Yes	No
I	Number of partners in this partnership ▶ _____		
J	Is this partnership a limited partnership (see the Instructions)?		
K	Is this partnership a partner in another partnership?		
L	Are any partners in this partnership also partnerships?		
M	Does the partnership meet **all** the requirements shown in the Instructions for **Question M**?		
N	Was there a distribution of property or a transfer (for example, by sale or death) of a partnership interest during the tax year? If "Yes," see the Instructions concerning an election to adjust the basis of the partnership's assets under section 754		

		Yes	No
O	At any time during the tax year, did the partnership have an interest in or a signature or other authority over a financial account in a foreign country (such as a bank account, securities account, or other financial account)? (See the Instructions for exceptions and filing requirements for Form TD F 90-22.1.) If "Yes," write the name of the foreign country. ▶		
P	Was the partnership the grantor of, or transferor to, a foreign trust which existed during the current tax year, whether or not the partnership or any partner has any beneficial interest in it? If "Yes," you may have to file Forms 3520, 3520-A, or 926		
Q	Check this box if the partnership has filed or is required to file Form 8264, Application for Registration of a Tax Shelter	☐
R	Check this box if this is a partnership subject to the consolidated partnership audit procedures of TEFRA	☐

Caution: 1986-87 Fiscal year partnerships see the Instructions for Form 1065 before completing page 1.

Income

1a	Gross receipts or sales $ _____ **1b** Minus returns and allowances $ _____ Balance ▶	**1c**	
2	Cost of goods sold and/or operations (Schedule A, line 7)	**2**	
3	Gross profit (subtract line 2 from line 1c)	**3**	
4	Ordinary income (loss) from other partnerships and fiduciaries (attach schedule)	**4**	
5	Taxable interest and nonqualifying dividends	**5**	
6a	Gross rents $ _____ **6b** Minus rental expenses (attach schedule) $ _____		
c	Balance net rental income (loss) ▶	**6c**	
7	Net income (loss) from royalties (attach schedule)	**7**	
8	Net farm profit (loss) (attach Schedule F (Form 1040))	**8**	
9	Net gain (loss) (Form 4797, line 17)	**9**	
10	Other income (loss)	**10**	
11	**TOTAL** income (loss) (combine lines 3 through 10)	**11**	

Deductions

12a	Salaries and wages (other than to partners) $ _____ **12b** Minus jobs credit $ _____ Balance ▶	**12c**	
13	Guaranteed payments to partners	**13**	
14	Rent	**14**	
15a	Total deductible interest expense not claimed elsewhere on return (see Instructions) . **15a**		
b	Minus interest expense required to be passed through to partners on Schedule K-1 (1065), 15a(1), 15a(2), and 15a(3) **15b**		
c	Balance ▶	**15c**	
16	Taxes	**16**	
17	Bad debts	**17**	
18	Repairs	**18**	
19a	Depreciation from Form 4562 (attach Form 4562) $ _____ **19b** Minus depreciation claimed on Schedule A and elsewhere on return (including Schedules K-1) $ _____ Balance ▶	**19c**	
20	Depletion (**Do not deduct oil and gas depletion.**)	**20**	
21a	Retirement plans, etc.	**21a**	
b	Employee benefit programs	**21b**	
22	Other deductions (attach schedule)	**22**	
23	**TOTAL** deductions (add amounts in column for lines 12c through 22)	**23**	
24	Ordinary income (loss) (subtract line 23 from line 11)	**24**	

Please Sign Here

Under penalties of perjury, I declare that I have examined this return, including accompanying schedules and statements, and to the best of my knowledge and belief, it is true, correct, and complete. Declaration of preparer (other than taxpayer) is based on all information of which preparer has any knowledge.

▶ _____ ▶ _____
Signature of general partner   Date

Paid Preparer's Use Only

Preparer's signature ▶		Date	Check if self-employed ▶ ☐	Preparer's social security no.
Firm's name (or yours, if self-employed) and address ▶			E.I. No. ▶	
			ZIP code ▶	

Schedule A — Cost of Goods Sold and/or Operations

1	Inventory at beginning of year	**1**	
2	Purchases minus cost of items withdrawn for personal use	**2**	
3	Cost of labor	**3**	
4	Other costs (attach schedule)	**4**	
5	Total (add lines 1 through 4)	**5**	
6	Inventory at end of year	**6**	
7	Cost of goods sold (subtract line 6 from line 5). Enter here and on page 1, line 2	**7**	

8a Check all methods used for valuing closing inventory:

    (i) ☐ Cost

    (ii) ☐ Lower of cost or market as described in regulations section 1.471-4

    (iii) ☐ Writedown of "subnormal" goods as described in regulations section 1.471-2(c)

    (iv) ☐ Other (specify method used and attach explanation) ▶ _____

  b Check if the LIFO inventory method was adopted this tax year for any goods (if checked, attach Form 970) . . . . ☐

  c If you are engaged in manufacturing, did you value your inventory using the full absorption method (regulations section 1.471-11)? ☐ Yes ☐ No

  d Was there any change in determining quantities, cost, or valuations between opening and closing inventory? . . . ☐ Yes ☐ No
If "Yes," attach explanation.

Schedule B — Distributive Share Items

	(a) Distributive share items		(b) Total amount
1	Net long-term capital gain (loss)	**1**	
2	Other net gain (loss) under section 1231 and specially allocated ordinary gain (loss)	**2**	
3a	If the partnership had income from outside the United States, enter the name of the country or U.S. possession ▶ _____		
b	Total gross income from sources outside the United States	**3b**	

Schedule L — Balance Sheets

(See the Instructions for Question M Before Completing Schedules L and M.)

		Beginning of tax year		End of tax year	
	Assets	**(a)**	**(b)**	**(c)**	**(d)**
1	Cash				
2	Trade notes and accounts receivable				
a	Minus allowance for bad debts				
3	Inventories				
4	Federal and state government obligations				
5	Other current assets (attach schedule)				
6	Mortgage and real estate loans				
7	Other investments (attach schedule)				
8	Buildings and other depreciable assets				
a	Minus accumulated depreciation				
9	Depletable assets				
a	Minus accumulated depletion				
10	Land (net of any amortization)				
11	Intangible assets (amortizable only)				
a	Minus accumulated amortization				
12	Other assets (attach schedule)				
13	**TOTAL** assets				
	Liabilities and Capital				
14	Accounts payable				
15	Mortgages, notes, and bonds payable in less than 1 year				
16	Other current liabilities (attach schedule)				
17	All nonrecourse loans				
18	Mortgages, notes, and bonds payable in 1 year or more				
19	Other liabilities (attach schedule)				
20	Partners' capital accounts				
21	**TOTAL** liabilities and capital				

Schedule M — Reconciliation of Partners' Capital Accounts

(Show reconciliation of each partner's capital account on Schedule K-1 (Form 1065), Question H.)

(a) Capital account at beginning of year	(b) Capital contributed during year	(c) Ordinary income (loss) from page 1, line 24	(d) Income not included in column (c), plus nontaxable income	(e) Losses not included in column (c), plus unallowable deductions	(f) Withdrawals and distributions	(g) Capital account at end of year

✩ U.S. Government Printing Office: 1987—493-154   23-0916750

SCHEDULES 7 AND K (FORM 1065), PARTNER'S SHARE OF INCOME CREDITS, DEDUCTIONS, ETC.

SCHEDULE K-1
(Form 1065)

Department of the Treasury
Internal Revenue Service

Partner's Share of Income, Credits, Deductions, etc.

For calendar year 1986 or fiscal year
beginning _____, 1986, and ending _____, 19____

OMB No. 1545-0099

1986

Partner's identifying number ▶

Partnership's identifying number ▶

Partner's name, address, and ZIP code

Partnership's name, address, and ZIP code

A(1) Is partner a general partner? . . . . . ☐ Yes ☐ No
(F.Y. Partnerships only) If "yes" to Question A(1):

(2) Does partner materially participate in the trade or business activity(ies) included in lines 1a, 7, 10, and 12? . . . . ☐ Yes ☐ No

(3) Does partner actively participate in the rental real estate activity(ies) included in lines 1b and 11d? . . . . ☐ Yes ☐ No

B Partner's share of liabilities
Nonrecourse. . . . . $ _____
Other . . . . $ _____

C What type of entity is this partner? ▶

D Enter partner's percentage of: **(i)** Before decrease or termination **(ii)** End of year
Profit sharing . . . . _____% _____%
Loss sharing . . . . _____% _____%
Ownership of capital . . . . . _____% _____%

E IRS Center where partnership filed return ▶ _____

F Tax Shelter Registration Number ▶ _____

G(1) (F.Y. Partnerships only) Did the partner's ownership interest in the partnership increase after Oct. 22, 1986? ☐ Yes ☐ No
If yes, attach statement. (See page 12 of the Form 1065 Instructions.)

(2) (F.Y. Partnerships only) Did the partnership start or acquire a new activity after Oct. 22, 1986? . . . . ☐ Yes ☐ No
If yes, attach statement. (See page 12 of the Form 1065 Instructions.)

H Reconciliation of partner's capital account:

(a) Capital account at beginning of year	(b) Capital contributed during year	(c) Ordinary income (loss) from line 1a below	(d) Income not included in column (c), plus nontaxable income	(e) Losses not included in column (c), plus unallowable deductions	(f) Withdrawals and distributions	(g) Capital account at end of year

---

Caution: *Refer to attached Partner's Instructions for Schedule K-1 (Form 1065) before entering information from this schedule on your tax return.*

	(a) Distributive share item	(b) Amount	(c) 1986 1040 filers enter the amount in column (b) on:
Income (Loss)	**1a** Ordinary income (loss)	/////	Sch. E, Part II, col. (e) or (f)
	b Income or loss from rental real estate activity(ies). (F.Y. Partnerships only)	/////	⎫
	c Income or loss from other rental activity(ies). (F.Y. Partnerships only)	/////	⎬ (See Partner's Instructions for Schedule K-1 (Form 1065))
	d Portfolio income not reported elsewhere on Schedule K-1. (F.Y. Partnerships only)	/////	⎭
	2 Guaranteed payments		Sch. E, Part II, column (f)
	3 Dividends qualifying for exclusion		Sch. B, Part II, line 4
	4 Net short-term capital gain (loss).		Sch. D, line 5, col. (f) or (g)
	5 Net long-term capital gain (loss)		Sch. D, line 12, col. (f) or (g)
	6 Net gain (loss) under section 1231 (other than due to casualty or theft)		Form 4797, line 1
	7 Other (attach schedule)		(Enter on applicable lines of your return)
Deductions	**8** Charitable contributions		See Form 1040 Instructions
	9 Expense deduction for recovery property (section 179)		(See Partner's Instructions for Schedule K-1 (Form 1065))
	10 Other (attach schedule)		(Enter on applicable lines of your return)
Credits	**11a** Credit for income tax withheld		See Form 1040 Instructions
	b Low-income housing credit (F.Y. Partnerships only) . .		⎫
	c Qualified rehabilitation expenditures related to rental real estate activity(ies). (F.Y. Partnerships only) (attach schedule)	/////	⎬ (See Partner's Instructions for Schedule K-1 (Form 1065))
	d Credit(s) related to rental real estate activity(ies) other than 11b and 11c. (F.Y. Partnerships only) (attach schedule)	/////	⎪
	e Credit(s) related to rental activity(ies) other than 11b, 11c, and 11d. (F.Y. Partnerships only) (attach schedule).	/////	⎭
	12 Other credits (attach schedule)		(Enter on applicable lines of your return)
Self-employment	**13a** Net earnings (loss) from self-employment		Sch. SE, Part I
	b Gross farming or fishing income		⎫ (See Partner's Instructions for Schedule K-1 (Form 1065))
	c Gross nonfarm income		⎭

For Paperwork Reduction Act Notice, see Form 1065 Instructions.

Schedule K-1 (Form 1065) 1986

SCHEDULE K
(Form 1065)
Department of the Treasury
Internal Revenue Service

Partners' Shares of Income, Credits, Deductions, etc.

▶ File this form if there are more than ten Schedules K-1 (Form 1065) to be filed with Form 1065.
▶ Attach to Form 1065. ▶ See Instructions for Schedule K (Form 1065) in the Instructions for Form 1065.

OMB No. 1545-0099

1986

Name of partnership

Employer identification number

	(a) Distributive share items	(b) Total amount	
Income (Loss)	**1a** Ordinary income (loss) (page 1, line 24)	1a	
	b Income or loss from rental real estate activity(ies). (F.Y. Partnerships only)	1b	
	c Income or loss from other rental activity(ies). (F.Y. Partnerships only)	1c	
	d Portfolio income not reported elsewhere on Schedule K-1. (F.Y. Partnerships only) . . .	1d	
	2 Guaranteed payments	2	
	3 Dividends qualifying for exclusion	3	
	4 Net short-term capital gain (loss) (Schedule D, line 4)	4	
	5 Net long-term capital gain (loss) (Schedule D, line 9)	5	
	6 Net gain (loss) under section 1231 (other than due to casualty or theft) . .	6	
	7 Other (attach schedule)	7	
Deduc- tions	**8** Charitable contributions (attach list)	8	
	9 Expense deduction for recovery property (section 179) (F.Y. Partnerships see the Instructions) .	9	
	10 Other (attach schedule)	10	
Credits	**11a** Credit for income tax withheld	11a	
	b Low-income housing credit (F.Y. Partnerships only)	11b	
	c Qualified rehabilitation expenditures related to rental real estate activity(ies). (F.Y. Partnerships only) (attach schedule)	11c	
	d Credit(s) related to rental real estate activity(ies) other than 11b and 11c. (F.Y. Partnerships only) (attach schedule)	11d	
	e Credit(s) related to rental activity(ies) other than 11b, 11c, and 11d. (F.Y. Partnerships only) (attach schedule)	11e	
	12 Other (attach schedule)	12	
Self- Employ- ment	**13a** Net earnings (loss) from self-employment	13a	
	b Gross farming or fishing income	13b	
	c Gross nonfarm income	13c	
Tax Preference Items	**14a** For property placed in service before 1987, accelerated depreciation on nonrecovery real property or 15-, 18-, or 19-year real property . . .	14a	
	b For property placed in service before 1987, accelerated depreciation on leased personal property or leased recovery property other than 15-, 18-, or 19-year real property . . .	14b	
	c Depreciation adjustment on property placed in service after 1986	14c	
	d Unadjusted passive loss (F.Y. Partnerships only)	14d	
	e Depletion (other than oil and gas)	14e	
	f (1) Gross income from oil, gas, and geothermal properties	14f(1)	
	(2) Deductions allocable to oil, gas, and geothermal properties . .	14f(2)	
	g (1) Qualified investment income included on page 1, Form 1065 . . .	14g(1)	
	(2) Qualified investment expenses included on page 1, Form 1065 . .	14g(2)	
	h Other (attach schedule)	14h	
Investment Interest	**15a** Interest expense on:		
	(1) Investment debts incurred before 12/17/69	15a(1)	
	(2) Investment debts incurred before 9/11/75, but after 12/16/69 . .	15a(2)	
	(3) Investment debts incurred after 9/10/75	15a(3)	
	b (1) Investment income included on page 1, Form 1065	15b(1)	
	(2) Investment expenses included on page 1, Form 1065 . . .	15b(2)	
	c (1) Income from "net lease property"	15c(1)	
	(2) Expenses from "net lease property"	15c(2)	
Foreign Taxes	**16a** Type of income - - - - - - - - - - - - - - - - -		
	b Foreign country or U.S. possession - - - - - - - - - -		
	c Total gross income from sources outside the U.S. (attach schedule) . . .	16c	
	d Total applicable deductions and losses (attach schedule)	16d	
	e Total foreign taxes (check one): ▶ ☐ Paid ☐ Accrued . . .	16e	
	f Reduction in taxes available for credit (attach schedule)	16f	
	g Other (attach schedule)	16g	
Other	**17** Attach schedule for other items and amounts not reported above. See Instructions . .		

For Paperwork Reduction Act Notice, see Form 1065 Instructions.

Schedule K (Form 1065) 1986

SCHEDULE K-1 (FORM 1065), PARTNER'S SHARE OF INCOME, CREDITS, DEDUCTIONS, ETC.

SCHEDULE K-1 (Form 1065)	**Partner's Share of Income, Credits, Deductions, etc.**	OMB No. 1545-0099
Department of the Treasury Internal Revenue Service	For calendar year 1986 or fiscal year beginning _____, 1986, and ending _____, 19___	**1986**

Partner's identifying number ▶   Partnership's identifying number ▶

Partner's name, address, and ZIP code   Partnership's name, address, and ZIP code

A(1) Is partner a general partner? . . . . . ☐ Yes ☐ No
(F.Y. Partnerships only) If "yes" to Question A(1):
(2) Does partner materially participate in the trade or business activity(ies) included in lines 1a, 7, 10, and 12? . . . . . . ☐ Yes ☐ No
(3) Does partner actively participate in the rental real estate activity(ies) included in lines 1b and 11d? . . . . ☐ Yes ☐ No
B Partner's share of liabilities
Nonrecourse. . . . . $ _____
Other . . . . $ _____
C What type of entity is this partner? ▶

D Enter partner's percentage of:

	(i) Before decrease or termination	(ii) End of year
Profit sharing	_____%	_____%
Loss sharing	_____%	_____%
Ownership of capital . . .	_____%	_____%

E IRS Center where partnership filed return ▶ _____
F Tax Shelter Registration Number ▶ _____
G(1) (F.Y. Partnerships only) Did the partner's ownership interest in the partnership increase after Oct. 22, 1986? ☐ Yes ☐ No
If yes, attach statement. (See page 12 of the Form 1065 Instructions.)
(2) (F.Y. Partnerships only) Did the partnership start or acquire a new activity after Oct. 22, 1986? . . . . ☐ Yes ☐ No
If yes, attach statement. (See page 12 of the Form 1065 Instructions.)

H Reconciliation of partner's capital account:

(a) Capital account at beginning of year	(b) Capital contributed during year	(c) Ordinary income (loss) from line 1a below	(d) Income not included in column (c), plus nontaxable income	(e) Losses not included in column (c), plus unallowable deductions	(f) Withdrawals and distributions	(g) Capital account at end of year

Caution: *Refer to attached Partner's Instructions for Schedule K-1 (Form 1065) before entering information from this schedule on your tax return.*

		(a) Distributive share item	(b) Amount	(c) 1986 1040 filers enter the amount in column (b) on:
Income (Loss)	1a	Ordinary income (loss)		Sch. E, Part II, col. (e) or (f)
	b	Income or loss from rental real estate activity(ies). (F.Y. Partnerships only) . .	/////	
	c	Income or loss from other rental activity(ies). (F.Y. Partnerships only)		(See Partner's Instructions for Schedule K-1 (Form 1065))
	d	Portfolio income not reported elsewhere on Schedule K-1. (F.Y. Partnerships only)	/////	
	2	Guaranteed payments		Sch. E, Part II, column (f)
	3	Dividends qualifying for exclusion		Sch. B, Part II, line 4
	4	Net short-term capital gain (loss).		Sch. D, line 5, col. (f) or (g)
	5	Net long-term capital gain (loss)		Sch. D, line 12, col. (f) or (g)
	6	Net gain (loss) under section 1231 (other than due to casualty or theft)		Form 4797, line 1
	7	Other (attach schedule)		(Enter on applicable lines of your return)
Deductions	8	Charitable contributions		See Form 1040 Instructions
	9	Expense deduction for recovery property (section 179)		(See Partner's Instructions for Schedule K-1 (Form 1065))
	10	Other (attach schedule)		(Enter on applicable lines of your return)
Credits	11a	Credit for income tax withheld		See Form 1040 Instructions
	b	Low-income housing credit (F.Y. Partnerships only)	/////	
	c	Qualified rehabilitation expenditures related to rental real estate activity(ies). (F.Y. Partnerships only) (attach schedule)	/////	
	d	Credit(s) related to rental real estate activity(ies) other than 11b and 11c. (F.Y. Partnerships only) (attach schedule)	/////	(See Partner's Instructions for Schedule K-1 (Form 1065))
	e	Credit(s) related to rental activity(ies) other than 11b, 11c, and 11d. (F.Y. Partnerships only) (attach schedule).	/////	
	12	Other credits (attach schedule)		(Enter on applicable lines of your return)
Self-employment	13a	Net earnings (loss) from self-employment		Sch. SE, Part I
	b	Gross farming or fishing income		(See Partner's Instructions for Schedule K-1 (Form 1065))
	c	Gross nonfarm income		

	(a) Distributive share item	(b) Amount	(c) 1986 1040 filers enter the amount in column (b) on:
Tax Preference Items	**14a** For property placed in service before 1987, accelerated depreciation on nonrecovery real property or 15, 18, or 19-year real property	/////	Form 6251, line 4c
	b For property placed in service before 1987, accelerated depreciation on leased personal property or leased recovery property other than 15, 18, or 19-year real property	/////	Form 6251, line 4d
	c Depreciation adjustment on property placed in service after 1986 .		} (See Partner's Instructions for Schedule K-1 (Form 1065))
	d Unadjusted passive loss (F.Y. Partnerships only)		
	e Depletion (other than oil and gas)		Form 6251, line 4i
	f (1) Gross income from oil, gas, and geothermal properties		See Form 6251 Instructions
	(2) Deductions allocable to oil, gas, and geothermal properties . . .		See Form 6251 Instructions
	g (1) Qualified investment income included in Schedule K-1, line 1a .		} (See Partner's Instructions for Schedule K-1 (Form 1065))
	(2) Qualified investment expenses included in Schedule K-1, line 1a .		
	h Other (attach schedule)		
Investment Interest	**15a** Interest expense on:	/////	/////
	(1) Investment debts incurred before 12/17/69		Form 4952, line 1
	(2) Investment debts incurred before 9/11/75, but after 12/16/69 .		Form 4952, line 15
	(3) Investment debts incurred after 9/10/75		Form 4952, line 5
	b (1) Investment income included in Schedule K-1, line 1a		} (See Partner's Instructions for Schedule K-1 (Form 1065))
	(2) Investment expenses included in Schedule K-1, line 1a		
	c (1) Income from "net lease property"		
	(2) Expenses from "net lease property"		
Foreign Taxes	**16a** Type of income _____	/////	Form 1116, Check boxes
	b Name of foreign country or U.S. possession _____		Form 1116, Part I
	c Total gross income from sources outside the U.S. (attach schedule) .		Form 1116, Part I
	d Total applicable deductions and losses (attach schedule) . . .		Form 1116, Part I
	e Total foreign taxes (check one): ▶ ☐ Paid ☐ Accrued . . .		Form 1116, Part II
	f Reduction in taxes available for credit (attach schedule)		Form 1116, Part III
	g Other (attach schedule)		Form 1116 Instructions
Other	**17** Other items and amounts not included in lines 1a through 16g and 18 that are required to be reported separately to you	/////	(See Partner's Instructions for Schedule K-1 (Form 1065))

	18 Properties:	A	B	C	
Property Subject to Recapture of Investment Credit	**a** Description of property (State whether recovery or nonrecovery property. If recovery property, state whether regular percentage method or section 48(q) election used.) .				/////
	b Date placed in service .				Form 4255, top
	c Cost or other basis . .				Form 4255, line 2
	d Class of recovery property or original estimated useful life .				Form 4255, line 3
	e Date item ceased to be investment credit property				Form 4255, line 4
					Form 4255, line 8

Other Information Provided by Partnership:

_____

_____

_____

_____

_____

INDEX

239